The Randolph Women ...
And their men

Ruth Doumlele

BOOK PUBLISHERS NETWORK

Book Publishers Network
P.O. Box 2256
Bothell • WA • 98041
PH • 425-483-3040
www.bookpublishersnetwork.com

10 9 8 7 6 5 4 3 2 1

Printed in the United States of America

LCCN 2009912349
ISBN10 1-935359-25-8
ISBN13 978-1-935359-25-8

Doumlele, Ruth.

    The Randolph women ... and their men / Ruth Doumlele. -- Bothell, WA : Book Publishers Network, c2010.

    p. ; cm.

    ISBN: ISBN13: 978- 1- 935359-25- 8; ISBN10: 1- 935359- 25-8
    Includes bibliographical references and index.

    1. Randolph family. 2. Women-- United States-- History. 3. Women-- Virginia-- History. 4. United States-- Social life and customs. 5. Virginia --Social life and customs. I. Title.

CT274.R34 D68 2010   2009912349
929/.20973-- dc22   1002

Editor: Vicki McCown
Cover Designer: Laura Zugzda
Typographer: Nina Barnett

To the memory of
John, "heart of my heart,"
and
Tony, who filled my life with his magic

and
for Suzanne,
a treasure beyond compare

CONTENTS

Illustrations

Acknowledgments

*W*hat a ride this has been—sharing the lives of these women, two centuries after their turbulent times. Reading their letters, I marveled at their eloquence in describing the most mundane events for their readers. And their men's were no less eloquent, from Gouveneur Morris's lyrical prose to John Randolph's diatribes.

The journey began in the Cumberland Court clerk's office, where I found the court order from Richard Randolph's trial. The trail led me to the Prince Edward Courthouse and Richard's will freeing his slaves, and from there to the Bizarre plantation cemetery, in an iron-fenced enclosure with cows grazing nearby.

There were so many helpful people along the way, beginning with the court clerks in these counties as well as those in Goochland, Chesterfield, and Lancaster. I am grateful to the staff in the Lipscomb Library at Randolph College, who provided a wonderful sanctuary to pore over the extensive records of John Randolph of Roanoke; the Swem Library at the College of William and Mary; the Alderman Library at the University of Virginia; and the archives at the Mary Ball Washington Museum and Library in Lancaster County. Staff members in my own neighborhood's Midlothian Library, as well as those at the Main Branch, Richmond City Library, were always eager to help. I could never have completed this book without the resources at the Library of Virginia, where Conley Edwards in the archives and Audrey

Johnson and Tom Camden in Special Collections guided me unerr-ingly. I was fortunate to live close to the Virginia Historical Society and its extensive Randolph family collections, where Dr. Nelson Lankford gave me good advice and Dr. Lee Shepard graciously checked the files to be certain that my material was used legally.

I am indebted to my professors at the University of Richmond in allowing this nontraditional student in the master's program to use much of the Randolph women's material. Dr. Frank Eakin and Dr. Margaret Denton were especially supportive, and Dr. Woody Holton, demanding professor and mentor, guided my narrative superbly.

Sabra Ledent tracked my progress with great editing and critiqu-ing; Jennifer McCord helped me define my priorities; Bob Reilly drew the Virginia plantations map; Jerry Stuart diagrammed the way to the Bizarre graveyard; and Jim Logios was my Apple/Mac guru.

I deeply appreciate Sheryn Hara's expertise and patience in bringing my efforts to fruition. Sheryn, the engine of Book Publishers Network, and her team are the great ladies of publishing.

A host of special people have been there for me, every step of the away. I thank fellow members of the Richmond Branch, National League of American Pen Women; the daughters in the Commonwealth Chapter, National Society Daughters of the American Revolution; a number of wonderful friends in the Powhatan County Historical So-ciety; and many others who have offered support and encouragement.

Finally, my deepest gratitude goes to my family. My husband, John, lived for years with eighteenth-century guests in the study. My chil-dren—Tony, who left us too soon, and his family, Leigh, Nick, and Kyra, and my daughter, Suzanne, with Tom, Randy, and Courtney, and now with Josh, Meredith, and Owen—were incredibly patient, as were my sisters Lois and Esther.

Thank you, thank you!

FOREWORD

It cannot be a coincidence that the Virginia colony began the production of tobacco and the importation – the word is inappropriate here – of women in the same year: 1613. Not that Englishwomen were put to work in the tobacco fields; no, the importation of another category of human beings, Africans, had begun in earnest. But the great Chesapeake tobacco plantations could never have operated without the European women who managed the households, raised the children, and – surprisingly often – brought immense wealth to the men they married. George Washington and Thomas Jefferson were the most famous of the Founding Fathers who remained outside the charmed circle of the inner gentry until they married wealthy widows.

Women were as important to the colonial struggle for home rule as they had been to the development of the colony. How could the boycotts of British merchandise – especially the pledge not to drink tea – have succeeded without the efforts of women? And it was women who spun the thread and wove the garments that patriots donned in place of what they had once imported from the mother country. When the conflict became a shooting war, women managed the farms of absent soldiers and statesmen, and they sometimes followed their menfolk right into the army. George Washington deserves praise for enduring the bitter winter at Valley Forge, but so does Martha, who was with him there the whole time.

And then, later, when the charmed vessel sank beneath the waves, the gentlewomen went down with the ship. The market for tobacco, as it turned out, was not inexhaustible, and the soil of Virginia was quite easily exhausted. Within a few decades of the great military victory at Yorktown in 1781, a combination of slackening demand and soil exhaustion led to a series of debilitating economic defeats. Some members of the gentry class held on by going into trade. Others sold off their human chattel, which inevitably meant the permanent separation of families. It was an ill portent that the category of well-to-do Virginians who seemed to hold on the longest was the lawyers – in particular those who agreed to represent British merchants suing for pre-revolutionary debts.

Yet every gentry family that tied its fate to the cultivation of tobacco was doomed to decline. The Randolphs were such a family. The union in 1680 of William Randolph of Turkey Island with Mary Isham of Bermuda Hundred produced nine children, and they in turn established the Randolph dynasty. Many of their descendants' names are among the most illustrious in American history: Thomas Jefferson, John Marshall, Robert E. Lee, Lady Nancy Astor, J. E. B. Stuart, and Thomas Nelson Page.

It was said, "No one was good enough for a Randolph except another Randolph," and the Randolphs married cousins and had children who married Randolphs. While intermarriage produced geniuses in some instances, deviant genes also generated serious character flaws and physical defects. The emergence of libertine traits and tempestuous dispositions triggered explosive events as the eighteenth century ended. John Marshall's grandmother, a Randolph of Tuckahoe, became a lunatic. Richard Randolph of Bizarre, married to a Randolph cousin, was considered one of the most promising men in Virginia, but he ruined his reputation by immoral behavior. His brother, John Randolph of Roanoke, never married, achieved prominence in Congress, and was seemingly headed for a pinnacle in government but destroyed himself by publicly turning on President Jefferson, a cousin, and President James Madison. As he descended into madness, his attempt to destroy his cousin Nancy Randolph failed. She fought back publicly, supported by her husband, New York statesman Gouverneur Morris. Thomas Mann Randolph married Martha Jefferson, a Randolph cousin. She worshipped her father, who controlled the marriage, and was unable to accept her husband as a true partner. He became an embittered recluse, never reaching his potential as congressman or governor.

"When I look back upon the past," John Randolph wrote, "the eventful history of my race and name . . . presents a tragedy that far outstrips in improbability and rivals in horrour all dramatic or romantic fiction."

Randolph was thinking primarily of the men of the family, but, if anything, his female cousins fell further than the men. As told here by the eloquent Ruth Doumlele, the story of the Randolph women is gripping, and it is also instructive. But most of all it is precisely what Randolph said it was: tragic.

Woody Holton, Ph.D.

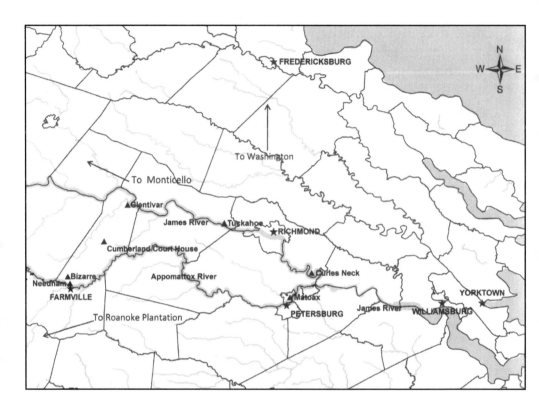

Map of Virginia Plantations, circa 1795

Introduction

❦

*T*he Randolph family heritage in Virginia began with the Indian princess Pocahontas. She became friends with the English settlers at Jamestown, particularly with Captain John Smith. During a severe famine, she and her people brought food to Jamestown, saving the settlement. Later, she was seized and held hostage by the English there. While in captivity, Pocahontas adapted well to their culture, learned English, and converted to Christianity. John Rolfe, a young planter, fell in love with her and their marriage on April 5, 1614, began the Peace of Pocahontas, a cessation of hostilities between the Indians and the English. John Rolfe took his wife and their son to England in 1616. Princess Pocahontas, now known by her Christian name, Rebecca, was presented at the English court. Her regal bearing impressed the king and queen and her fun-loving disposition charmed the formal English. As she and her husband prepared to return to America, Pocahontas became ill, died, and was buried at Gravesend in 1617. Her son, Thomas, was educated in England and then returned to America to claim his heritage. His marriage to an English woman, Jane Poythress, produced a daughter, Jane, who married a Bolling. Their children married Blands, who married Randolphs, the many descendants of William Randolph I of Turkey Island.

William Randolph emigrated to Virginia in the last half of the seventeenth century and built his home, Turkey Island, on the James

River east of Richmond. The large home, named for the wild turkeys that roosted in the chimneys, lasted until the Civil War, when fire from Union gunboats destroyed it.

Already a big landowner, William acquired more land and possessions from property seized after Bacon's Rebellion. Randolph's social position and acquisitions were enhanced even more by his friendship with William Byrd II of Westover, and his marriage in 1680 to Mary Isham of Bermuda Hundred brought him even more wealth. His prized tobacco went to merchants in England to be sold, and its proceeds purchased furniture, silk, slaves, and indentured servants. William Randolph helped to found and charter the College of William and Mary in 1693 and became a trustee.

Mary Isham Randolph bore seven sons and two daughters who received land and property. One son, Henry of Longfield, settled in England. Sir John became master of Tazewell Hall. His son Peyton was the first president of the Continental Congress; a grandson, Edmund, served as a governor of Virginia, a U. S. secretary of state, and U. S. attorney general. Other sons were Edward of Bremo, William II of Chatsworth, Thomas of Tuckahoe, Richard of Curles, and Isham of Dungeness. The daughter of William I, Mary, married John Stith, a president of William and Mary College in Williamsburg, and Elizabeth married Richard Bland.

All built elegant plantation homes along Virginia rivers. The home of Richard of Curles was ninety-five by twenty-six feet, two stories, with a sixty-foot colonnade connecting it with other buildings.

Their descendants married Randolphs who married first, second, and third cousins until the family genealogy resembled a "tangle of fish hooks." It was said that "no one was good enough for a Randolph except another Randolph." Family traits of pride and acquisitiveness were at times exacerbated by the tempestuous willfulness of the Pocahontas bloodline; and this intense interbreeding produced character flaws, hereditary disease, and personality distortions. Virginians at odds with the Randolph traits commented, "If God had been the God of Virginia, he would have struck William Randolph of Turkey Island with sterility." Even so, the Randolph courage, richness of intellect, and eloquence also produced geniuses, statesmen, and generals.

This true story of the Randolph women and their men examines the intertwining of several Randolph families of the Revolutionary War and post–Revolutionary War era.

Thomas Randolph of Tuckahoe married Judith Fleming. Their daughter, Mary, was found in flagrante delicto with Reverend James Keith. She followed him, when he was banished for fornication with a gentlewoman, to a distant parish. They were married, and she became the grandmother of John Marshall, chief justice of the United States.

Thomas's son Thomas Mann Randolph married Ann Cary, a cousin from the Isham Randolph line. She descended from Pocahontas through Richard of Curles's marriage to Jane Bolling. With the Randolph fascination for men, she was described as beautiful, spirited, and articulate. Sir John Leslie, on his stay at Tuckahoe, wrote that she "exalted his opinion of the whole sex." They produced three sons—Thomas Junior, William, and John—and seven daughters—Mary, Elizabeth, Judith, Ann Cary (Nancy), Jane, Harriet, and Virginia. Thomas Mann Randolph, Jr. married his cousin, Martha Jefferson.

Mary Randolph, called Molly, shown in a St. Memin silhouette to have been a handsome woman, married her cousin, David Meade Randolph. They built a "city plantation," Moldavia, in Richmond. In the spacious home with its octagonal ballroom, they entertained with "sumptuous repasts" and "grand and glorious balls." Molly was referred to as the "Queen of the Realm," by Samuel Mordecai, a nineteenth-century historian, for her fabulous entertaining. Moldavia had stood for more than a century when it was demolished around 1900. Later, Molly opened a boarding house and became a successful businesswoman. While living in Washington, D. C., she published the first American cookbook, which included numerous recipes from the Tuckahoe menus.

Judith Randolph inherited her mother's beauty and her attraction to men. A distant cousin, Peter Randolph of Chatsworth, described her on a visit to Tuckahoe to "storm the citadel of her virtues and accomplishments." He spoke of her "angelic majesty . . . her beauty in its meridian splendour . . . and the magical influence of a beautiful woman on the soul." Sir John Leslie spoke to Judith's brother of his love for her, his "burning affection tinctured with sadness," because she did not reciprocate. In what later became a great tragedy, she married, at a young age and unwisely, her cousin, Richard Randolph of Matoax and Bizarre.

Ann Cary Randolph, called "Nancy," a few months younger than Judith, was sunnier, more athletic. A descendant, Francis Biddle, described her as being "full of the delight of living, hot-blooded, careless, haphazard." Historian A. J. Eckenrode described her as "handsome, determined in character, and infinitely courageous." Her letters chronicle the sad events of her life—evicted from Tuckahoe, living subserviently with various relatives, penniless in a nonexistent job market for a woman of her training and social standing. Her seduction and impregnation by her brother-in-law, Judith's husband, Richard, reduced her to a "trull," a fallen woman. She found happiness for a few years as the wife of northern aristocrat and statesman Gouverneur Morris.

Nancy's January 1815 letter to John Randolph was described, in 1888, "as a literary performance, this letter . . . is entitled to rank as one of the finest specimens of English composition anywhere to be found, equaling, if not exceeding in vigor and point as well as elegance in form of expression, the celebrated letters of Junius."

Her husband, Gouverneur Morris, referred to her as "that fortune, my wife," and "the bounty of Him who gilds with a celestial beam the tranquil evening of my day."

Jane Randolph married her cousin Thomas Eston Randolph of Dungeness, a wealthy planter who later lost his fortune. Harriet married Richard Hackley of New York, whom Jefferson appointed as consul at Cadiz, Spain. He returned with a Spanish mistress, causing his wife to leave him and Martha Randolph to refer to him as a "mean rascal and a fool."

Martha and Tom Randolph reared his youngest sister, Virginia. She married her cousin, Wilson Jefferson Cary, and after his death at a young age, she wrote articles and books to help support herself and their children. She wrote of a smoldering problem, "Slavery is indeed a fearful evil, a canker in the bud of our National prosperity." Her daughter carried on a family tradition when she married a northern cousin, the son of her sister Nancy and Gouverneur Morris.

⚮

Frances Bland descended from William Randolph I through his daughter Elizabeth. When she married a cousin, John Randolph, a descendant of Richard Randolph of Curles, her father-in-law was a first cousin and her husband's mother-in-law was also his aunt. John built Matoax for her, which sat high above the Appomattox River near Petersburg and was noted for its extensive library. She was described as "a woman of superior personal attractions who excelled all others of her day in strength of intellect for which she was so justly celebrated." The "tawny," stately beauty was fearless as British troops advanced during the Revolution, wearing her husband's steel-hilted dagger in her stays. She bore three sons—Richard, Theodorick, and John—before her husband died. She later married St. George Tucker.

The sons were educated at boarding schools and universities. Richard was described as a man of "great personal beauty, a character out of a Roman novel, excelling in strength of intellect." He was said to "have extensive and useful accomplishment with commanding and extraordinary talent." He destroyed his future and Nancy's reputation when he seduced her and they were tried for the murder of her infant.

Theodorick attended college in New York City, adopted a dissolute lifestyle, and died of consumption at age twenty-one.

John Randolph of Roanoke became known as the most eloquent man of his time. He was erratic and brilliant, an ardent states rightist. While Thomas Jefferson said, "I am a citizen of the world," John Randolph said, "When I speak of my nation, I mean the Commonwealth of Virginia." His rapier-like verbal attacks seldom missed their mark. Although seemingly destined for greatness in public life, he destroyed his career when he publicly turned on President Jefferson. Even so, when he spoke at the end of his career in 1829, it was reported "the gallery was crowded to suffocation" to hear him. "The thrilling music of his speech fell upon the ear like the voice of a bird singing in the pause of a storm."

Thomas Jefferson was descended from Isham of Dungeness through his daughter Jane, who married Peter Jefferson. Thomas Jefferson married Martha Wayles Skelton and their two daughters were Martha and Maria. Martha was "homely," six feet tall and angular, "a delicate likeness of her father," with a frank and affectionate manner. She married her cousin Thomas Randolph Jr. of Tuckahoe, a skilled horseman, hard-working, dedicated to his family. Her unusual and extreme love for her father doomed their happiness, leaving Thomas sad and embittered. Maria was beautiful, simple, and reserved, "the fairest flower which my eyes ever beheld." She married her cousin John Eppes and died young in childbirth.

To the Randolph coat of arms, Nil Admirari (Wonder at Nothing), John Randolph of Roanoke added Fari Que Sentiat (Do What You Feel), an appropriate representation of this family's response to their environment and time in history.

CAST OF CHARACTERS

The Families

Matoax-Bizarre-Roanoke

Frances Randolph Tucker	Widow of John Randolph, wife of St. George Tucker
St. George Tucker	Her second husband

Children:

Richard Randolph (Dick)	Frances's son – married Judith Randolph of Tuckahoe
Theodorick Randolph (Theo)	Frances's son
John Randolph (Jack)	Frances's son
	Later John Randolph of Roanoke
Fanny Tucker	Frances and St. George Tucker's daughter – married John Coalter
John St. George Randolph (Saint)	Richard and Judith's son
Tudor Randolph	Richard and Judith's son
Lelia Carter Tucker	St. George Tucker's second wife

Tuckahoe

Colonel Thomas Mann Randolph Master of Tuckahoe
Ann Cary Randolph   His wife

Children:
Mary Randolph (Molly)   Daughter – married David Meade Randolph
Elizabeth Randolph   Daughter – married Robert Pleasants
Thomas Mann Randolph Jr.   Son – married Martha Jefferson
William Randolph   Son – married Lucy Randolph
Judith Randolph   Daughter – married Richard Randolph
Ann Cary (Nancy)   Daughter – married Gouverneur Morris
Jane Randolph   Daughter – married Thomas Eston Randolph
Harriet Randolph   Daughter – married Richard Hackley
John Randolph   Son – married Judith Lewis
Virginia Randolph   Daughter – married Wilson Cary

Gabriella Harvie Randolph   Second wife of Colonel Thomas Mann Randolph
                             Later married Dr. John Brockenbrough

---

Monticello

Thomas Jefferson   Master of Monticello, minister to France,
                             Vice President and President of the United
                               States
Children:
Martha Jefferson   Daughter – married Thomas Mann Randolph, Jr.
Mary (Maria)   Daughter – married John Wayles Eppes

Other characters:

Joseph Bryan	Congressman, friend of John Randolph
John Coalter	Tutor to Tucker children, husband of Fanny Tucker
Maria Cosway	Friend of Thomas Jefferson in Paris
Adele de Flahaut	Friend of Gouverneur Morris in Paris
Mary Randolph Harrison	Cousin and friend of Judith Randolph, wife of Randolph Harrison
Randolph Harrison	Master of Glentivar
Nathaniel Macon	Congressman, friend of John Randolph
Dolley Madison	Wife of James Madison
James Madison	Fourth president of the United States, friend of Thomas Jefferson
John Marshall	Supreme Court justice, defense attorney for Richard Randolph
Gouverneur Morris	Minister to France, husband of Nancy Randolph
David Meade Randolph	Husband of Mary Randolph
Creed Taylor	Statesman, jurist, a Bizarre neighbor
Sally Taylor	Wife of Creed Taylor
William Thompson	Friend of John Randolph
Maria Ward	Fiancee of John Randolph, friend of Judith Randolph

"I look forward with great impatience to March.
I am afraid to flatter myself with the hope of seeing you sooner.
. . . every sentiment of tenderness. . .
centered in you and no connexion found since
that could weaken a sentiment interwoven with my very existence"

January 22, 1798
MARTHA JEFFERSON RANDOLPH TO THOMAS JEFFERSON

"When I look back upon the past,
the eventful history of my race and name . . .
presents a tragedy that far outstrips in improbability
and rivals in horrours
all dramatic or romantic fiction"

JOHN RANDOLPH OF ROANOKE

"Perhaps some wind may yet waft you over the bosom of the Atlantic
and you shall become acquainted with my wife,
and you shall see that fortune –
fortune No, – the word befits not a sacred theme, –
let me say the bounty of Him,
who . . . gilds with a celestial beam
the tranquil evening of my day."

GOUVERNEUR MORRIS TO JOHN PARISH

The Trial
April 29, 1793

A lthough regular Cumberland County court days had passed, a crowd had assembled outside of the courthouse to hear details of this case, a previously unheard-of event in the county. Not only would it be a scandalous scene involving one of the local gentry, but defense attorney Patrick Henry would make a rare appearance. For those unable to crowd into the courtroom, a sentry climbed a tree near a window to view the proceedings and pass the information to those below. The mood swung from those who waited to see the whoring, adulterous husband, Richard Randolph of Bizarre, get his just due, to others who felt that "God himself would think twice before dooming one of his quality!" He was accused of feloniously murdering a child said to have been his and his sister-in-law's, Nancy Randolph.

Inside, the county justices and the attorneys waited.

The twenty-three-year-old prisoner entered the courtroom with the sheriff, walking the gauntlet of angry citizens and well-wishers. He exuded the description of having "great personal beauty," of being a "character out of a Roman novel." With flashing dark eyes and tawny hair pulled back with a ribbon, he wore buckled shoes, cotton stockings, knee breeches, waistcoat, and coat. Of his legal counsel, only the well-dressed Alexander Campbell, precise and somber, appeared to be an appropriate associate. John Marshall, with dark, penetrating eyes, wore baggy breeches and a foulard that was slightly askew. "Old Pat" was dressed in dark countryman's breeches and coat, with tiny spectacles perched on his nose. He thoroughly enjoyed the adulation and reverence of the spectators and was always a crowd-pleaser.

∽

Dick Randolph's brother, Jack Randolph, sat on the front row. Two handsome women sat with him. Judith Randolph, Dick's wife, in the middle trimester of pregnancy, had been described as "a beautiful woman . . . who transported" her suitor with rapture. Her younger sister, Nancy, sat with her. Their brother, Tom Randolph, sat with his wife, Martha, across the courtroom, glaring at Dick with hatred.

The long months of vicious gossip, speculation, and accusation would end soon with the determination whether Dick, and possibly Nancy, would be tried later before a jury. The minutes of this proceeding would not be recorded; the order book would indicate only whether the prisoner was found guilty and would stand trial or be released.

∽

The Commonwealth opened with a deposition from Carter Page of The Fork plantation, the husband of Mary Cary Page, Judith and Nancy's aunt.

He had seen Miss Nancy and Mr. Randolph together frequently, had seen them kissing at Bizarre. The previous May, he noticed an increase in her size and wondered if she were pregnant, but he knew of no criminal act between the two. They did not try to conceal their affection for each other, and there was no other reason to believe that she was pregnant.

∽

Martha Jefferson Randolph, the daughter of Thomas Jefferson, President Washington's secretary of state, was called. She was poised and at ease. In response to a justice's question, Martha explained that around September 12, at Mrs. Richard Randolph's request, she had suggested a remedy for Miss Nancy's colic.

"I recommended gum guaiacum, an excellent remedy for the colic, but cautioned that it could also cause an abortion."

Later, Miss Nancy's aunt, Mrs. Page, requested some of the medicine for her niece. She sent some a few days later. One of the justices asked whether she believed that Miss Nancy was pregnant.

"I suspected that she was."

"Did you send enough to cause an abortion?" Henry asked.

"Yes, but I know of cases where even more has been given to pregnant women without harm," she answered.

❧

Mary Cary Page, the sisters' "Aunt Polly," considered herself the family matriarch, although she was only twenty-six years old. Her father, Archibald Cary, and Patrick Henry were political enemies and Cary had once threatened to "thrust a dagger" through Henry's heart.

On a visit to Bizarre, she testified, Mrs. Randolph had told her that Mr. Randolph and Miss Nancy were company only for themselves, but that he was generally out on his plantation and her sister was upstairs in her room. But Mrs. Page's suspicions were aroused when she noticed how fond Mr. Randolph and Miss Nancy were of each other. After Miss Nancy's shape changed, and she began to complain of disorders, she refused to undress and go to bed in her aunt's presence. Suspicious of her niece's condition and anxious to learn more, Aunt Polly peeked through a crack in the locked door and observed that Miss Nancy was undressed and appeared to be pregnant. Later, when she heard gossip that Miss Nancy had been delivered of a child, she went to Bizarre and asked to examine her in order to contradict the report. Miss Nancy refused, saying that if her denial were not enough, she would give no further satisfaction.

Patrick Henry relished the opportunity to cross-examine Archibald Cary's daughter and discredit her testimony.

He asked whether Miss Nancy had ever undressed for bed in her presence. Mrs. Page replied no, admitting that her refusal was not unusual.

"Your purpose in going to the door and eavesdropping on your niece's conversation was only one of concern?" he asked with a skeptical but deferential smile.

"Yes."

"And you peeped through the crack, also, to observe?"

"Yes."

Seizing his opportunity, Henry asked coyly, "And pray, madam, which eye did you peep with?"

The question infuriated the witness and before she could reply, Henry turned to his audience in the courtroom and thundered "Great God, deliver us from eavesdroppers."

Spectators roared with laughter. The sentry in the tree by the window passed the remarks down to Henry's audience outside the courtroom. Their hero had not lost his touch. And the witness's testimony had been discredited as being frivolous.

Randolph Harrison was careful and deliberate in his testimony.

"Yes," he replied, "I had observed improprieties between Mr. Randolph and Miss Nancy but had too high an opinion of them to be suspicious."

He described the Randolphs' visit to his home, Glentivar. He met them outside of his home and handed the ladies out of the carriage. Miss Nancy had her great coat buttoned around her, and he observed no sign of pregnancy. She complained of not feeling well and lay down on the bed and after dinner retired to her room upstairs. After supper, Mrs. Harrison and Mrs. Judith Randolph went up to check on her; she was still ill but told her sister she had taken essence of peppermint for colic.

During the night, Mr. Harrison and his wife were awakened by loud screams and a servant came to their door to ask for laudanum for Miss Nancy. Mrs. Harrison went upstairs to see Miss Nancy and, finding she was better, returned shortly. Later, they heard steps on the stairs and assumed it was Mr. Randolph and thought he had sent for a physician. Servants had gone up and down the stairs several times.

The next day, he and Mr. Randolph went in to lay a fire in her room. Miss Nancy was in bed and very pale. There was a disagreeable odor in the room. After their guests left on Saturday, Mr. and Mrs. Harrison were told by a Negro woman that Miss Nancy had miscarried. Six or seven weeks later, he investigated a report that a birth had been deposited on a pile of shingles. He found the shingle and observed that it had been stained.

Henry asked whether the disagreeable odor was one that would be attributed to childbearing. The witness imputed it to a cause totally different. The ladies' behavior later was the same as before, he told Henry. On a later visit to Bizarre, everything seemed as usual, except that Mr. Randolph appeared somewhat "crusty."

❧

Mary Harrison was called next. After months of Judith's denials and expressions of misery, she was sympathetic to her friend. Her testimony was the same as her husband's until after dinner, when she went upstairs. Miss Nancy seemed unwell and her sister told her to take her gum guaiacum. Mrs. Randolph went to bed and Mrs. Harrison came downstairs. When she went upstairs after the screams, Mrs. Harrison found Mrs. Randolph sitting up in bed with a candle burning and said that her sister must have the hysterics.

"I went to the door but found it fastened by a bolt. Then I recalled that the catch was broken and the door would not remain closed without being fastened. I knocked and Mr. Randolph opened the door at once. He asked me not to bring the candle in; Miss Nancy had taken laudanum, was in great pain, and the light hurt her eyes. I put the candle down and went into her room. Miss Nancy, her seven-year-old sister, Virginia, and a Negro girl about fifteen were in the room. I stayed for a while but Miss Nancy seemed better and I left."

The next day, she found blood on the pillowcase and on the stairs. The sheets and bed quilt were gone. Miss Nancy was in bed, very pale, with blankets drawn up close. After her guests' departure, Mrs. Harrison found an attempt had been made to wash the bed but she had to remove the feathers to wash the ticking.

She noticed no resentment or alarm in Mrs. Randolph that might be expected if her sister had had a child and she suspected her husband was the father. She was uneasy only because her sister was sick.

A midwife testified of examining the bed and finding appearances of a possible birth or abortion. She conceded, when questioned by Henry that another problem could have the same effect.

∾

Mrs. Brett Randolph testified that, although she had never noticed any ill will between the sisters, Mr. Randolph was very attentive to Miss Nancy, more so than to Mrs. Randolph. On the visit to the Harrisons' home, Miss Nancy wore a close gown without any attempt to conceal her shape. Mrs. Randolph thought she was large enough to admit the possibility of a pregnancy. When she saw Miss Nancy next, her size was diminished. Ill health may have produced the change.

∾

Archibald Randolph, Mary Harrison's brother, told the justices that about eighteen months earlier he had entertained suspicions that Mr. Randolph and Miss Nancy were too fond of each other. Before this event happened he had relinquished those suspicions. He had not noticed any increase in her size at the Harrisons' home. She seemed weak and asked for his help to go upstairs. He noticed a disagreeable odor but had no suspicion of it until Mr. Peyton Harrison, Randolph Harrison's brother, told him that she had had a child or had miscarried.

Peyton Harrison informed the court that he too had perceived a fondness between Miss Nancy and Mr. Randolph. Henry asked why he would repeat slaves' gossip of such a matter. Mr. Harrison replied that, as a friend, he felt it was his duty to pass the information on to Mr. Archy.

Jack Randolph testified on behalf of his brother. Spectators noted the lack of similarity in their looks. Now almost twenty years old, he had flaxen hair, was tall, thin almost to the point of emaciation, and beardless. His voice was high and squeaky but his elocution was superb. His brother, Theodorick, now deceased, had told Jack of his engagement to Miss Nancy, while Jack was studying in Philadelphia. His brother and sister-in-law had told him that Miss Nancy was in low spirits after his brother's death.

"The most perfect harmony existed in the family, and I often observed how much fonder Mrs. Randolph was of Miss Nancy than of her other relations. That fondness had increased."

Jack was with her a lot, and observed that she never wore stays and continued to dress in her usual manner. He attributed her ill health to an obstruction. He sat in the room with her at the Harrisons' home and noticed the disagreeable odor but did not detect it on the way home in the carriage.

Brett Harrison visited at Bizarre without ceremony, saw perfect harmony between the family members, and found no reason to suspect a pregnancy or criminal act.

Testimony in Dick's hearing ended. The justices accepted the testimony in Dick's hearing as Nancy's also.

Except for one significant addition.

Judith Randolph, because she could not testify for her husband, gave a deposition for her sister that was designed to exonerate her husband. The decision was hers, and hers alone, and she committed perjury.

She was awake the entire night, she said, because of her sister's illness. Just before Mrs. Harrison came upstairs, Judith left Miss Nancy's room and awakened her husband. She asked him to drop some laudanum for her sister. He was reluctant, but he went in to her sister.

She maintained that a child could not have been taken out of the room without her knowledge, and she was confident that no such thing happened. Her husband did not go downstairs until after daybreak.

⚮

John Marshall later prepared the detailed notes of evidence that outlined the basis for the defense, explaining the circumstances in the foregoing testimony, "examining them without favor or prejudice."

He listed five areas of concern: the fondness of Mr. Randolph and Miss Nancy for each other; the appearance of pregnancy; the request for gum guaiacum, knowing it to be a medicine to produce abortion; the events at Mr. Harrison's; and Miss Nancy's refusal to comply with the request of Mrs. Page for an examination.

Mr. Randolph's and Miss Nancy's fondness for each other was due to her special circumstances. Having grown up in ease and indulgence, with every wish granted, she had been left with no home, few possessions, and relatives who had little patience. His brother, her fiancé, had died, after which he and his wife had extended to her their home's hospitality. His special attention was appropriate and they would have concealed their feelings for each other if they had been guilty. Mrs. Randolph was present and never found their actions inappropriate.

⚮

The small increase in Miss Nancy's size could be attributed to several causes. When the Pages noticed this increase in May, Miss Nancy, if pregnant, would have been in the third or fourth month; a pregnancy would not have been noticeable until then. By the first of October, she would have been about eight or nine months and ready to deliver.

Although Mrs. Brett Randolph suspected Miss Nancy was pregnant in September, she did not mention an increase in size. Nor did Mr. and Mrs. Page, who saw her at the same time. Mr. and Mrs. Brett Randolph saw Miss Nancy frequently, and although Mrs. Randolph noticed she was larger, she agreed that there could be another reason.

Mr. John Randolph found no reason for suspicion, nor did Mr. Archy Randolph.

If she had been close to a delivery, it would have been apparent to everyone.

Mr. Randolph Harrison, who helped her out of the carriage, denied that she had any appearance of pregnancy.

The increase in size first noticed in May must have been caused by an ailment that, unlike a pregnancy, would not cause continual growth.

❧

Gum guaiacum is a medicine used not only to cause abortion but also to remove obstruction. If Miss Nancy were near delivery, the use of this drug would have been unnecessary; she would have sought abortion earlier in the pregnancy and taken the drug at home without fear of discovery.

The illness at the Harrisons' could have been from either cause. There was no attempt to conceal the pain. Mr. Randolph was in the room at the request of his wife and his request not to bring a candle into the room was natural for a person who had taken laudanum.

The blood and the appearance of the bed and covers were due to another cause and aroused no suspicion until a servant reported a miscarriage. The servants apparently were aware of the suspicions, and anything unusual would have seemed to be proof. No one would have placed a birth on a pile of shingles.

Mrs. Randolph had no apprehension except for her sister's health. Miss Nancy immediately resumed her horseback riding when she returned to Bizarre. There was the most perfect family harmony.

❧

Miss Nancy has reason to regret her refusal to allow Mrs. Page's examination. Any innocent person may have refused.

Although there is some reason for suspicion, even Miss Nancy's enemies must admit that every circumstance can be explained without imputing her guilt.

"Candor will not condemn or exclude from society a person who may only be unfortunate," concluded Marshall.

❧

The gentlemen justices ruled:

"It is the opinion of the court that the said Richard Randolph is not guilty of the felony wherewith he stands charged and that he is discharged out of custody and may go hence . . ."

Dick Randolph was detained at the courthouse for two more days; the other Randolphs of Bizarre left. Judith was distraught with humiliation at the public exposure, while Nancy attributed the cries of adulation as Patrick Henry left the courthouse to shouts of joy for Dick's freedom, "expressed in shouts of exultation." The noise shut out the sisters' quarreling voices to everyone but Jack, who rode postilion as he and his cousin Robert Banister accompanied them.

On April 30, 1793, Dick Randolph gave Patrick Henry a note for £140 pounds, due May 30, 1793. Henry assigned the note to William Andrew, who later sued and won judgment with costs and interest, on July 28, 1794.

Martha Randolph wrote her father, Thomas Jefferson, who was in Philadelphia, "They have been tried and acquitted, tho their lawers [sic] gained more honour by it than they did."

Cumberland Court April 25th 1793 qr sesn

The Court is adjourned untill Court in Course. The minutes of the proceeding being read were signed.

Benjamin Wilson

At a court held for Cumberland county the twenty ninth day of April one thousand seven hundred and ninety three for the examination of Richard Randolph who stands committed and charged with feloniously murdering a child said to be born of Nancy Randolph. — Present

> Mayo Carrington, Thomas Nash, William Macon
> Nilson Patteson, John Holman, Ben Allin
> Joseph Carrington, Henry Skipwith, Joseph
> Michaux, Anderson Cook, Cary Harrison   } Gentlemen Justices
> Walter Warfield, Benjamin Wilson Codrington
> Carrington, Archer Allen & Nath Carrington

The Court being thus constituted the prisoner was led to the bar in custody of the sheriff to whose care by he was before committed, for the felony aforesaid and being charged with the same denied the fact, Whereupon sundry witnesses were sworn and examined touching the premises and the prisoner heard in his defence. On consideration whereof and of the circumstances relating to this fact, it is the opinion of the Court that the said Richard is not guilty of the felony where with he stands charged and that he be discharged out of custody and go hence thereof without day. — Signed.

Joseph Carrington.

County Court Order Book 1792 - 97

A Copy-

Teste:

Carol O. Henshaw, Deputy Clerk,
Circuit Court, Cumberland County, Virginia.

Court Order, April 29, 1793, Cumberland County, VA
Order Book 18, 1792-1797

1787

O n a warm, sunny day in late June, two men rode westerly from Richmond through lush countryside. One was young and fashionably dressed, while the older man was clad simply. They turned onto the lane leading to Tuckahoe plantation, where tall cedar trees flanked the mile-long drive from the whitewashed gates to the brick-and-frame mansion. It had been built on a bluff, high on the north side of the James River.

The older man, Dr. Thomas Currie, came for a professional visit to the plantation's mistress, Ann Cary Randolph. The younger man, Peter Randolph of Chatsworth, came to "storm Miss Judah's (Judith's) citadel," to court a Randolph daughter. At two in the afternoon, they reached Tuckahoe where Judith was "doing the honors of the table."

"Miss J's beauty was in its meridian splendor . . . I was transported with rapture," Peter later described the visit to a friend. "I sat down to dine but could scarcely swallow a mouthful . . . my hand trembled, my heart palpitated." Later, Judith played the harpsichord and Peter found the "musick . . . inspired by some deity."

Judith Randolph would have the same effect on other men throughout her life.

With great distances between plantations and slow travel, guests came for days and sometimes weeks. Peter, a Randolph cousin, planned a three-day stay, for by then they would have seen all of his clothes.

He arrived in a "genteel riding coat, white waistcoat, nankeen breeches, white stockings and half boots," with a red coat, black silk breeches, and an "elegant dimmity waistcoat" in his wardrobe. Peter was a dandy.

⸎

Plantation mistress Ann Cary Randolph had come to Tuckahoe as a beautiful, spirited, and articulate girl when she married Colonel Thomas Mann Randolph in 1761. By 1786, they had ten living children. There were two older daughters, Mary and Elizabeth, who were already married and two older sons, Tom and William. Judith was the oldest daughter at home; Nancy was twenty-two months younger. The other children were Harriet, Jane, John, and Virginia, the youngest.

Judith was a dark, sultry beauty, with mood swings, while Nancy was sunny and athletic. Her long, dark hair framed her face with large expressive eyes. She raced her brothers and sisters on horseback over Tuckahoe's vast acreage along the river. Women of the time were often fearless and skillful riders.

But few women studied away from home. Judith complained to her second cousin Martha Jefferson about the lack of educational opportunities for women in Virginia, particularly at Tuckahoe because the plantation tutor was in Scotland with her two brothers. She envied Martha, who studied at a Catholic abbey in France. Martha lived in Paris while her father, Thomas Jefferson, served as U.S. minister to France. In Virginia, daughters studied literature, French, and rudimentary arithmetic, taught by a tutor. Instructors came to teach ballroom dancing; musicians gave pianoforte and harpsichord lessons. Their mothers taught needlework and social etiquette. They were expected to learn the skills of proficient plantation mistresses: taking care of the sick, both family and slaves, keeping plantation books, and maintaining contact with others through letter writing.

Women married early with only a brief period between childhood and marriage to enjoy balls, parties, and courtship. Southern men expected their wives to be skillful in home management, gracious in conversation, decorous with men outside of the family, and productive in bed. After her marriage, Ann showed remarkable proficiency in all these skills. She was a gracious and tireless hostess to the many guests invited to Tuckahoe. In 1782, the Marquis de Chastellux, who had served with the French during the Revolution and published a book on his travels in America, wrote of his visit to Tuckahoe and its prodigal hospitality.

Sons studied geography, mathematics, science, and philosophy. Most sons attended the College of William and Mary in Williamsburg, but Colonel Randolph sent Tom and William, accompanied by their tutor, Thomas Elder, to the University of Edinburgh in Scotland in 1784. When Elder returned, he reported that William preferred people, and a social life, to academia. Tom, Elder said, was a scholar and a gentleman. After William went to London on a spending spree, the Colonel, who had mortgaged one of his plantations, Varina, to pay for their education, promptly ordered William home. Tom stayed on in Edinburgh and formed a close friendship with John Leslie, a mathematician and alumnus of St. Andrew's University.

❧

Tall green oaks shaded the Tuckahoe manor house. A boxwood maze enclosed gardens of verbena, marigolds, and poppies. The house had north and south wings connected by an elongated salon that separated the two sections with arched doorways. There was a glittering chandelier, a spinet, harpsichord, chairs, and four sofas. Family portraits decorated the walls. Furniture, china, and plate had been ordered from France and England. A frieze with flowing flowers and vines on the Georgian paneling on the north stair was the only example of such carving in Virginia. The rooms were paneled in walnut and pine. A guest once described a room as "an apartment all done in velvet and gold and a bed decorated like a feast day." A library featured books such as *Tom Jones,* a titillating novel by Henry Fielding, and *Pamela, Virtue Unrewarded* and *Clarissa Harlowe,* both inspirational epistolary works of Samuel Richardson.

Paired frame buildings flanked the mansion. One, the schoolhouse, was where Thomas Jefferson had studied as a small boy when his family lived with the Randolphs. The other building was the plantation office. Colonel Randolph had built elaborate stables along the rear, and one was especially equipped for his favorite horse, a dappled grey named Shakespeare; his groom lived there as well. The outdoor kitchen was behind the house and the lane used for rushing food from the fireplace there to the dining room inside was referred to as "battercake alley."

Tuckahoe's prosperity came from the tobacco, produced by slaves, that was shipped to England. There tobacco merchants arranged for its sale. The proceeds, after the exorbitant fees charged for service and commissions, were used to purchase silk gowns, shoes, and nankeen breeches for family members, furnishings for the mansion, and beautiful horses for the Colonel. The horses were for his use, for his guests, and were given as gifts to his children.

The daughters' every wish was gratified as they matured into womanhood. Musicians came in to play at the dances that Judith, her best friend and cousin, Mary Randolph of Dungeness, and others led up together. Nancy, in early adolescence, read her books, rode her horse, and watched, awaiting her turn in the social sphere.

The plantation had no incursions from the British during the Revolutionary War. Virginians whose homes had been burned and slaves stolen rancorously noted that Tuckahoe was spared because of the Colonel's earlier entertainment of British Major-General John Phillips and General Lord Charles Cornwallis.

Tuckahoe even had its resident ghost, a young woman in white seen sobbing and fleeing along the east walk. She was said to be Mary Randolph, one of the Colonel's aunts. She had fallen in love with the Dungeness overseer, but because of the difference in their social status, their romance was forbidden. They ran away and were married. When they were found on Elk Island, above Tuckahoe, Mary was brought back home. Two stories were told about her. One said she was forced to marry a minister much older than she, and the ghost was Mary fleeing from her elderly bridegroom. The other story said she was a licentious young woman and was found in flagrante delecto with the Reverend James Keith. He was banished by the Anglican Church to a distant parish. Mary followed him and they were married. After the birth of several children, she heard a rumor that her first husband was alive and searching for her. She became so fearful that her children would be labeled bastards that she lost her mind. Her daughter married Thomas Marshall, and one of their sons, John Marshall, became chief justice of the United States. Thus, the chief justice was the grandson of an insane woman.

MATOAX AND BIZARRE

In the spring of 1787, Frances Tucker brooded over her pregnancy, the seventh since her marriage to St. George Tucker in 1778. She

MJ 1

BIZARRE

NEAR HERE IS THE SITE OF BIZARRE, OWNED IN 1742 BY RICHARD RAN- DOLPH OF CURLES. IN 1781, HIS GRAND- SON, JOHN RANDOLPH OF ROANOKE, TOOK REFUGE AT BIZARRE WITH HIS MOTHER ON ACCOUNT OF ARNOLD'S INVASION. JOHN RANDOLPH LIVED HERE UNTIL 1810, WHEN HE MOVED TO ROANOKE IN CHARLOTTE COUNTY.

CONSERVATION & DEVELOP-   MENT COMMISSION 1933

Bizarre Historical Marker, Farmville, VA.
Virginia Department of Historic Resources

lashed out at Tucker in a letter, blaming him for her predicament. The only methods of birth control—abstinence and coitus interruptus, both requiring his cooperation—were practices that she never suggested. When he received her letter, he returned to Matoax to assuage her concerns. After his departure, Frances was reconciled to the pregnancy, promising to "conceal every circumstance that might trouble you."

She shouldered heavy responsibilities exacerbated by his frequent absences; his legal work required frequent travel. Frances supervised the care of four young children—Fanny, Harry, Tudor, and Beverley— at home. Her sons by her first marriage, to John Randolph—Dick (Richard), Theo (Theodorick), and Jack (John)—were away at school. She was also responsible for plantation operations at Roanoke, Matoax, and Bizarre, left by John Randolph to his children. Each location had its overseer, but Frances was manager.

Frances, the daughter of Theodorick Bland of Cawsons, a descendant of William Randolph I of Turkey Island, was considered a woman of superior personal attractions and thought to be "exalted in strength of intellect." Her brother, Dr. Theodorick Bland, thought her voice was so lovely that she could "charm a bird out of a tree."

In 1769 she married John Randolph of Matoax, also descended from William Randolph I, and both were descended from Pocahontas. John built their home on a grassy knoll overlooking the Appomattox River, near Petersburg. The spacious manor house, which he called Matoax after Pocahontas's tribal name, was flanked by beautiful groves and was noted for its extensive library. Frances had three sons, and a daughter who died, before her husband died in 1775, leaving her a widow at age twenty-three. She returned home often to Cawsons and visited friends on other plantations. While in Williamsburg, the tall, dark, statuesque widow met St. George Tucker, from Bermuda, who had gone into law practice in Virginia. Her good looks, intelligence, and refined manners captivated him. After their marriage in 1778, Tucker moved to Matoax and bonded quickly with his wife's sons. Their first child, Fanny, was born in 1779 and Harry was born in 1780. A young orphan, Maria Rind, lived with them to help with the younger children.

In early January 1781, the Tuckers learned of Benedict Arnold's landing with British troops at Westover and their march to Richmond.

Matoax would be in Arnold's path and Tucker acted quickly to remove his family out of harm's way by taking them to Bizarre, the Randolph plantation in Cumberland and Prince Edward counties. Frances, with week-old Harry, Maria Rind, and little Fanny, rode in the family chariot, driven by Syphax. Her three sons, accompanied by the slave Essex, traveled on horseback; Tucker was outrider. After the family was settled at Bizarre, Tucker joined volunteers commanded by General Robert Lawson and left to fight the British.

On a march through the area, the British had destroyed everything they could not carry away with them, and Frances, still recuperating from Harry's birth, faced a daunting situation. She had to arrange for food and clothing for both her family and the slaves. Then she faced another crisis.

Baron von Steuben, fighting with the Americans, was routed from Point of Fork in Fluvanna County and planned to retreat to Prince Edward. General Lawson and his volunteers refused to join in retreat and St. George Tucker sent Frances an urgent message. Leave Bizarre.

"Lose no time . . . to remove yourself and our little ones out of the way."

She left by midnight that night, wearily packing for the forty-mile journey to Roanoke plantation in Charlotte County. A mare foaled ("folded," she wrote Tucker), the babies screamed, and seven-year-old Jack watched his mother as she hurriedly threw his father's valuable papers into a pillowcase and thrust his steel-hilted dagger into her stays. Jack asked why.

"My son," she replied, "your mother will never be insulted." Frances was fully prepared to protect her family and her honor.

At Roanoke, in a smoky two-room cabin, she tried to cope, supervising the slaves who had accompanied her, the nursing baby, a toddler, and Dick, Theo, and Jack. The three boys, without a tutor or male influence, ran wild.

"I wish I had a tutor to make me mind my books. I am such a perverse boy I want to play instead of read," Theo wrote Tucker.

Frances Tucker's letters to her husband contained assurances of her devotion such as "My lips have not been touched since yours blessed them."

St. George Tucker, later attached to troops led by Lafayette, wrote her of the fifth anniversary celebration of the Declaration of Independence in Williamsburg. The Marquis de Lafayette hosted an officers' dinner that was followed by a feu de joie and a military review. Later, recuperating from a fever, Lafayette heard that Washington had arrived. Despite the fever, Lafayette left his bed, mounted his horse, and raced to greet his friend and commander.

"He embraced General Washington with an ardor not easily described," Tucker wrote Frances of Lafayette's greeting.

When Tucker learned that the British would be under siege at Yorktown and the danger was past, he allowed his family to leave Roanoke.

"We were never so glad as when we got your letter to return to Bizarre," Theo reported.

❧

Tucker spoke French fluently and served as an interpreter between the French and Continental officers at Yorktown, and he, with his brigade, witnessed the surrender ceremony. Cornwallis did not appear; he sent a message that he was ill. As the British band played "The World Turned Upside Down," the French and American troops faced each other in long lines. The British marched between them, their eyes turned toward the French. They refused to acknowledge surrendering to the Americans. Incensed, Lafayette ordered the drum major to strike up "Yankee Doodle." The lively music so startled the British troops that they involuntarily looked to the Americans.

❧

The family was reunited at Matoax. With the courts open again, Tucker returned to his law practice and travel, but he was home often enough that Frances found herself pregnant again. After another son, Tudor, was born in 1782, the Tuckers sent Dick, Theo, and Jack to Walker Maury's school in Orange County. Maury was unctuous and servile to the parents but abused and humiliated his pupils. He routinely lashed Jack every Monday. The beatings, reported by Dick, appalled his parents, who sent Jack to visit Tucker's family in Bermuda.

Frances's problems did not abate with Jack away. She gave birth to another son, Beverley, and while she was recuperating in 1784, Theo ran away from Maury's school, now in Williamsburg. Benjamin

Harrison, of a nearby Tidewater plantation, had given Theo cash to take the stage to Frances's sister in Petersburg. Maury's report to the family did not mention his harsh treatment, only that Theo had been "assuming airs." Elizabeth Banister persuaded Theo to return, but the situation deteriorated. Maury reported that Theo had been disobedient since his return.

In 1785, Tucker, to give Frances a respite, took the entire family and a favorite riding horse for a visit with his parents in Bermuda. The visit was a pleasant interlude, but the travel arrangements, particularly on the return, weakened Frances, frail with another pregnancy. Passengers on the ship were responsible for food and quarters for themselves and their servants, and oversight of these arrangements fell on her. According to Jack, their "return on a long and boisterous voyage in a miserable sloop" depleted her strength. Sometime after their return home, her baby died at birth.

Jack and Theo returned to Maury's school, and Dick entered the College of William and Mary.

Tucker took his wife to New York City for medical treatment and they were away during July and August 1786. While in the North, Tucker visited New Jersey College (now Princeton University) to check its suitability for his stepsons' enrollment. When they returned home, they found that Theo had run away again and this time he refused to return. John Banister reported that "Maury made a violent attack upon Theo, who repelled him." Maury had then called in an usher to assist in the beating. According to Jack later, "the shocking barbarity of Maury towards my brother Theodorick drove him away from school." Frances promptly removed Jack from Maury's too and hired a tutor to operate a small school at Matoax.

⊰≫

Soon, Tucker was off again, to Annapolis, Maryland. He, James Madison, and Edmund Randolph were Virginia delegates to the Annapolis Convention, mandated to recommend the adoption and addition of commercial guidelines to the Articles of Confederation. The Articles had been submitted to the thirteen states in November 1777 for ratification, which did not take place until 1781. The reluctance in ratification indicated their inadequacy. John Adams referred to them as a "rope of sand," and George Washington found them "wanting energy."

By September 1786, the Annapolis Convention, unable to formulate satisfactory revisions, recommended a general convention to study comprehensive amendments.

Jack and Theo Randolph entered New Jersey College in March 1787. George Wythe, Dick Randolph's law professor at William and Mary, had been named chancellor of Virginia. He moved to Richmond, and freed his slaves. Dick admired the celebrated Wythe, but the Tuckers were unable to persuade him to go to Richmond to continue his law studies. He preferred Williamsburg, informing his mother that he needed to be still more on guard with respect to his morals. Temptation won out, however, for he later told of the lady who received him in bed at Mr. Wythe's home. When Frances heard of his association with "dissolute companions," she sent him North, over his protests. He grumbled to his mother about his dislike of the North, where people did not even know their neighbors' names.

Frances hoped that life would be easier, with her sons away, after she hired John Coalter, a young man from Augusta County, as a tutor for the younger children.

Her troubles continued, however, as yet another pregnancy advanced. After a serious illness in October, she had a nasty fall in November, injuring her foot, and the injury did not heal. Dr. Bland treated his sister's injury initially, then sent to Petersburg for advice and even wrote Dr. McClurg in Richmond, requesting help. The remedy prescribed was a "pediluvium, if she could stand it." This was a special footbath of hot water and brandy in which rosemary or some other aromatic herbs had been boiled.

Her situation was exacerbated later when a Bizarre slave appeared at the door. He had run away to get to Frances and tell her of the extreme and repeated cruelty of the overseer to the plantation slaves. This overseer had driven off many of the more valuable slaves who refused to accept his treatment. Although Frances was expecting Tucker's return home, she did not hesitate. She wrote him a letter describing the situation and left immediately for Bizarre, "where anarchy reigns." She could no longer leave "the miserable creatures a prey to the worst part of mankind." She had to mitigate, as much as she could, "the pangs of their cruel situation."

Thomas Jefferson 1743-1826,
Library of Virginia

Ending her letter with "adieu my best beloved till I have the happiness of embracing you again . . . ," she set out in cruel wintry weather over terrible roads on her mission. There is no record of what was accomplished at Bizarre, but she returned to Matoax a critically ill woman. Her last letter asked her husband not to return home early on her account, but that he "wait till court rises."

In mid-December, she went into labor and a daughter was born. Tucker, optimistic that she would regain her health, wrote her sons, his "ever dear boys," of their sister, "born last evening." He advised them not to come home for Christmas in such terrible weather. Within a few days, however, his optimism gone, he wrote to Dr. Witherspoon, saying his wife was worse and asking that her sons be sent home immediately.

"We had gone to New York to spend a little money at Christmas, when a letter arrived, summoning us home to our mother's deathbed," Jack wrote.

MONTICELLO AND PARIS

While Martha Jefferson studied at the Abbaie Royale in Paris in 1787, she awaited the arrival of her younger sister, Mary, from America, whom she had not seen for nearly three years. Martha lived at the convent six days a week and returned home on Sunday. She wore a red uniform with muslin cuffs and a tucker. Fellow students called her "Jeffy." In addition to her regular studies, Jefferson had arranged for lessons on the harpsichord and art classes. Tall and angular like her father, she had reddish brown hair, blue eyes, and a fair complexion. Although not a beauty, Martha was described by Nabby Adams, John Adams's daughter, as a "sweet girl, delicacy and sensitivity are read in every feature."

❧

Thomas Jefferson was the son of Virginia aristocrat Jane Randolph and a Welshman, Peter Jefferson, a surveyor. Instead of family inheritance, Peter's property came from a royal land grant of two thousand acres in Albemarle County on the Rivanna River. Thomas's father died when he was fourteen, and after boarding school, he entered the College of William and Mary in 1760. He was elected to the House of Burgesses in 1769. Jefferson fell in love with Martha Wayles Skelton, and they were married on New Year's Day 1772. They lived in a one-room cabin at Monticello while Jefferson planned and began construction of their Palladian home. Her first child, Martha, was born the next September.

Jefferson entered politics through his writing, an illegal essay outlining the colonists' grievances, "A Summary View of the Rights of British America." He served in the Continental Congress in 1775 and wrote both the state constitution for Virginia and the Declaration of Independence before resigning his seat and returning to Monticello.

His wife, tiny and frail, was not suited for the rigorous demands of child-bearing. She lost two sons and one daughter before giving birth to her fifth child, Mary, who survived.

Jefferson succeeded Patrick Henry as Virginia's governor. In early 1782, after the British surrender at Yorktown, he isolated himself at Monticello to await his wife's next confinement. Chastellux visited him in April and wrote of Jefferson's personality, a mixture of aloofness and charisma. At first, he found Jefferson serious and cold, then a "spark of electricity" passed between the two, and they felt the days they were together passed as if in minutes.

A daughter, Lucy Elizabeth, was born to Martha on May 8, 1782, and she never recovered. Not a religious man, Jefferson had the inscription "If in the House of Hades, men forget their dead, Yet will I even there remember my dear companion" carved on her headstone in Greek.

∽

Deaths among women and infants in the South were much higher than in the North. Early marriages and frequent pregnancies depleted a woman's strength. Nursing a baby was usually a woman's only means of birth control. Sometimes it worked and sometimes it did not. If a mother nursed her baby, she might not become pregnant until it was weaned. If the baby died or the mother was unable or chose not to nurse, the pregnancies were closer together. If married at sixteen, a woman might have seven children by age thirty.

∽

After Jefferson's election by the General Assembly to Congress in June 1783, he took his eleven-year-old daughter Martha with him and enrolled her in a boarding school in Philadelphia. Jefferson and his eldest daughter forged a bond during their years together that neither his loves, her husband, or her children ever penetrated.

Jefferson's great opportunity to travel abroad came when he was appointed to join John Adams and Benjamin Franklin in Paris. They were authorized to negotiate treaties with the European countries. This would satisfy Jefferson's yearning to travel abroad, and be a life-changing experience for the little girl whose home was on an isolated mountain in Virginia. Martha and her father sailed on a new ship, the *Ceres,* on July 5, 1784. They arrived by channel boat at Le Havre and set out for Paris. They traveled, awed, through Rouen, where Joan of Arc had been tried and burned. At Nantes they climbed 365 steps to a church. Martha was overwhelmed by all that she saw, and she wrote home of the "pretty statues and windows of check glass of the most beautiful colors that form all kinds of figures." At St. Germain-en-lay, she was fascinated by the fourteen water wheels and the acres of ducts and pumps that formed the Machine de Marly. These raised the Seine River to reservoirs, supplying the Grandes Eaux at Versailles.

Finally, they reached Paris, the largest city she had ever seen, and Jefferson rented quarters on the Cul-de-Sac Taitbout. They found their American wardrobe ill-suited in this sophisticated city. Martha wrote that "we were obliged to send immediately for the stay maker, the mantilla maker, the milliner and even a shoemaker before I could go out." Usually docile with adults, Martha adamantly refused the services of a coiffeuse, a friseur, to tease her hair. She insisted on turning "my hair down, in spite of all they could say," thus avoiding a three-to-four-hour ordeal.

Jefferson became à la mode. He powdered his hair and ordered expensive clothes, including lace cuffs and ruffles, knee breeches and buckles, and even a sword. He rented a pianoforte and bought a fancy new chariot. Well read, personally attractive, and with beautiful manners, he became a sought-after bachelor. With Martha away at school for six days a week, he entertained lavishly and beyond his means for the salary he was paid. The Jeffersons became good friends with John and Abigail Adams, their daughter Nabby, and son John Quincy. The two women accompanied Jefferson to the Abbaie to visit Martha, who quickly adjusted to her environment and was soon more fluent in French than her father.

Both Jefferson and the Adams were equally shocked at the libertine behavior of the Parisian women. "Conjugal love has no existence among them," Jefferson wrote home. Half the children born in Paris were illegitimate, and so many were abandoned that special places in the city were set aside for their collection.

Jefferson had left both of his younger daughters with his wife's family, the Eppes. Both he and Martha were heartbroken when they received word, through Lafayette, in January 1785 that his youngest daughter, Lucy, had died. He wanted his other daughter, Mary, to come to France, but negotiations between him and the Eppes family would take two years.

A Monticello slave, James Hemings, had come with them to learn French cooking, and William Short, a young Virginia planter and politician, came to serve as Jefferson's secretary. Jefferson hired a French maître d'hotel, Petit, and a valet.

Benjamin Franklin, tired and ill, wanted to return home. And the British finally consented to receive a U.S. minister to the Court of St. James. Within weeks, Adams and Jefferson were separated in 1785, when Adams was appointed to England and Jefferson replaced Franklin as minister to France. Martha had parted reluctantly with her American friends, but now wrote them that she was very happy at school. Jefferson and Martha soon moved to more prestigious quarters on the Rue Napoleon on the Left Bank. Martha described it as being "very elegant, even for Paris, with an extensive garden court, outbuildings in the handsomest style."

Her father became the most popular foreign minister at court, "the plainest man in the room and the most destitute of ribands [sic], crosses and other insignia of rank . . . the most courted and attended to."

❦

In 1786, Jefferson entered into a romantic adventure that would surpass any other in his life. That summer, artist John Trumbull visited Jefferson in Paris to sketch and plan his magnificent painting "Signing of the Declaration of Independence," and to paint Jefferson's part in it. Knowing of his admiration of beautiful and unusual architecture, Trumbull persuaded Jefferson to visit the Halle Aux Bleds, Paris's new grain market. Here Trumbull introduced Jefferson to Richard and Maria Cosway, husband and wife artists from England. Maria was petite, blonde, and beautiful and, like Jefferson's deceased wife, played the harpsichord. She was years younger than her foppish husband; her mother, a widow without money, had arranged the marriage. It was believed that Maria despised her husband, who was cruel to her and was said to prefer boys to women. She painted landscapes and her husband painted miniatures. They had come to Paris because he had a painting assignment.

Jefferson, enthralled with this elfin girl-woman, acted as host and guide during the ensuing weeks. Most of the time the Jefferson and Maria were alone while her husband painted. Jefferson stopped writing and delegated much of his ministerial work to his secretary. Given the moral tone of Paris during the period, they most certainly became lovers. Biographer Fawn Brodie wrote that the insistence of writers to believe that Jefferson remained continent "is a curiosity, considering the letter exchange pertaining to Cosway's visits to Paris." Other biographers thought differently, saying there was no reason to think the relationship was anything but platonic or a superficial flirtation. But Dumas Malone, in his masterful work, wrote that Jefferson "fell deeply in love during that golden September."

Jefferson misled Martha about Maria and their time together. While strolling with Maria, he fell and injured his wrist; Martha explained the incident to others, saying he was on a ramble with a friend, and then left him to seek help.

When the Cosways left Paris, Jefferson and another friend accompanied them for a way in their carriage. After returning home, Jefferson wrote what would become one of the most compelling love letters in history, "A Dialogue Between my Head and my Heart." In more than four thousand words, it was written with passion and constraint, using opposition to each other. In the Dialogue, Head tells Heart that he is "the most incorrigible of all beings that ever sinned." Heart responds that "this is not the moment to upbraid my foibles, I am rent into fragments by the force of my grief." Head accuses Heart of imprudence in "placing affection on subjects you must soon lose." Heart responds, "when Heaven has taken from us some object of our love, how sweet it is to have a bosom wheron to recline our heads."

The letter began a remarkable correspondence that would last, intermittently, for forty years. More than one hundred years would pass before the family allowed copies of his letters and Maria's letters to him to be made public. Since all the letters were kept, Brodie felt that "this was one love affair he was clearly willing to share with history."

Jefferson, aware that his mail by post was often opened, sent this letter to London by Trumbull. Maria responded by promising to return to Paris in the summer of 1787. He replied, "I am always thinking of you," and she responded, in a cold, damp London winter, "Night thoughts, the pain of separation, when the imagination is well warmed up, one could cool off in a river."

≫

In January 1787, the Eppes family sent Mary to Paris. They used a ruse to get her on board the ship. Several children went aboard with her but left and the ship went to sea with only Mary aboard, accompanied by a fourteen-year-old-quadroon slave, Sally Hemings. Mary became so attached to the captain, Andrew Ramsey, that when he took her to John and Abigail Adams in London and left, she wept. Abigail wrote Jefferson of his daughter's arrival, and they looked forward with anticipation to seeing their friend again. He, however, was expecting Maria Cosway to arrive and sent Petit to pick up his daughter, citing the weight of ministerial business. Adams promptly wrote Jefferson of his disappointment that he had not come for his daughter.

Mary was a beautiful child, small-boned like her mother, with dark curly hair and large brown eyes. Her beauty and sweet disposition charmed everyone who knew her. Abigail took her shopping for new clothes, and the two formed such a strong bond that when Petit, who spoke no English, came, Mary sobbed again and clung to her American friend. Abigail insisted that Mary remain with them until she was willing to leave. Even then, their parting was painful. Mary had left the Eppes family, the only home she remembered, in Chesterfield County, Virginia, traveled to Norfolk, sailed across the Atlantic Ocean to England, visited with strangers until a strange man who spoke no English came for her, then sailed with him across the English channel to Paris to be reunited with a father and sister whom she did not remember. Mary Jefferson arrived on July 15, 1787, two weeks before her ninth birthday.

She became a boarding student at the Abbaie with Martha, who was six years older than she. Martha was not only a devoted sister, but she became Mary's best friend and surrogate mother. Although devoted to her family, Mary never achieved the degree of intimacy with her father that Martha had. She soon insisted on using the French version of Mary, and henceforth she was Maria.

Sally Hemings was reunited with her brother James and, because slavery was unlawful in France, Jefferson paid salaries to the two while they were in Paris.

Richard Cosway refused to visit Paris again, but Jefferson continued to urge Maria to return.

"Come and we will breakfast every day a l'Angloise, hie away to the desert, dine under the bowers of Marly, and forget they we are ever to part again."

The temptation was too great for Maria to resist; she slipped way and arrived in Paris without her husband. For the first few weeks, she and Jefferson visited Paris's parks and gardens, and Petit made discreet arrangements for intimate dinners together, repeating the idyll of the previous summer. Then Trumbull's news, that Richard Cosway was enraged by his wife's departure and suggested Jefferson scold Maria, ended their time alone. Jefferson tartly responded that he had not as yet invented a scolding machine, but Maria was frightened. She arranged their visits so that they were "surrounded by a numerous cortege" or else spent their time together in his home. When she came, his secretary, William Short, arranged to be away. They planned a final breakfast together, but when he arrived at her hostess's home, she had already left. She left a note for him, saying, "To bid you adieu once is sufficiently painful."

From London, Maria apologized for some failure on her part. "Perhaps I don't know how to go about it. I am perfectly sure 'twas my fault but my misfortune." The letters taken together suggest an obsession and fear of pregnancy. Brodie wrote of "some kind of failure in the act of love."

GOUVERNEUR MORRIS

Gouverneur Morris had served brilliantly in the American cause. An educated man, he worked in practical ways to champion freedom of religion and of the press and to fight the institution of slavery. He was born in 1752, graduated from college at age sixteen, and was admitted to the bar at age nineteen. In later years he developed great oratorical skills, and his diaries and letters attest to his gift as a writer.

Forced to make a choice between the colonists—with George Washington at the head of the Continental Army—and the British, Morris stood with the patriots. His mother and a half-brother remained loyal to England. His friendship with Washington had developed when he served in the Provincial Congress. Morris then served in the Continental Congress but was unable to serve in the military because of an injury. In 1766, boiling water tipped from a teakettle had scalded his arm and it withered, with extensive scar tissue. As a civilian, he worked with others on a revision of the supply system to alleviate the desperate situation in the army.

Gouverneur Morris was thirty-five years old in 1787, tall and striking in appearance, with blue eyes, brown hair, and a melodious voice. With otherwise excellent carriage, his most prominent feature was not an actual part of his body, but a peg leg. In 1780, he had been thrown from his carriage by runaway horses. His leg, caught in one of the wheels, was amputated by physicians. Efforts to adjust to an artificial leg were unsuccessful, but he wore the peg leg with great aplomb. The loss of his leg psychologically affected Morris for the rest of his life, but it did not diminish his popularity with women.

Gouverneur Morris served with Robert Morris, a friend but not a relative, seeking to extricate the country from economic collapse. They established a national bank to secure private resources to bolster public credit. He then drafted a plan for funding the public debt, called "the single most important state paper on public credit ever written prior to Alexander Hamilton's "First Report on Public Credit." Publication of this paper later impressed leaders of the need to reinforce the Articles of Confederation.

When the Constitutional Convention opened in Philadelphia on May 25, 1787, Gouverneur Morris was one of seven Pennsylvania delegates. He spoke 173 times, more than any other delegate except James Madison. He changed the Preamble to a more stately form, "We, the people of the United States, in order to form a more perfect union..." etc. Madison later wrote of Morris's genius.

"He added, what is too rare, a candid surrender of his opinion, when the lights of discussion satisfied him, that they had been too hastily formed, and a readiness to aid in making the best of measures in which he had been overruled.

"The finish given to the style and arrangement of the Constitution fairly belongs to Gouverneur Morris," Madison wrote.

The final document was signed on September 17, 1787. Congress issued a call for ratification, and the thirteen states scheduled conventions to debate whether to approve or disapprove the instrument.

Gouverneur Morris came to Richmond with Robert Morris in the fall of 1787. Having played such an important role in the formation of the Constitution, he was interested in the voting on its ratification. Moreover, Virginia was the biggest shipper of tobacco overseas, and he and his business partner, Robert Morris, hoped to arrange tobacco contracts between the growers and French business interests.

1788

Frances Tucker's Randolph sons were with her when she died on January 17. She was interred in the family cemetery and the inscription on her tombstone read:
"IHS Francescae Tucker Blandae conjugis St. Georgii Tucker. Qui desidero sit modus?" (How can one be moderate in mourning?)

Jack and Theo returned to school in the North and enrolled at Columbia College in New York City. Dick stayed in Virginia; he planned to go to Richmond to hear the ratification debates.

⚬

In June 1788, Richmond, the capital of Virginia, was astir with excitement as planters and their families arrived for two big events. One was the annual meeting of the Richmond Jockey Club, where, in addition to beautiful horses racing at the tracks, lovely women and handsome men would attend parties and glide across the floor at fancy balls. A far more serious occasion awaited the 170 delegates who would participate in the debates on the new Constitution. Among them were Colonel Thomas Mann Randolph and St. George Tucker.

Richmond, twenty miles east of Tuckahoe on the James River, became the capital of Virginia in 1780 when Thomas Jefferson, governor of Virginia at the time, moved the capital there from Williamsburg to escape British troops. In January 1781, however, British cavalry and infantrymen landed down river and, led by Benedict Arnold, marched to Richmond to ransack and plunder. Jefferson and other government officials escaped. He took his wife, newborn baby, and two daughters to safety at Tuckahoe.

In 1788, Richmond's population was around 2,500 with about 300 homes. Most of the homes were frame, the townspeople were trades-men, and merchants clustered around Richmond's seven hills. Several inns, such as the Indian Queen and Eagle Tavern, were frequented mostly by men. Stores such as Hollingsworth and Johnson and Com-pany, stocked dry goods. Wright Southgate offered "plain and fancy silks," brocades, camlets, and jewelry. Mrs. Gilbert's Coffee House, "where a body could meet a body," was popular.

Virginia's new capitol, high on Shockoe Hill and crowning the skyline, neared completion. Thomas Jefferson had commissioned the French architect Charles Clerisseau to draw plans based on a Roman temple, the Maison Carrée.

The ratification debates would be held in Academy Hall, the only building in Richmond large enough to hold the delegates and spec-tators. "The Old Church," St. John's, was over on Church Hill. Here Patrick Henry had given his fiery "Give me liberty or give me death" speech, and he was returning to Richmond to fight again. His oratory was eagerly awaited, as he opposed ratification. Among others inter-ested in the debates were Gouverneur Morris and Robert Morris, who brought his wife and daughter with him. Colonel Randolph brought his family, a momentous event for Judith.

Members of the Jockey Club sweated in the June heat as they drank and bet at the race tracks. The women sipped cool drinks in shaded rooms and played loo and whist. Mary Morris, Robert Morris's wife, excelled in these card games with the expertise learned in New York and Philadelphia salons.

❧

Younger women discussed ball gowns and headdresses. Under an open robe a woman wore a chemise, corset, petticoat, and a "bum roll" fastened to the inside edge of the back waistline of the un-der gown. The open robe was gathered to the waistline of the low, round-necked bodice. The front of the bodice, cut away at a sharp angle, was fastened to the corset. Sleeves were tight, long, and edged in short frills. A large folded handkerchief covered the shoulders, crossed the bosom, and was tied at the back. A wide ribbon or sash was worn around the natural waist and tied in a bow at the back. White and bright colors, such as orange, scarlet, emerald green, and bright blue were preferred. Shoes were low, with small heels, and were worn with white stockings.

A woman's hair was curled with the sides wide and full, and the back arranged in a long, full queue, looped up and tied or allowed to hang in a cluster of ringlets down the back. Outdoors, she wore a large-brimmed hat, trimmed with feathers or ribbons.

Young men were as careful in their attire as the women. Boys sometimes wore corsets until about ten years old to improve their carriage into the upright fashionable shape. The feet were always turned out, making an eighteenth-century gentleman stand firm and easy. Clothes were cut to give a trim and narrow line to the figure. The waistcoat, either fancy or plain, terminated a little below the natural waist. They wore knee breeches and skintight stockings with calf-length boots, usually white, enhancing the appearance of well-turned calves. Stockings were either white, colored, or striped. Shirts were worn with stock collars and had wrist frills. Wigs were worn powdered or unpowdered. A queue was usually turned up on itself and tied with a narrow black ribbon.

Wine and whiskey flowed at the parties and balls.

When the couples danced, the ladies' silks and brocades rustled and trailed behind them. They danced the minuet, gavottes that required precise, schooled movements, and reels with instructions from a dance master. Two to four musicians played the fiddle, oboe, trumpet, cello, or hammered dulcimer, along with the harpsichord or pianoforte.

⚯

Judith later recalled the joy of her teens, as she led up a dance, perhaps in Richmond, "with heart as light as air."

Then, into this mixture of pleasures and solemnity rode Richard Randolph of Matoax and Bizarre, resembling a "Roman god." He met his second cousin, beautiful Judith of Tuckahoe. With his good looks and erudition, he dazzled, and she, who had turned away other suitors, was impressed. She soon had another conquest. Other romances began in Richmond as well; Robert Morris's daughter met and later married John Marshall's brother.

At age nineteen, Dick had not completed his education and had financial problems that concerned his stepfather. He and his two brothers had inherited the plantations and slaves from their father. Unfortunately, everything was collateral for a pre-war debt owed to tobacco merchants Hanburys of London. Collection of the debt could not be enforced until the Constitution was ratified.

Many Virginians had a valid reason for opposing ratification. In addition to large debts incurred by the planters to the British tobacco merchants, there were other problems. Thirty percent of the taxpayers owned no land, thrusting a large tax burden on the landholders, especially planters with vast acreage and large numbers of slaves who, because they were considered personal property, incurred a tax for their owners. Bonds that had been sold were paid for with tax collections; bond speculation flourished. One writer to a newspaper complained that both the speculators and the British debt must be paid, and that "they have taken Virginia without the fere of a gun." Sheriffs confiscated land when they were unable to collect taxes and foreign financiers were reluctant to lend money because land security was doubtful. British merchants still exploited Virginia planters, extracting sizable profits as middlemen. Both the debtor and the creditor elements, those against ratification and those for it, were present as delegates began the ratification debates.

⤝

As the debates began, Patrick Henry led the opposition. His concern centered on the need for prior amendments, a bill of rights that many delegates considered crucial to the Commonwealth. James Madison and John Marshall led the proponents for ratification, insisting that each state would want its own bill of rights, an agreement would never be reached, and the union would be dissolved. Henry spoke on the eighteenth day of the twenty-three-day session, mesmerizing his listeners.

"The splendid maintenance of the president, and the members of both houses, and the salaries and fees for swarms of officers and dependents on the government will cost this continent immense sums. After satisfying their uncontrolled demands, what can be left for the states? Not a sufficiency even to defray the expense of their internal administration."

With his notes in his hat and his hat in his hand, James Madison skillfully directed arguments to delegates less committed. Governor Edmund Randolph changed sides, announcing that he would support ratification with confidence that the bill of rights would be adopted later. Some delegates never forgave him. After days of contentious wrangling, they voted. Many feared that Patrick Henry would lead a walkout if his side lost. The final vote count was eighty-nine for ratification and seventy-nine against. Henry stood and apologized for having taken up so much time, saying, "I will be a peaceable citizen. My head, my hand and my heart shall be at liberty to retrieve the loss of liberty and remove the defects of the system in a constitutional way."

It was over; Virginia, the largest and most heavily populated state, joined ten others that had already ratified.

The delegates dispersed. The Jockey Club members left, going home to Westover, Wilton, and Shirley in the Tidewater; Stratford Hall and Corrotoman on the Northern Neck; and Tuckahoe and Dungeness in the Piedmont.

⤝

Tom Randolph was unhappy in Edinburgh after William returned to America and asked for permission to also return home. John Leslie urged him not to withdraw, to instead take a holiday, perhaps visit their friend Josiah Wedgewood at the Wedgewood potteries. But Tom refused, he wanted to come home, and he did, arriving at Tuckahoe in June. He was eager to bring his friend John Leslie over and Colonel Randolph arranged for Leslie to come as plantation tutor.

⤝

Dick Randolph followed Judith to Tuckahoe and they were together for most of July and August, but always with a chaperone. For a woman, courtship was a golden period, the highlight of her life. Women enjoyed the rituals of flirtation and coquetry and writing and telling friends of their amorous agonies or joys. The happiness of courtship was a bridge between post-puberty and the responsibilities of marriage and motherhood. A woman's power as absolute monarch ended with her subjugation after her marriage. A double standard regarding sex existed. Men philandered, usually with women of a lower class, but women in planters' families were expected to be chaste. A woman who was discovered to have had a sexual encounter before marriage could have ruined her life. Virtue was paramount, woman's most precious commodity, chastity was crucial, and in courtship she assumed the primary burden of restraint.

During his visit to Virginia, Gouverneur Morris accepted Colonel Randolph's invitation to Tuckahoe. The Colonel wanted Morris's advice on the collectibility of his British debt. He had paid over ten thousand pounds on Archibald Cary's debt and Virginia law prevented further collection. But Ann Cary Randolph was ill, and her husband wanted to take her to New York for medical treatment. He asked Morris whether in New York the British could exert more legal pressure to collect. Morris felt certain that this would be the case, but, as a courtesy, he wrote and asked his friend Alexander Hamilton to find out. Morris mentioned appreciatively "the amiable, bear in mind that word, Mrs. Randolph."

Morris would have observed, in addition to Ann Randolph, Tom, recently returned from Scotland and already restless, and the current Tuckahoe beauty, Judith. He would scarcely have noticed Nancy, not yet thirteen years old, engrossed in her books, her French lessons, and her horse. She could not have been oblivious to the handsome, aristocratic visitor with the peg leg. Twenty years later, ill and penniless in a hostile environment, she remembered him and sought his help.

John Leslie arrived from Scotland in August and became tutor to all the children at Tuckahoe, but it was Judith who caught his eye.

❧

Jack and Theo Randolph were in New York City during that state's debates over ratification. New York barely managed to ratify and only through Alexander Hamilton's efforts. The vote was thirty to twenty seven. Nonetheless, there was a great celebration in New York City afterward, which the Randolphs witnessed. A grand procession wound from Bridewell through Wall Street to Federal Green. Tables were set up "like sticks of a fan to represent the states which acceded," and the president and members of Congress were seated around them where eight thousand people dined together.

Tucker wrote his stepsons in New York:

"You will have heard that the Constitution has been adopted by this state."

Recovery of the British debts could no longer be postponed, and there was a "moral certainty that your patrimony will all go to satisfy the unjust debts from your papa to the Hanburys." They could rely only on their personal ability and exertion for future success.

❧

Tucker was shocked to learn that Judith and Dick were already con-templating marriage. He sent Dick back to college in New York by packet boat from Norfolk in fifty-two hours, a record time. Tucker then wrote to Ann Randolph of his concern that Dick was only nine-teen and that he had not as yet completed his education. Ann replied quickly. She was not surprised; she had expected the proposal. She hoped to keep her daughters single until they were old enough to make a proper judgment, since a woman's happiness depended entirely on the husband with whom she united.

"As young people cannot have a sufficient knowledge of the world . . . they are apt to be sour when the delirium of love is over, and reason is allowed to reascend her throne."

Although John Leslie had not been impressed with America's wil-derness, Tuckahoe charmed him and Ann Randolph exalted his opin-ion of her whole sex. But his beautiful student Judith won his heart. He fell in love, but she scarcely noticed him.

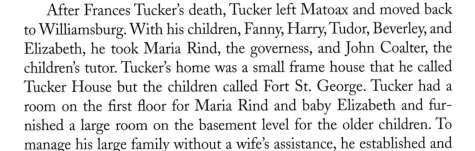

After Frances Tucker's death, Tucker left Matoax and moved back to Williamsburg. With his children, Fanny, Harry, Tudor, Beverley, and Elizabeth, he took Maria Rind, the governess, and John Coalter, the children's tutor. Tucker's home was a small frame house that he called Tucker House but the children called Fort St. George. Tucker had a room on the first floor for Maria Rind and baby Elizabeth and fur-nished a large room on the basement level for the older children. To manage his large family without a wife's assistance, he established and required adherence to strict guidelines of conduct.

John Coalter enrolled in law school at the College of William and Mary. Tucker "settled" his tuition fees, arranged for him to live next door with the Wickhams, and provided the use of his own law library. In return, Coalter tutored the Tucker children for three hours each day.

With his good looks and sharp intellect, Dick Randolph shone bril-liantly at Columbia, both among students and those in social circles. Among the latter was Anne Bingham, who had lived in Paris where she and Thomas Jefferson had become friends. William Bingham built a pa-latial home in Philadelphia where his wife entertained in the European manner. Anne sent a message to New York. She wanted "that manly and most elegant youth, Richard Randolph, to be my Master of Ceremonies at my Annual Ball." A decade earlier, she had selected the "Tall Boy," handsome Gouverneur Morris before he lost his leg, for the same honor.

Tucker said no, he would not allow Dick to make the trip to Philadelphia. Dick consoled himself at not being able to accept Mrs. Bingham's invitation by taking one Kitty Ludlow to bed in New York.

⚬⚬

On December 17, 1788, Gouverneur Morris sailed from Philadelphia for Europe. He had a letter from his friend, George Washington, in his pocket and an authorization to participate in trade negotiations for the United States.

John Adams prepared to return to America and become vice president under George Washington, but before he left, Jefferson joined him in Amsterdam. Without instructions from Congress on how to proceed, the two somehow, apparently through personal integrity, arranged a loan from Holland for the United States.

Afterward, Jefferson toured the region and found an angry letter from Maria Cosway when he returned to Paris in April 1788. He answered right away, apologizing for not having written her during his trip.

"At Dusselforf I wished for you much. I surely never saw so precious a collection of paintings. Van de Werff's painting of Sarah delivering the concubine Agar to Abraham was delicious.

"At Heidelberg I wished for you too."

He interpreted her anger as proof of her esteem, "but I love better . . . soft testimonials of it. . . . You must therefore now write me a letter teeming with affection, such as I feel for you."

Maria replied that she would not visit Paris that year. "I am afraid to question my Lord and Master on the subject." Instead, she suggested that he come to England, where "we may do it better."

Jefferson became aware of Martha's growing interest in becoming a nun and her "tendencies toward the Catholic religion." Her father, while not outwardly opposing her interest, had tried to distract her. Although reluctant to leave his post at such a critical juncture, he requested a leave of absence to take his daughters back to America.

⚬⚬

Jefferson commissioned John Trumbull to make miniature copies of his portrait, based on "Signing of the Declaration of Independence," for Maria Cosway and his friend Angelica Church. Sensing jealousy in Martha, William Short, Jefferson's secretary, wrote secretly to Trumbull and asked him to make one also for Jefferson's daughter, "a very clever, gallant thing to do." Of the three, Martha's was said to be the best likeness.

⚓

A bad harvest and a severe famine were followed by the coldest winter on record.

Jefferson's thermometer registered 50 degrees below freezing. The French were literally starving and freezing to death.

1789
Paris

S hortly after Gouverneur Morris arrived in Paris in February, he met with Jefferson and Lafayette, finding Lafayette "full of politics" and Jefferson "cold as a frog."'

At court, Morris became almost as popular as Jefferson. At a palace function in Versailles, he met Madame Adele de Flahaut, the beautiful wife of a count. She was twenty-eight and her husband was sixty-three. The brown-eyed beauty, with her curled and powdered hair, and the peg-legged American were instantly attracted to each other. He visited her frequently at her apartment in the Louvre.

His competition, in addition to her husband, was Charles de Tallyrand. Adele's affair with the latter had produced a son, Charles, who bore the de Flahaut name. Tallyrand and Morris sometimes encountered each other at Adele's apartment. Her husband's apartment was on the floor above.

∽

On April 18, 1789, Jefferson received a letter from Martha, asking permission to become a nun. Instead of answering, he drove to the convent and spoke privately with the abbess of his concern. Then he met Martha, who was in a "fever of doubts and fears." Gently, he told her and Maria to pack their belongings and he took them home. Her school days were over, although Jefferson engaged Abbe Edgeworth to tutor them privately.

Maria Cosway 1759-1838,
Library of Virginia

Jefferson never spoke of the incident, but made a special effort to placate Martha, spending over seven hundred francs on new clothes for her and paying forty-eight francs for a watch. Together they attended important functions, including dinners at Versailles. Many years later, Martha described her interest in the Catholic order to her children.

The Commonwealth of Virginia had commissioned a marble statue of General Washington for the rotunda of the new capitol. Jefferson engaged Jean Antoine Houdon, who came to Mount Vernon and fashioned a life mask and recorded body measurements. When he needed a live model in Paris, Jefferson selected Morris to pose. The sessions began in June, lasting to the end of the year.

Morris and Adele became lovers that summer. Their passion demanded gratification—in her apartment with her husband nearby, in Morris's carriage, even in public gardens. The driver carefully averted his eyes, but Morris recorded the details in his diary.

"It is a matter of natural . . . curiosity to wonder what this lady wore . . . to be able to behave so naughtily," observed Swiggett, Morris's biographer.

Violence escalated throughout France, especially in Paris. So many people were being beheaded, à la mode, that Jefferson wrote of the need to check his own head in the mornings. He and Morris were dining with aristocrats on July 14, 1789, when they received word that the Bastille had fallen. The two American men were on opposing sides. Morris was sympathetic to the monarchy, while Jefferson and Lafayette viewed a revolution as the means of establishing a democracy in France, but neither envisioned the ensuing blood bath.

One evening Morris ordered his carriage after dinner and walked a short distance while awaiting its arrival. A mob appeared with the head and body of a nobleman with whom Morris had recently dined, triumphantly displayed. The man's head was "on a pike, the body dragged naked on the earth."

"Gracious God, what a people," Morris wrote.

James Hemings's young sister Sally was now sixteen years old. The quadroon beauty was the daughter of Betty Hemings, who had long been the concubine of Jefferson's father-in-law, John Wayles, and was probably his wife's half-sister. In addition to paying her wages, Jefferson spent 216 francs within a few weeks on her clothes. He paid for her vaccination and, while he traveled, paid for her board and washing with a French family. Differing opinions down through the years persist on whether she became his concubine while in France, and she was said to have been pregnant when she returned to America.

Permission to return home arrived. Jefferson expected to return to Paris for several years and wrote Maria Cosway of his departure, hoping that Angelica Church could persuade her to come to America for a visit.

"For the way will ever be wrong that will lead us apart."

In September 1789, Jefferson booked passage on the *Clermont* for his family and the Hemingses. His packing list included Martha's guitar and harpsichord and books for James Madison, Franklin, and Washington.

He wrote Maria, "Adieu, my very dear friend. Be our affections unchangeable and if our little history is to last beyond the grave, be the longest chapter in it that which shall record their purity, warmth, and duration."

His last letter before sailing promised, in his planned April 1790 return, that "Spring might give us a meeting at Paris with the first swallow."

They sailed from Le Havre in October. He would never return or see Maria Cosway again.

TUCKAHOE AND MATOAX

Colonel Randolph canceled plans to take his wife to New York for the much-needed medical treatment. So, the woman who had impressed Gouverneur Morris with her amiability and who had exalted John Leslie's opinion of the whole sex, died at Tuckahoe on March 13, 1789, at the age of forty-four. She was interred in the family cemetery and Judith, Nancy, and Jenny (Virginia) scratched the date on the windowpane in a bedroom.

After his mother's death, Tom Randolph went to New York to be "in the thick of the political happenings"—the inauguration of his fellow Virginian, George Washington, as the first president of the United States.

Washington and John Adams were certified as president-elect and vice president-elect on April 6. The Randolphs of Virginia were well represented at the historic inaugural event on April 30, 1789. Dick, Theo, Jack, and Tom were all there, as were Frances Tucker's brother, Dr. Theodorick Bland, and St. George Tucker's brother, Dr. Tudor Tucker. Dressed in their best clothes, they viewed the ceremony in Federal Hall. Jack could see Washington from his position, but Washington spoke so softly that he was unable to hear him take the oath to enforce the Constitution. James Madison had written the inaugural address, and Washington must have read it before.

"Although tall and commanding in outward appearance, Washington seemed agitated and embarrassed. He trembled several times, could scarce make out to read. . . . Left rather an ungainly impression," as someone later described the occasion.

However, he attracted wild and widespread admiration.

"Men and women in a sloop sang an elegant ode to the tune of 'God Save the King.' The shores were crowded with onlookers, the water was full of porpoises and vessels were all decked out. There was a press of spectators to see the country's chief."

⤖

Afterward, Tom returned to Tuckahoe. He and John Leslie went on a botanical jaunt through the Blue Ridge Mountains and during their trip, Leslie confided to Tom his "burning affection tinctured with sadness" for Judith. This, and his disappointment with America, convinced him to return to Scotland. When he arrived there, he sent Tom a gift of the works of Hume, Herodotus, and Hesiad. Although he and Tom corresponded for more than twenty years, they never saw each other again.

John Leslie had a brilliant career. In 1802, his explanation of capillary action was the first to be consistent with today's theory. Two years later he published An Experimental Inquiry into the Nature and Propagation of Heat, and was elected to the Chair of Mathematics at the University of Edinburgh. In 1810 he froze water using an air pump. In 1819, he transferred to the Chair of Natural Philosophy and was knighted in 1832.

Summer vacation ended, and Theo and Jack returned to Columbia College without Dick. Soon, Theo wrote Tucker that he had been ill during the hostile northern winter, and suffered "much for the need of

St. George Tucker 1752-1827,
Library of Virginia

a servant." Instead, Tucker gave him an allowance of 300 pounds per annum in New York money, which had a higher value than Virginia's. Theo felt lonely and abandoned, but was also spoiled, weak, and undisciplined. The money provided opportunities for personal indulgence that he was unable to resist. Morally unacceptable companions caused him to neglect his studies and begin drinking. Tucker wrote him of his dismay in hearing that Theo had been seen in a "state of intoxication in Corrie's even in the A.M." He reminded his stepson of the planned trip to the University of Edinburgh. Theo begged to enroll in medical school in Philadelphia, where he would be closer home, but Tucker refused to consider the option.

⋙

Dick and Judith were inseparable, and when Tucker learned that her father had given approval for their marriage, he wrote the Colonel.

"Dick tells me that you have given your consent to the nuptials. I had hoped that he would attain his full age before taking this step."

Dick was "unappraised about her dowry," and Tucker wanted to know whether the Colonel planned to make any financial provision for his daughter.

⋙

The Jeffersons and Hemingses arrived at Norfolk in mid-November. The ship caught fire, but it was contained, and the Jeffersons' eighty packing cases, including six sofas, fifty-nine upholstered chairs, and draperies, escaped damage.

Their first stop was at Eppington, where Maria's reunion with the Eppeses, whom she remembered lovingly as family, was especially poignant. While there, Washington's courier delivered word that the Senate had approved Jefferson's appointment as secretary of state. Washington personally urged acceptance. Jefferson had other plans, both at Monticello and in returning to France, but he acquiesced reluctantly.

The family, with young John Eppes, traveled on to Richmond. Here for the first time, Jefferson saw Virginia's beautiful new capitol, not yet stuccoed. After the General Assembly honored Jefferson, the family continued to Monticello, stopping at Tuckahoe. Jefferson consoled the Colonel on his wife's death, but the Colonel assured him of his intent to remarry and have more children.

Tom and Martha renewed their childhood friendship; she had referred to him then as Sir Tom of the Tree Top Towers. He was dark and swarthy, tall like Martha, a superb horseman, and a brilliant conversationalist. Jefferson was obviously pleased with the attachment.

After the Jeffersons' departure, Tom argued with his father. He asked the Colonel to deed him one of the plantations, but the Colonel refused. He wanted to remarry, have more children and divide his land evenly among them. Tom, furious, followed Martha to Monticello.

The Colonel gave permission on December 28 for Dick and Judith's nuptials, and they were married on December 31 at Tuckahoe. Tucker traveled from Williamsburg for the event and wrote of the bountiful feast presented after the ceremony. They had choices of mutton, beef, venison, turkey, oysters, lobster, prawn, and salmon. For dessert there were custards, tarts, apple pies, syllabus, jellies, ice cream, and ripe and candied fruits.

Tucker's poetic description concludes with:

"Our cynic cries – 'how damned absurd

To take such pains to make a —.'"

Dick and Judith's married life began with the honeymoon at Presqu'ile, the plantation home of her sister Molly and David Meade Randolph. Judith would not allow Dick into the nuptial bed; she made him sit up all night in a corner of their room.

"To shew her power, she later boasted about it," according to Nancy.

1790

*D*ick Randolph took his bride home to Matoax, near Petersburg, the third largest city in Virginia, after Richmond and Williamsburg, and a community of parties, theater, and horse racing. Dick was now the master of his household, and he supplemented Frances Tucker's furnishings with orders of rugs and tables from abroad. He and Judith entertained lavishly and often. Numerous guests consumed large amounts of alcohol and provisions, initially paid for from his limited income. When he had exhausted this, he borrowed wherever he could. After the purchase of a carriage from England took him further into debt, creditors refused his requests for loans. They appealed to Tucker, who stepped in and strongly advocated that Dick and Judith move to Bizarre plantation, where they could live less lavishly.

❧

Tucker's problems continued with Theo, who socialized and ignored his education. Tucker devised various errands to take him away from his companions and admonished him to prepare for the trip abroad. Nothing worked. Weak and rudderless away from home, Theo continued as before.

"In two years," according to Jack, "my brother had undermined his constitution and destroyed his health."

They returned to Virginia in the summer, and Theo never went back to school.

Martha Jefferson Randolph 1772-1836,
Library of Virginia

Mary Randolph, Judith's cousin and best friend, married her cousin, Randolph Harrison, and they moved to Clifton, in Cumberland County. When Mary received word of Judith's move to Bizarre, she was aghast—the social darling from one of the finest homes in the area moving to the isolation of Prince Edward and Cumberland. Judith sought to allay Mary's concern, saying the move was her idea.

"He (Dick), ever indulgent to my wishes, would have continued at Matoax but for my strong solicitation for our removal."

Judith was happier and now lived closer to Mary. She, married only ten months and Mary, fewer than six, were already conversing in matronly terms about anticipated pregnancies.

"Let me know when you expect to be confined," Judith wrote. She returned with her sister Molly to Presqu'ile at the end of the year to be confined, but the incident proved to be a false alarm. She was not pregnant.

~

While at Monticello, Tom proposed marriage to Martha. They had much in common. They were cousins, both older children, and were akin to expatriates in their own country. Her time abroad, more than five years, and his own, four years, made them more cosmopolitan, causing a disconnect with the flavor of plantation happenings and community life.

Jefferson gladly acquiesced to the union. Tom's "talents, disposition and connections" made him Jefferson's best choice. Too, he probably felt assured that Tom would not threaten his and Martha's close relationship. Jefferson set the wedding date for February 23, before his departure for New York to assume his duties as secretary of state. Colonel Randolph declined to attend, citing an attack of gout. The nuptials took place at Monticello, a festive event, although not as elaborate as Dick and Judith's. A Negro family provided musical entertainment, and the local Episcopal minister performed the ceremony. Martha wore the white satin wedding dress purchased in Paris by her father. The newlyweds accompanied Jefferson as far as Richmond, where he left for the North. Here he began the supervision of their marriage that would eventually estrange the couple. He urged them not to linger too long in Richmond. They left on the customary round of honeymoon visits to relatives' plantations along the river.

Jefferson traveled by carriage to New York and joined President Washington, Vice President John Adams, Secretary of the Treasury Alexander Hamilton, Attorney General Edmund Randolph, and Chief Justice John Jay.

He wrote Martha of his unhappiness at his separation from her, begging, " . . . continue to love me as you have done." Martha assured him that her happiness would never be complete without his company, although her husband omitted nothing that could make her happier. She tried to please Tom in everything, she assured her father, making all else secondary except her love for him.

The Colonel deeded Tom the 950-acre primitive and remote plantation in Varina, near where Pocahontas and John Rolfe had spent their honeymoon. Martha despised the primitive remoteness of Varina, and Jefferson wanted his daughter to live close to him at Monticello. He urged Tom to buy land from his father at nearby Edgehill and build there. Tom, anxious to please his wife, began negotiations. Jefferson gave his daughter one thousand acres at Poplar Forest in Bedford County and twenty-five slaves.

❧

Jefferson heard that Maria Cosway was pregnant. Maria wrote him, fearing that he had forgotten her. His return letter congratulated her, saying that, while Europe may be the place to have babies, America was the place to raise them.

In ending his letter, he assured her, "Je vous aimerai toujours" (I'll always love you).

❧

Colonel Randolph found a bride that summer, eighteen-year-old Gabriella Harvie, daughter of neighbor John Harvie. She was in love with someone else and resented marrying a man nearly three times her age. To win her, the Colonel made tough concessions. He sold part of the Edgehill land to Harvie. Then Gabriella balked at going to Tuckahoe where the Colonel had children at home almost as old as she.

To placate her, the Colonel attempted to arrange a marriage for Nancy, the oldest daughter at home. His efforts were disastrous for both of them. Nancy refused to comply with "bestowing my hand when my heart revolted." Given the choice of an unwanted marriage or leaving Tuckahoe, she left, taking her youngest sister, Virginia, and her personal slave, Polly, with her. They visited Aunt Polly, their mother's sister at the Fork plantation and from there they went to their sister Molly and her husband, David Meade Randolph, at Presqu'ile plantation. Maria Jefferson visited there, too, as did Theo and Jack Randolph. At the boggy, low-lying, malaria-infecting plantation, Nancy charmed them all, including the Randolph brothers. Theo, worldlier and older, clearly had an edge, but Jack would never again feel the intensity of this first love and he would not surrender. He continued to pursue Nancy after the summer ended.

Theo, knowing that he would never return to school, requested a friend to send his trunks and books home to Virginia.

❧

Jefferson's letter informed Tom and Martha of Nancy's ejection (through no fault of her own) from Tuckahoe. Martha and Tom, still smarting from his father's refusal to sell Edgehill to him, were furious at Gabriella's high-handed manner, but Jefferson tried to soothe their feelings.

"Love and cherish what is good ... and keep out of the way of what is bad."

They were angered even more when Colonel Randolph and Gabriella were married in September at her parents' home and the bride refused to have any of the groom's family present.

❧

Martha was pregnant and never communicated the news to her father. By December, about four weeks before her delivery, Jefferson inquired pointedly about her condition.

"Perhaps you think you have nothing to say to me. I suspect you may have news to tell me of yourself of the most tender interest. . . . Why silent then?"

1791

I n late January 1791, Martha's first child, a daughter, was born. She learned quickly that her father's description of childbirth as "hardly more than a knock on the elbow" was seriously inaccurate. She described labor and delivery as a "horror of a trial . . . severe under the most favorable circumstances."

Babies were born at home, attended by either doctors or midwives. Unlike in the North, where women in labor were given rum for pain, on Virginia plantations laudanum was administered. Northern midwives believed that laudanum prolonged labor. Female friends and relatives came for the confinement and often stayed until the mother returned to her normal routine. Women literally faced death with the birth of each child. Men were not present at a delivery, because of both choice and custom, but most remained nearby or on the plantation and were notified after the birth had taken place.

Maria was home during the birth, lodged upstairs

"She is very well now," Maria wrote her father about Martha, "and the little one also. . . she is very pretty . . . has beautiful deep blue eyes and is a very fine child."

The news pleased Jefferson. "You announced you were become . . . a mother . . . the keystone of matrimonial happiness."

The new parents asked him to name the baby, and he gave her the name of Tom's mother, Ann Cary.

Martha readily learned housekeeping, parenting, and managing the house slaves.

※

While Jack was in Philadelphia studying, his law course came second to his social life and his preoccupation with Nancy. His heart remained with her in Virginia, and he wrote her frequently. He confided the intensity of his feelings to Henry Rutledge of South Carolina, his friend from his Columbia College days.

"A pin for existence without her. But I will drop a subject which never fails to demand the tribute of a sigh."

He then confessed sins of dissipation with another friend and student, Joseph Bryan of Georgia. A month later, Jack still daydreamed of the girl in Virginia; his sentiments would never change. But he lost her. When she and Theo became engaged, Jack was devastated at the news. He returned to Virginia on vacation and confronted Nancy at Presqu'ile. Leading her to the portico, he leaned against one of the pillars and burst out with his surprise at the news. He hoped that it was not true. He felt Theo unworthy of her.

"You made many assertions derogatory to his reputation," she later reminded him, "some of which were false." Nancy found his "stormy passions . . . mean selfishness . . . unacceptable."

Stung by her rejection, Jack retreated to Philadelphia and gave Henry Rutledge, who was in a similar situation, advice that Syphax had given, "If there's no hope, find a second mistress to light up another flame to put out this."

Tucker sent Theo to Bermuda with his brother, Dr. Tudor Tucker, hoping the change of climate would help him regain his health—a vain effort. Dr. Tucker wrote that Theo was no better, to prepare for the worst.

※

Life at Fort St. George was changing. John Coalter, the children's tutor, completed law school and went into legal practice in Staunton. He and Maria Rind, the Tucker governess, planned to marry, and she was in a hurry. She joined John Coalter in Staunton and they married, but within two years she died in childbirth.

※

Tucker had met Lelia Skipwith Carter, the widow of George Carter of Corrotoman and the daughter of a British baronet. A charming and

wealthy woman, Lelia had been described as being "a prodigy of learning." As a widow, Lelia could own property, buy and sell slaves, but
could not vote. Widows and single women enjoyed more privileges
than married women because husband and wife were considered one
entity and a husband's authority remained absolute. His one restriction
was the size of the club he could use to beat his wife. When Lelia and
Tucker were married in October 1791, Lelia relinquished control of
her property and took on a great responsibility for another's woman's
children. Along with her own children, Charles and Mary Carter, she
joined Fanny, Harry, Beverly, Tudor, and Elizabeth at Tucker House.

～⨍～

Dick and Judith took Nancy home with them to Bizarre. Dick surprised her one morning by coming to her room, falling to his knees, and
begging her to listen to him and not alarm anyone. He was unhappy;
he knew that his wife did not love him, and he described his amorous
adventures in Williamsburg with Betsy and in New York with Kitty.
Nancy was devastated by his attempt to seduce her and burst into tears.
Dick, professing his friendship, hastily left the room when Nancy's servant brought water.

"Oh, my poor father," she wept, "what has your wretched marriage
brought on your child?" She wrote her father, asking him to send a
carriage for her, but his wife sent word back that the horses were lame
and unable to travel though everyone knew that she had used the horses
and carriage for friends' visits.

After Theo's return, Dick begged her not to marry anyone, the idea
disturbed him so.

"Then, he endeavored to shake my principles," Nancy later disclosed. Judith was pregnant; she expected their first child in the spring.
In that winter of misery, Nancy had no home and no confidant.

"I might have married Archy Randolph, General Lee, or Ben Harrison in the spring."

"Dick had one fault of great magnitude. He was the victim of his
marriage with a cold hearted, malignantly haughty woman," Nancy
told Tucker later.

In November, the British debts case was heard in Federal District Court in Richmond. Patrick Henry, John Marshall, Alexander Campbell, and Attorney General James Innes represented the planters in the case. The case was continued to a later date when one of the judges died, leaving the Colonel's and the Randolph sons' indebtedness still unresolved.

~

President Washington's nomination of Gouverneur Morris to replace Jefferson as minister to France went to the Senate on December 21, 1791. Legislators wrangled for weeks, denying Washington's plea for speedy confirmation. James Monroe and Henry Lee were among those most vehement in bitter opposition and the battle went into the new year.

1792

After eighteen days of contentious debate on Gouverneur Morris's nomination as minister to France, senators were convinced that President Washington would not withdraw Morris's name and finally confirmed him by a vote of 17—11 in mid-January. Jefferson reviewed Washington's letter informing Morris of the confirmation. The final version was honest but personally friendly.

"Your abilities were asserted," but Morris's conversations and conduct had caused serious opposition. "Of my good opinion and of my friendship you may be assured."

Morris promised to observe "circumspection of conduct," then proceeded, inappropriately for a diplomat, to shelter French aristocrats from seizure. He ended his three-year affair with Adele de Flahaut, and his reports to Washington were prompt and accurate with shrewd observations. Henry Lodge wrote, "The two years which followed his appointment as minister make one of the most brilliant chapters in the diplomatic history of the United States."

Morris counseled the king and wrote a proposed constitution for France. It was not adopted. While in France, Morris recorded, in a dozen bound vellum volumes, details of France's disastrous attempts to equal America's success in revolution. In the midst of mob violence and terrible atrocities, he sought to fulfill a mission that now had few pleasures. He was the only foreign minister who did not ask to be recalled from the troubled country.

✂

Beverley Randolph completed his term of office as governor and returned to Cumberland. He enjoyed his home routine more than the bustle of Richmond, and his public career had left him nearly penniless. Tucker proposed to visit him in the spring, but without Lelia. In January, Randolph teased his friend about coming without his "rib," asking whether "sweet Lelia's power to supply the place of firewood would make it too warm."

Randolph mentioned that Theo had brought him the letter and may have imparted his suspicion of what was happening at Bizarre with Dick and Nancy. Theo thought himself better, but "his appearance by no means justifies the opinion." Judith wrote Tucker that Theo was the same "poor fellow," but by February he was no longer able to stand without assistance. He died on February 14.

✂

As Martha and Tom returned from Varina on the way to Monticello, they picked up their mail at Bizarre. From Monticello, she wrote her father of the "disagreeable journey of three months through deep snow and dismal weather."

"I never saw the end of anything with more pleasure in my life."

She had good news as well. The Colonel had finally sold Tom the remaining land at Edgehill, along with the slaves.

Jefferson soon tired of the long journeys between Monticello and Philadelphia. He delayed his departure until President Washington left for Mount Vernon, then instructed Tom to send a pair of wagon horses to Jones Tavern, seventeen miles from Montpelier and fourteen miles from Monticello. He would meet the driver and horses at Jones on the twenty-second and be home later that day. Thus, the trip between Philadelphia and Monticello took eight days overland.

✂

Dick's efforts to seduce his wife's naïve sister succeeded, probably during the "gander months," the last months of pregnancy, when some husbands typically sought sex outside of marriage. Judith was too far advanced in pregnancy to ride, and Nancy and Dick enjoyed morning horseback rides along the Appomattox River. Judith complained to Aunt Polly that Dick and Nancy were company only for themselves, and when Mary and Randolph Harrison visited, they noted "imprudent familiarities" between Dick and his young sister-in-law.

"Poor Dick possessed some noble qualities, and if he had not married so unhappily before he was old enough to have his principles fixed, he would have been an ornament to human nature," Nancy later recalled.

Judith gave birth to her first child in March, a son whom they named John St. George. They called him Saint because of his placid disposition.

Martha visited, too, and noted the situation. She told her father that Judy had a fine son and that Nancy was coming to Monticello for a visit. Before the Monticello visit ended, Martha, who was pregnant again, suspected with horror that Nancy was also.

Nancy returned to Bizarre and discussed her situation with Dick, who reassured her. Her situation was the same as Judith's in late 1790, he told her, a weight gain and a false pregnancy. But rumors flew about the suspected pregnancy, their attention to each other, and their having been seen kissing. Aunt Polly came from the Fork for a visit and, one evening, peeked in Nancy's bedroom door. Nancy was undressed and seemingly far enough along in pregnancy to show.

❧

Jack developed scarlet fever, and while returning from Philadelphia, recuperated in Richmond before continuing to Williamsburg to meet his new stepmother. In late pregnancy in stifling summer heat, Lelia, challenged with supervising her two children, five stepchildren, and the slaves, had little patience with her husband's sharp-tongued stepson. In an exchange of opinions, he called Lelia a "shrew," then came on to Bizarre.

Lelia and Tucker's son, Tutee, was born in late August.

❧

William, Judith's and Nancy's brother, married Beverley Randolph's daughter, Lucy, on September 11, 1792. No one from Bizarre attended the wedding because they suspected William of spreading rumors about Nancy and Dick. Instead, the women were with Martha when Thomas Jefferson Randolph was born on September 12. During their visit, Judith asked Martha about a remedy for Nancy's colic. Martha suggested gum guaiacum, but warned that it had been known to cause abortions. The next week, Aunt Polly requested some of the herb and Martha sent it to Nancy around September 20.

⤜⤛

Mary and Randolph Harrison moved into their new home, Glentivar, in Cartersville.

On Monday, October 1, 1792, the Randolphs of Bizarre came to visit the Harrisons.

Archy Randolph, one of Nancy's suitors and Mary's brother, came too. Glentivar was a long carriage ride from Bizarre, and the party arrived just before the mid-afternoon dinner. Randolph Harrison came outside to the circular driveway to welcome the guests and to help Judith and Nancy from the carriage.

Nancy joined the others for dinner but, ill, retired shortly afterward. She did not return for supper. The hostess and Judith later went upstairs to check on her. Nancy shared a room with Virginia, her seven-year-old sister, that opened across a stairwell from Dick and Judith's room. Nancy assured them that she had taken her medicine and expected to feel better soon.

According to the custom that single male guests do not sleep in the house, Archy and Jack stayed at an overseer's house or a tavern.

Mary had a new baby, too, and after her guests retired, she tucked in the sick child and she and her husband went to bed. They were drifting off to sleep when they heard a loud scream, which they attributed to Judith. Then a servant came and asked for laudanum for Miss Nancy. Mary sent the laudanum, lit a candle, and went upstairs. The door to Nancy's room was closed and Mary found Judith in her own room, sitting up in bed. When asked what happened, Judith thought Nancy must be having hysterics; the colic would not make her scream so. Mary went to Nancy's door and called. Dick was in the room and said she had taken laudanum and the light hurt her eyes. Mary stepped inside and stayed for a while until Nancy seemed to feel better, then went back downstairs.

Later the Harrisons heard footsteps on the stairs and, from the weight and tread, they thought it was Dick going for a doctor. Servants went up and down the stairs several times. When Mary went upstairs the next morning to check on Nancy, there was blood on the stairs and on a pillowcase. The sheets and bed quilt were missing and Nancy had the blanket drawn up around her neck.

She stayed in her room for a day or so, and when she came downstairs, asked for Archy's support. Both of the Harrisons, Jack, and Archy noticed a foul odor on Nancy and in her room. After the Randolphs left for Bizarre, Mary was shocked when a servant told her that Miss Nancy had miscarried. About six or seven weeks afterward, Harrison found that a birth had been deposited on a pile of shingles between some logs.

He and Mary visited Bizarre about three weeks later and found the family as usual, except that Mr. Randolph was "somewhat crusty."

⚬⚬⚬

Word spread from the slaves on the plantations to the inns and saloons and then back to the plantation owners. In this culture, friends and neighbors often overlooked a man's liaison with a woman of a lower class and even with a mulatto, but this was different. Men smirked and commented on Randolph and his little whore; she had had a baby at the Harrisons' and he had killed it and disposed of the remains. Not only was this a terrible blot on Nancy's character, but since she was his wife's sister, she was considered his sister also, making their relationship incestuous.

The rumors reached Martha and Tom, and she later told her father, "It is painful . . . to be obliged for so near a connection." Tom was furious about the gossip.

⚬⚬⚬

Jack knew nothing of the gossip until he visited the Banisters at Battersea in Petersburg. Here his cousin Robert gave him "the first intelligence of what was alleged to have happened" at Glentivar.

⚬⚬⚬

After Christmas, the Bizarre family visited in Williamsburg. Tucker House was a shelter from the gossip and gave Dick an opportunity to discuss his options. He firmly denied that a birth had taken place. Tucker closed ranks. He kept Jack nearby, sending him to William and Mary instead of Philadelphia. It was probably the wrong decision. Jack's anger with his brother exacerbated his nervous resentment. He and another student quarreled over the pronunciation of a word and resolved it with a forbidden duel on a field outside of town. Jack missed on the first shot but found his mark on the second, wounding but not killing his opponent. Jack escaped unscathed. To escape the scandal of Jack's sure dismissal, Tucker withdrew his stepson.

Jack's love for his brother had degenerated into hate by this point. During dinner one evening, he threw a knife at Dick's head.

"If passion had not diverted your aim," Nancy reminded him later, "your brother much earlier would have been consigned to the grave."

1793

*T*ucker urged Dick to enlist Colonel Randolph's help in stifling the gossip. If William Randolph were the instigator, who could deal better with him than his own father? Hoping that the Colonel would insist on a public denial, Dick, Judith, Saint, Nancy, and Jack visited Tuckahoe plantation in March. Dick suggested a possible suit of slander against William, and the Colonel assured Dick of his help. Hoping the "villainy of traducers would soon be exposed," Dick planned to take his family, including Nancy, north for the summer. Judith was pregnant again, he had promised not to pursue the matter further, but he felt obliged to resolve this "base atrocious calumny."

Even Elizabeth Pleasants, Judith's older sister, heard the gossip and demanded an explanation. The rumor was false, Judith assured her, condemning the "vile wretch" with whom it originated.

The family wanted publicly to prove the falsity of the accusation and went first to Williamsburg and then to Matoax. They waited in vain for a public denial from William. Finally, Dick and Tucker sought legal counsel. Dick engaged his friend, Alexander Campbell, who lived in a strange little house on the corner of Fifth and Franklin Streets, and a distant cousin, John Marshall, whose countrified appearance and simple manners were offset by his handsome brick home in Richmond.

They recommended a novel approach. Because Virginia laws were being revised, several statutes had been suspended in late 1792 for nine months. A directive stated that "County justices were to hold a court for an examination of the fact, which shall consider whether the case as it may appear to them, the prisoner may be discharged from further prosecution" or tried in a county or district court. The statute suspension meant that Dick could request an inquiry, or examination, to determine whether he should be placed on trial.

Dick published a letter in the April 3 issue of the *Richmond Gazette and Advertiser* advising the public that his character had been the subject of conversation, that he had been imputed with crimes at which humanity revolts. He would present himself before "the bar of the public." He planned to go to Cumberland Court and render himself a prisoner to answer any alleged charges.

"Let not a pretended tenderness toward the supposed accomplice [Nancy] . . . shelter me. That person will meet the accusation with . . . fortitude," he wrote.

⤝

"What have I not suffered," since they last met, Judith wrote Mary Harrison. "You know not how your letter mortified me." She was afraid that her friend was now lost to her.

Both Campbell and Marshall felt that they had a solid case to argue for Dick. He could not testify, as he could incriminate himself, and Nancy's situation was unique. Since she could incriminate herself, her testimony was inadmissible. Judith could not testify for or against her husband, as legally they were one person. Slaves' testimony was inadmissible.

Dick and Tucker were not so sure that the case was solid and decided on another measure.

They wanted a folk hero lawyer, one who would rely on emotion rather than the exact letter of the law, in the small county court. Dick sent his cousin Brett Randolph to engage Patrick Henry, instructing him to offer a seventy-pound retainer. Brett rode to Henry's home, Long Island, in Campbell County, more than fifty miles west of Cumberland. Henry refused; the distance was too far, he was too old, and he was preparing to argue the British debts case again in May. Dick refused to take no for an answer and sent Brett, saddle-sore and weary, back to double the offer. Henry reconsidered the offer. With fourteen children, one a widow, and numerous grandchildren, he could not refuse. He promised to arrive the day before the hearing.

Marshall's records show only expenses for the period, with no offsetting income. He arranged for Charles Lee to handle his cases in Fredericksburg District Court during the time he was in Cumberland. Alexander Campbell did not charge for his services. They worked on the case at the Effingham Hotel in the village. The Effingham served as the unofficial center of operations for attorneys having business during court sessions. An abundance of food and conversation was always available.

❧

At Tucker's request for an explanation, Judith described Nancy's illness as a trifling complaint in the stomach, that she persuaded Dick to get up and administer some medicine. He had not gone downstairs during the night, and the rumored events could not possibly have happened.

Nancy wrote a letter, too, acknowledging the miscarriage and naming Theo as the father. She gave the letter to Dick to use to exonerate himself. Dick read it, and then showed her a letter he had received from Tom. Her brother threatened to "wash out with blood any stain on my family. . . . I defy you to transfer the stigma to your deceased brother." Dick threw her letter into the hot coals in the fireplace and watched it burn before leaving for the courthouse.

❧

At Cumberland Courthouse, the sheriff arrested Dick and placed him in jail, held without bond. His hearing was scheduled for April 29. He would either be set free or held for trial, and three crimes could be imputed—incest, adultery, and murder. He could die on the gallows. If he were found guilty, Nancy could be tried on the same charges and likely would face the same fate.

❧

Court day was a big event in the county. Residents from all over the county came, and for some of them, it was the only time when friends visited together. They brought baskets of food to share along with family news and gossip. Dick's examination would take place four days after court day, when county cases were heard, but already the curious were making plans to attend.

❧

Jack rode his horse Star to Cumberland to see Dick, probably to take fresh clothing for the court appearance. and returned to Matoax.

The next day he and his cousin Robert Banister brought Judith and Nancy to the hearing.

Fourteen of the sixteen Cumberland gentleman justices conducted the inquiry. They were appointed by the governor and were selected from the most prominent families, and had tremendous legislative, judicial, and administrative powers. The justices would hear the evidence and ask questions; there would not be a prosecutor. Patrick Henry would cross-examine for the defense, and he and Marshall would make closing arguments, with Campbell's assistance.

After all of the testimony had been heard or presented, the court's decision was given. The gentlemen justices ruled that "the said Richard Randolph is not guilty of the felony wherewith he stands charged— that he be discharged out of custody and may go hence."

AFTER THE TRIAL

St. George Tucker was at court in Fredericksburg during the trial. Thirteen-year-old Fanny Tucker wrote him from Williamsburg, "Dick sent sixteen yellow jasmine plants," for Tucker's garden. "Tutee [her half-brother] has two teeth."

Tucker published an affirmation of support for Dick in the May 5, 1793, *Richmond Gazette and General Advertiser Broadside,* noting their connection and the charges, saying "nothing short of a fair, open and judicial inquiry into the truth of the charges . . . could effectually wipe them off. . . . A resolution not to attempt to anticipate the public adjudication imposed on me a rigid silence, except to a few . . . friends from whom I sought to be informed of the extent of the charges. He appeared at the Cumberland Court, was arrested by a warrant from a magistrate, was committed to prison without bail, tried before an examining court . . . and acquitted."

"The public mind is not always convinced by the decisions of law . . . there lies an appeal to a court of honor."

Tucker's plea for vindication had little effect on the general public.

Martha and Tom returned to Monticello after the trial where she found a letter from her father in Philadelphia confirming that gossip about Dick and Nancy had reached outside of the state. He was uneasy because he realized how unhappy the situation must have made others.

"Everyone stands on the merit or demerits of their own conduct."

He expressed pity for the victim (Nancy), "whether it be error or slander . . . I see guilt but in one person and not in her."

He implored his daughter to provide Nancy comfort that would "become balm to her wounds." He hoped Martha would be not only supportive, but preserve her "afflicted friend in . . . peace and love."

Martha did not reply until May 16, because of a "house full of company," but her point of view was not as benign as her father's.

She spoke of the "infinite anxiety, both to Mr. R. and myself for many months." She believed others pitied the "poor deluded victim more than she herself," "the villain had successfully corrupted her mind and destroyed her reputation . . . she alone is tranquil and seems proof against every other misfortune . . . but that of separation from her vile seducer."

⚮

Earlier, Martha had not believed the reports were true, because her opinion of R.R .(Richard Randolph) was "most exalted."

⚮

Jefferson was tired of the feuding between himself and Alexander Hamilton. He felt that Washington favored Hamilton. Hamilton smarted under Jefferson's coldness. Washington was unable to conciliate the differences between the two men.

In July 1793, Jefferson wrote a letter of resignation to the president. He wished to return to "scenes of greater tranquility." He agreed to stay in office until the end of the year.

He learned that Maria Cosway had entered a convent. He "thought that enthusiasm would have prevented her from shutting up her adoration of God within walls of a cloister . . . that she would rather have sought the mountain top. How happy should I be that it were mine."

⚮

Tom finally obtained the deed to the land and slaves at Edgehill and began planning the home he would build there, very close to Monticello.

⚮

Dick, Judith, and Nancy returned to Matoax. Judith had established a position from which she would never deviate, even to her closest friend,

Mary. She was implacable in any admission of wrongdoing that could reflect on her family. Even while reiterating her husband's innocence to Mary, she confessed her despair and fear of the future, that her mind had been in the most perfect state of misery. She could never have suffered so much had she doubted her husband's innocence. The diabolical machinations of his and Nancy's enemies had caused the problems.

The Randolphs of Bizarre were in a situation with no happy solution. Judith's public position forced her to take Nancy back into her home, and Dick was trapped in a loveless marriage with no escape.

"The ardor of his feelings would not have injured him had he married any other kind of woman than the remarkable one that fell to his lot," Nancy wrote Jack many years later.

Nancy, whom Judith would repeatedly revile as "the blasterer of my happiness," was doomed as a social outcast.

"The charge was very public and excited much attention . . . a part of the family avowed their belief in her guilt," John Marshall informed Gouverneur Morris in 1809. "The consequence was that this ill-fated young woman ceased to appear in public."

The existence of sexual virtues between men and women was paramount in the code of conduct among the families along the riverbanks of Virginia. The perceived break in this code would nearly destroy Dick and Nancy. Young men on Nancy's social level avoided her. Her withdrawal from "polite society" relegated her to a life of drudgery and obscurity. For Dick, the consequences were nearly as far-reaching.

※

Jack visited Tucker in Williamsburg, where he copied John Marshall's notes of evidence on Dick's examination in Cumberland. He stopped at Matoax before returning to Philadelphia, where he found his friend Joseph Bryan already awaiting him at their boarding house. The two became men of pleasure, "plunging into the gaiety that fills the mouth with blasphemy."

※

Dick and Judith learned that their handsome, docile son, Saint, was a deaf mute. Dick blamed himself because of a history of hearing impairment in his line. Misfortunes persisted when Judith had her baby. The little boy, whom they named Alexander, possibly after Dick's friend Alexander Campbell, died soon after birth.

Colonel Randolph's health deteriorated, hastened by the proud man's shame at the scandal. Martha told her father that divisions among the family increased daily, with the "old gentleman" in the thickest. Tom's father's imprudence in handling the family situation had to have widened the breach, although Tom had attempted to conciliate the factions.

"He is the link by which so many discordant parts join."

Although the Colonel was only fifty-two years old, his father-in-law, John Harvie, took over and made a will for him on November 5, 1793, and appointed himself guardian of the children at Tuckahoe—his grandson Thomas Mann II along with step-grandchildren John, Jane, and Harriet. Harvie moved the Colonel to Belvedere, his town plantation in Richmond, and summoned the children from Randolph's first marriage to their father's bedside. He died on November 20.

Nancy was at the Harvie home when the melancholy event occurred. The daughter whom he had mistreated so shamelessly by evicting her from Tuckahoe was the child who was with him when he passed over.

"My arm was between the pillow and the head of my much beloved parent when he expired."

Gabriella Randolph refused to allow her shamed stepdaughter to attend the funeral. Not everyone felt such animosity toward Nancy, and afterward Gabriella's mother attempted to compensate for her daughter's behavior by having Nancy stay for a visit. While she tried to "extract a temporary antidote to care from the plaintive notes of a well-tuned harpsichord," a friend of the Harvie family invited Nancy for a visit that lasted four months. After exhausting her Richmond invitations, she returned to Bizarre.

William and Tom were made executors of the Colonel's will and much of the burden of settling the estate, which was deeply in debt, became Tom's responsibility. In addition to the three British prewar debt claims against it, there was the mortgage on Varina. Colonel Randolph's will stated that he had already "made ample provision for my wife, Gabriella, and through her for my youngest son, Thomas Mann." Tuckahoe descended to Gabriella's son and passed out of Ann Cary Randolph's family. The Colonel left his Middle Quarter Plantation to his son John and his Dover Island Mill and land to his five younger daughters—Judith, Nancy, Jane, Harriet, and Virginia.

With Harvie now guardian of the children at Tuckahoe and Judith and Dick rearing Virginia, Nancy was the only child left with no legal status. The stepfather of her seducer, St. George Tucker, applied to Henrico County to become her guardian. For Nancy, this was a fortuitous event. Tucker became her benefactor and her confidant, and their long friendship would sustain her for more than twenty five years.

᪐

After Gouverneur Morris's appointment as minister to France, he rented ministerial quarters at 488 Rue de la Planche, in Faubourg St. Germain, for thirty-five hundred francs annually. Then he purchased silver, linens, and china appropriate for the American minister. They, and later purchases of furniture and rugs in France, were used to furnish his home, Morrisania, in New York.

᪐

The Third Estate, the national assembly, created a national constitution for France, stripping the king of his powers, and Morris advised the king not to accept it. Then, with Adele de Flahaut helping him with the technical French, Morris drafted a constitution that he thought would work for France. The king, because he either would not or could not consider the proposed constitution, accepted the national one instead. Morris informed Washington that the king's life and crown depended upon his making himself popular. He was unable to do so and, instead, was tried for treason and convicted, but by a close margin.

Morris wrote President Washington of the king's execution.

The king died with dignity on the guillotine in the Place de la Revolution. Earlier, he had expressed forgiveness for his persecutors and prayed that his people might benefit by his death. He mounted the scaffold and made two efforts to speak but an officer ordered a drum beat. The executioner threw him down in haste and let the axe fall before his neck was properly placed and he was mangled.

The distress and mourning in France at the king's death was unexpected and the execution changed America's attitude toward the Revolution.

Riding through Paris, Morris witnessed mobs literally tearing apart men he knew. A Madame de Lamballe was beheaded, and her head displayed atop a pole, "her pubic hair cut off and worn by some men as a moustache."

Morris was arrested because he did not have his papers with him; armed men entered and searched his home. He took into his home aristocrats fleeing from execution who sought shelter in the only foreign legation in the city still open. Among them were Adele de Flahaut and her son, Charles. Her husband had already been executed, but she was successful in sending Charles to safety in England and later went there herself.

"The path of life in Paris is no longer strewed with roses," Morris wrote Jefferson.

⤝

Lafayette sought to escape France but was captured and imprisoned by the Austrians. Morris sent the sad news to Washington, saying, "He has spent his fortune on a revolution and is now crushed by what he had put into motion."

⤝

Later in 1793, Queen Marie Antoinette, whose hair had turned white during the long months of her ordeal, was executed. She arrived at the place of execution by tumbril, wearing a simple white gown, with a blouse tying at the wrists, and a bonnet. She had had the dress smuggled into prison for her. She accidentally stepped on the executioner's foot and murmured, "Pardon, monsieur," as he removed her bonnet and cut off her hair. She was decapitated with an axe, and her body and severed head were loaded onto a cart and taken to a cemetery. No grave had been prepared for her, and she was tossed out and left lying on the ground, her head between her legs.

1794

*I*n January, Tucker was appointed Nancy Randolph's guardian, although she continued to live with Dick and Judith. When she returned to Bizarre from Richmond in March, she could not accept Tucker's invitation to Williamsburg due to a smallpox epidemic, unable even to get a letter posted. There had been numerous epidemics of the deadly, highly contagious disease, but most people dismissed vaccination of the cowpox virus, demonstrated by Edward Jenner as an effective vaccine. Jefferson had been vaccinated years earlier and Tom planned to have Ann, Jeff, and Virginia receive the cowpox vaccination as soon as they were old enough.

⤝

Martha eagerly awaited her father's return from Philadelphia. She had been "cruelly disappointed" to learn of the delay; she had set her heart on seeing him, hoping never again to be disappointed by his absence. Maria had already returned from school in Philadelphia in the fall of 1793 because of the yellow fever epidemic.

The real reason for Jefferson's resignation was the ongoing feud between him and Alexander Hamilton. They clashed in political theory—Jefferson adhering to an agrarian philosophy, while Hamilton favored commercial and manufacturing interests. They also differed on the recognition of the new French republic. Jefferson had tried unsuccessfully to remove Hamilton, urging James Madison to attack him

publicly, to "cut him to pieces." The feuding became acute, causing un-
easiness among other cabinet members, and Washington was unable to
effect conciliation.

Jefferson prepared for his departure and, at Tom's suggestion,
shipped his books and furniture by boat, a safer mode of transit, in
late December 1793, expecting to arrive at Monticello by January 15.
When Jefferson left Philadelphia on January 6, John Adams, weary and
exasperated by the cabinet feud, noted his departure as "good riddance
of bad ware."

Washington appointed another Virginian, Edmund Randolph, to
replace Jefferson as secretary of state. Randolph agreed to instruct several young men, including Jack Randolph and Joseph Bryan of Georgia, in law. Rather than studying, however, they "commenced men of
pleasure," partying and gambling. In early 1794, Jack met and married
Hester Hargrove, a "woman from an incompatible background." It was
believed that Edmund Randolph and Joseph Bryan rescued Jack from
an "unsuitable marriage" by sending her to England. Jack described it
vaguely as "an act of friendship as no one had ever rendered another."
But many years later, and after Joseph Bryan's death, Jack described
such an incident to his niece, who had married Bryan's son. Interest-
ingly, in Jack's account, it was he who saved Bryan, not the opposite.

As the yellow fever epidemic gripped Philadelphia, Bryan returned
to Georgia and Jack came back to Virginia. His education ended in
April 1794. Family members believed that a severe case of mumps had
destroyed Jack's virility. Although he was twenty years old, his soprano
voice remained high, at times an uneven falsetto. His torso did not grow,
but his arms and legs became enormously elongated, giving a grotesque
appearance. Although nearly beardless, his face lost its formerly attractive, somewhat feminine features, becoming gaunt and emaciated.

Matoax's taxes were unpaid, and an unsupervised overseer was in
charge of discontented slaves. When Tucker suggested that Dick and
Jack sell their home plantation, they eagerly agreed. The sale brought
1,600 pounds for the 603 acres, with the Randolphs retaining rights to
the family graveyard where their parents were interred.

⚮

Judith was unrelenting in her refusal to forgive those whom she
blamed for Dick's catastrophe and her humiliation. She even threat-

ened her friend Mary that, if ever she found that Mary had spread "the vilest of reports," their friendship, almost her greatest happiness, would be terminated. This, she said, would be sacrificed to the reputation of the man—whom she called "the best of husbands"—and whose kindness "demands every return which it is in my power to make." Judith was as "thin as a lath" (a narrow strip of wood) after the trial and the loss of her baby.

In June, she found that rearing her sister Virginia was too great an undertaking for her in everything but affection. She sent Virginia to live with Martha and Tom; her brother's "amiable wife" was in every way qualified for the task. Judith felt as much anguish, she wrote Mary, in parting with "Virgin" as she had in the loss of her own dear babe.

⤜⤛

Mary Harrison, pregnant again and facing a long, hot summer, complained of her large size and thought she was carrying twins. Judith said size had nothing to do with it; she had seen women carrying twins who appeared smaller than others with only one. She hoped Mary's apprehensions were groundless.

"Two at once! God forbid! One is enough in all conscience. You and I, my dear, fulfill the destiny of our creation fast enough in that way."

Judith parried Mary's question concerning being pregnant herself. She scarcely knew how to answer her friend's interrogatories; she was always "entirely ignorant of it until it was too obvious to be doubted." As there was no pregnancy for her that year, she and Dick probably had not resumed sexual relations after Alexander's birth in mid-1793.

At Mary's next confinement, her twins were boys, two of her fourteen children.

Years later, Nancy recalled events of that turbulent summer after Jack's return. He divided his time between the Petersburg racetracks, his cabin at Roanoke in Charlotte County, and Bizarre. He and Judith clashed; he resented her treatment of his brother.

Nancy reminded him of one scene.

"Returning from a morning ride with your brother, you told me you found it would not do to interfere between man and wife."

Evidently Jack had suggested Dick go to Connecticut for a divorce, to which Dick made no reply and spoke not a word after.

"How often you have declared your detestation of her conduct as a wife and her angry passions," Nancy continued. "'I have heard,' said you, 'that Mrs. Randolph was handsome and perhaps, had I ever seen her in a good humor, I might have thought so; but her features are so distorted by constant wrath that she has to me the air of a fury.'"

&

In Virginia, divorce was available only through a special act of the General Assembly, not the courts. The few divorces that were granted were usually to men whose wives had run away or who had been exposed in an adulterous relationship. Men and women of the upper class seldom resorted to the public humiliation of seeking the special separation that was available through the courts. Wives endured physical abuse with little recourse available and husbands endured emotional or physical abuse in private.

Years later Jack confided to Fanny, "I have seen the most amiable and worthy of mankind received with cold and austere looks, his affection merely tolerated, his friends slighted, his house that the master would have made the temple of hospitality cold and repulsive, himself feebly striving against his situation and, at last, sinking under it, the whole man changed, countenance, voice, manners, dress."

&

Martha welcomed her father back at Monticello, believing that he had given up public life; but soon he was working to advance the cause of the Republican Party. In August, his best friend, James Madison, married Dolley Payne Todd, a young vivacious widow whose husband and new baby had died in the yellow fever epidemic. She and Madison had been introduced by Aaron Burr. Many wondered why the desirable Dolley would want the little man with the lisp, but she was deeply attached to her "Jemmy." Dolley was a Quaker and when she married Madison the Religious Society of Friends cast her out of the sect.

&

Martha worried about Tom. Since his marriage, he had handled Monticello's affairs while his father-in-law was away and while managing his own plantation, Varina. Additionally he had endured the trauma of Nancy's trial and disgrace and his father's death. Now with the British debts pressing upon him and his role as executor of his father's will demanding his time and efforts, his health wavered. He placed the Dover plantation and grist mill on the market for sale and divided the proceeds from the mill operation among his sisters, Judith, Nancy, Jane, Harriet, and Virginia, sending Nancy's share to Tucker.

Doctors diagnosed his condition as gout, but the symptoms were those of acute depression. In August, he and Martha left Ann and Jeff with Jefferson at Monticello while they went to New York for treatment. Martha was reluctant to leave but felt her duty was to her husband. When they returned to Virginia, they stayed at Varina, not returning to Monticello until Christmas.

⤫

Nancy wrote Tucker, requesting a few guineas from Tucker for the stage from Bizarre to Monticello for Christmas. When she returned to Bizarre, Judith was pregnant once again.

1795

The Tuckers entertained their Bizarre guests during their New Year's visit to Williamsburg, where it was always social season. Virginia aristocrats enjoyed its social season readily, eagerly accepting invitations to Judge and Mrs. Tucker's soirees to meet Dick Randolph, his beautiful wife, Judith, and her sunny, vivacious sister, Nancy. Most guests overlooked the scandal of Dick's illicit seduction of Nancy. After all, they were the Randolphs of Virginia, and this culture often excused male sexual irresponsibility.

But Nancy bore the brunt when a guest "overstepped the bounds of acceptable behavior" toward her. She was blamed and was not allowed to return to Bizarre. Homeless again, she explained to Tucker from Rocky Mills that "Mr. Lee" feigned entire ignorance of the cause of her displeasure at first, then recollected himself and apologized, entreating her never more to think of his unwarrantable conduct.

❧

Tom and Martha dug in at Varina while Ann and Jeff were in Jefferson's care at Monticello. Tom had found everything at Varina in a "ruinous condition; the expected 3000-bushel crop of wheat had dwindled to 800 and the corn was at the mercy of thieves, hogs and birds." He discharged the overseer and took over the plantation management, in addition to executing Jefferson's directives. The crop failure problem was exacerbated when he learned that the tobacco crop at Poplar

Forest had been miniscule. Tom finally hired a new overseer, and he and Martha returned to Monticello while Jefferson made his spring visit to Poplar Forest.

In late May, Martha and Tom were off again, searching for a cure for Tom's stress and depression. Martha was pregnant again when they left for Warm Springs and Sweet Springs.

Virginians who were financially able visited the springs for both its therapeutic and social benefits. The high season ran from July 15 to September 1. Lord Fairfax had given land for Warm Springs, and the General Assembly had sold lots for the town layout in 1775. Warm Springs featured a theater, billiards, and boxing, as well as horseback riding for the ladies. Gambling was popular as were card games such as faro, whist, and loo. Sweet Springs was known for ardor, where the "water excited the animal passions and inspired the mind with pleasurable sensations." Balls, held every week, featured Virginia reels, square dancing, and occasional cotillions.

Carriages traveled along rough mountain roads that at times were so steep that passengers had to leave the carriages and walk. After a tormenting trip from Warm Springs to Sweet Springs, Martha went into labor. Her third child, a daughter whom she named Ellen Wayles, died within a few days after birth. After Jefferson learned of the infant's death, he had her returned to Monticello and interred in the family cemetery.

Jefferson wrote Martha that Nancy was homeless again. "She is now with Mrs. Carrington in Richmond." He suggested that they invite her to come to Monticello for a visit, provided her company was desirable.

⁕

As Nancy languished, awaiting a return to Bizarre, "that dear sequestered spot," her letters to Tucker were of homesickness and loneliness. She had been ill; she consoled him on the death of Tudor. She had sewn a dress of Virginia cloth, which she hoped three-year-old Tutee would travel in. She hoped the Tucker children would stop in Richmond on their next trip to Bizarre.

"I long ardently to see you all."

Instead of the silks and satins from overseas, Nancy replenished her wardrobe from inventory at Mewburn's General Merchandise Store, enough to last her a year. Tucker paid from the Dover Mill proceeds.

In Cumberland and Prince Edward, Dick sought to cement his friendship with Creed and Sally Taylor, their closest neighbors, at Needham. Needham and Bizarre were two miles apart, but a side road shortened the distance. Taylor, a local attorney and brilliant jurist, organized the Needham Law School, the second oldest in Virginia after William and Mary. In his moot court system, students argued hypothetical cases and served in various courtroom roles.

The Taylors preferred Nancy's company to Judith's and rarely visited Bizarre when she was away. Dick's messages to them at first were formal, even while asking to borrow "a reasonable amount of spiritous liquor," emphasizing that Taylor "not disfurnish yourself."

Then as he coaxed them to a sterile Bizarre, the invitations became warm and considerate.

"When are we to promise ourselves the pleasure of seeing you?"

While Nancy was away and the Taylors were unresponsive, Dick's entreaties continued. When the Taylors did not invite them to dinner, he and Judith invited themselves. He wrote that they were "dining with you tomorrow, amidst the hurly-burly, I forgot to tell you."

The Taylors declined an invitation, " a pleasure long denied" and Dick offered to set a more neighborly example than they had been shown and would dine with them tomorrow.

"However, if you are otherwise occupied, do not stand on ceremony, but let us know."

James and Dolley Madison visited Monticello that summer, where Jefferson was in the process of a major renovation. He planned to double the space, and introduce French architectural features, such as beds in alcoves, French doors, and parquet floors. He professed to being only a farmer and builder but read the newspapers assiduously for their national political content.

Nancy was overjoyed when Dick and Judith allowed her to return to Bizarre. It would be a busy fall for, in addition to the usual harvesting, Judith prepared for her lying-in. After Nancy returned, the Taylors found time in their busy schedules for visits to Bizarre.

In September, Tucker and Lelia's son, Tutee, died.

Judith's baby was due that month. As a woman approached the end of her pregnancy, her confinement began. With the onset of labor pains, the midwife or physician was called. The second stage of labor brought a full dilation of the cervix and what eighteenth-century practitioners called "forcing or bearing pains." This active stage required the mother to assist in expelling the child. Wrote one young mother, "When they said, 'push,' she began to push, sending her mind into her abdomen, becoming a great muscle, forcing the burden out. Slithering and then rushing on a tide of blood, the baby was born."

Theodorick Tudor Randolph was born on September 17, 1795, physically healthy with no apparent hearing or speech problems.

By November, Dick had been admitted to the bar to practice law in both Cumberland and Prince Edward counties. There is no record, however, that he had any cases or practiced.

❧

Jefferson had a young visitor from South Carolina in November—Henry Rutledge, son of Edward Rutledge. Young Rutledge had been to Boston, New York, and Philadelphia and returned south by way of Monticello, with a letter from his father for his friend Jefferson. Jefferson "pestered Henry with questions about what is passing in the world." When Rutledge left, he headed for Bizarre, where he planned to visit with Jack Randolph, his Columbia College friend.

Jack, a "mere lounger," went from one racetrack to another. Roanoke plantation was his retreat and residents of Charlotte, Prince Edward, and Cumberland counties watched the expert horseman on Jacobin, his favorite horse, frequently travel the forty-mile route between Roanoke and Bizarre. Henry Rutledge arrived at Bizarre while Jack was away, but had an opportunity to meet the girl that Jack had loved so deeply during their student days together. He saw a typical spinster, although only twenty-one years old, relegated to child care and routine household tasks, a captive source of labor without a wife's social and psychological benefits. For everyday attire, she wore the country woman's bonnet and gowns from fabric produced in the weaving room on the plantation.

Rutledge left Jack a note, urging him to visit South Carolina. Jack took the note with him to Roanoke for Christmas, returned to Bizarre by December 27, then back to Roanoke on the twenty-ninth. From

Bizarre, he replied to Rutledge's note, remembering the love that had possessed him five years earlier.

"You have seen the sad relic of her for which I wished to live. I cannot trust my pen on the subject. . . . You inquire after my plans. I have none, my dear Henry, I exist in an obscurity from which I shall never emerge."

Jack accepted Rutledge's invitation "where I hope to embrace the friend of my youth, the sight of whom will ten thousand times repay this tedious journey." He planned to visit Joseph Bryan in Georgia, too, and prepared an itinerary, with distances and times between stops to refresh himself and rest Jacobin, since he would travel on horseback.

To all whom it may concern, I Richard Randolph Junior of Bizarre, in the County of Cumberland, of sound mind and memory, as declare this writing, written with my own hand, and subscribed with my name, this eighteenth day of February in the twentieth year of American Independance, to be my last will and Testament, in form & substance as follows.—

In the first place — To make retribution, as far as I am able, to an unfortunate race of bondmen, over whom my ancestors have usurped and exercised the most lawless and monstrous tyranny, and in whom, my countrymen (by their iniquitous Laws in contradiction of their own declaration of rights, and in violation of every sacred Law of nature; of the inherent, unalienable & imprescriptible rights of man; and of every principle of moral & political honesty) have vested me with absolute property:

To express my abhorrence of the theory, as well as infamous practice of usurping the rights of our fellow creatures, equally intitled with ourselves to the enjoyment of Liberty and happiness:

To exculpate myself, to those who may perchance to think or hear of me after death, from the black crime, which might otherwise be imputed to me, of voluntarily holding the above mentioned miserable beings in the same state of abject slavery in which I found them receiving my patrimony, at lawful age; To impress my children with just horror at a crime so monstrous & indelible, to enjoin them in the last words of a fond father never to participate in it, in any the remotest degree, however sanctioned by Laws (framed by the tyrants themselves who oppress them,) or supported by false reasoning, used always ... to veil the sordid views of avarice, and the lust of power:

To declare to them and to the world, that nothing but uncontroulable necessity, forced on me by my father; (who wrongfully, bound over ... to satisfy the rapacious creditors of a Brother — who for this purpose, which he falsely believed to be generous, mortgaged, all his slaves to british Harpies, for money to gratify pride & pamper sensuality; by which mortgage the said slaves being bound, I could not exercise the right of ownership necessary to their Emancipation; and being obliged to keep them on my land was driven reluctantly to

Richard Randolph's will, February 18, 1796,
Prince Edward County, VA Will Book 1, page 4

1796

While visiting Henry Rutledge in February 1796, Jack and Sir John Nesbit, a visitor from Edinburgh, Scotland, raced, each riding his own horse. The ladies watching found Sir John more exciting, and, although Jack won the race, "Sir John won their hearts."

Jack rode on to Georgia to see Joseph Bryan. There a vivid experience would affect his later congressional career. He witnessed the indignation of Georgians at their legislators after corrupt lawmakers engineered the sale of over 35 million acres of land, through which ran the Yazoo River—territory that later became Alabama and Mississippi—to land speculators for less than one and a half cents per acre. Georgians were enraged, lynchings were threatened, the legislature rescinded the sales, and huge bonfires were held to burn the certificates.

Purchasers appealed to Congress, and ten years later, in the House of Representatives, Jack and Bryan together would fight Jefferson against making any concessions in the monumental Yazoo frauds.

※

After Dick learned that his cousin, Anna Eaton Dudley, Frances Tucker's niece, and her three children were destitute in North Carolina, he went there and brought them back.

"A planter's support of family was not unusual," historian Catherine Clinton wrote. "As long as these family members had any blood or marriage connection, he was obliged to support them with unfailing loyalty."

The Dudleys' arrival at Bizarre increased the work and responsibility for Judith, contrary to the popular belief that Southern plantation mistresses led lives of luxury and ease. Life on Virginia plantations was demanding. Bizarre was no exception.

The plantation routine included a morning ritual. The cook, with baskets on both arms, accompanied Judith or Nancy to the locked smokehouse to select the meat to be served that day. In the storeroom for staples, such as flour, sugar, and stored vegetables, they measured out the exact proportions needed. Rounds were made to the sick or injured including the overseer, his family, and the slaves.

In the spinning and weaving house, work on blankets, socks, and slaves' clothing was supervised. Shoes were ordered from Richmond. Judith and Nancy, both expert seamstresses, cut and sewed the children's clothes, including their gowns, underwear, and bed linens. The unbecoming bonnets to shade them from the sun were made by stitching narrow slats of wood into wide brims to maintain rigidity.

In February, Dick wrote his will. The phrasing of its text conveyed a subliminal impression that the writer may have expected to die early.

"I, Richard Randolph, Junior of Bizarre . . . do declare this writing, the eighteenth day of February in the twentieth year of American independence, to be my last will and testament.

"I give and bequeath to my wife, Judith Randolph, all my personal estate . . . I likewise, devise, give and bequeath to my said wife all my real estate . . . in full confidence that she will do the most justice to our children."

He wanted them independent as soon as they were of age and asked Judith to educate them as well as her fortune would enable her.

"I request my wife frequently to read this my will to my tenderly beloved children, that they may know something of their father's heart when they have forgotten his presence."

The remaining paragraphs of the will would have serious consequences after his death.

Jack returned to Bizarre from his 1,800-mile trip. Poor Jacobin brought his master home safely and then died. Jack attributed the death to Carolina distemper, but it may have been simply exhaustion.

Shortly thereafter, Jack and Dick left for Petersburg to visit with the Banister cousins, assorted friends, and nearby racetracks. Jack became ill and Dick stayed with him until he recuperated, then headed home, stopping off at the federal courts in Richmond.

⤝⤞

Meanwhile, at Bizarre the always-delicate domestic peace was endangered. Mrs. Dudley, noting the volatile situation between the mistress and her sister, was deferential to Judith and critical of Jack's selfishness. When Nancy confronted her on the rifts she caused, Mrs. Dudley informed her that Nancy alone would see her "unveiled."

Dick arrived home on June 5 and soon fell critically ill. Judith treated him from the drug chest. Although his condition worsened, she did not send for a physician. In the past, she had had a doctor prepare various concoctions, such as jalop and calomel, for Saint and herself.

⤝⤞

On June 11, a stranger arrived at Bizarre. Benjamin Henry Latrobe, an English architect and artist, had emigrated to America and was in Virginia doing a study on river navigability. He stayed overnight with Bizarre neighbors, the Skipwiths at Horsdumonde and left to meet the superintendent of the river project, lost his way and his clothes in the woods, and in early afternoon found himself at the gate to Bizarre.

He waited until heavy rain and stares from observers in the house persuaded him to approach Bizarre.

"Another French name but not quite applicable . . . for there is nothing bizarre about it that I can see."

The family welcomed him with Southern plantation hospitality. Although very ill, his host sent a slave to look for his clothes and insisted that Latrobe stay overnight. Latrobe dined with the melancholy family while thunder and lightning joined the downpour outside. He suggested that his hostess send for a physician for Dick, but she refused, saying no one would come out in such a storm. The physician was summoned the next morning, however, before Latrobe's departure, seven days after Dick had become ill. The doctor's prognosis was not encouraging.

Latrobe rode on to Petersburg, where he sketched "from memory of Miss Nancy Randolph." A wide countrywoman's bonnet covered part of her face, a long curl drifted down her back, and an enigmatic half smile played against a classic profile.

⁂

Dick summoned Nancy to his chamber and sent his servant, Toney, on an errand.

"He seemed very unhappy and I tried to soothe him. He extracted silence from me, not to reveal anything to damage his sons' names. I promised, as he asked, to protect his memory and the Saint and Tudor from slander. He seemed comforted."

At Mrs. Dudley's urging, Nancy wrote Tucker that his stepson was on the brink of death.

"This is a scene of much wretchedness, Dick does not know a creature."

Judith made no effort to locate Jack, but Nancy scrawled a hasty note: "Mr. Davis (at the general merchandise store) will oblige me by sending this immediately." Inside she had a message.

"My dear Jack, Dick is on the brink of death, I write come Jack come or it will be too late."

Jack never received the note and when he returned home, it was too late.

Dick died at 4 a.m. on Tuesday, June 14. Toney was sent to find Jack but missed him on the way when he stopped to feed and water his horse. Jack reached home four days after his brother's funeral.

Each person reacted differently to Dick's death.

With her nephew now deceased, Mrs. Dudley moved out of the house the day before the funeral.

Nancy wrote her friend Mary Johnston, who lived at Cherry Grove: "Your goodness can never be effaced. I supposed long ago that I had ascertained all the evils which await one in the dreary shade of adversity . . . my presence now operates like a reproachful conscience on a sister and for that, I am treated like a culprit . . . it is the crisis of affairs . . . the last paroxism of tyrannic power exulting over patient endurance."

⁂

Jack wrote his stepfather: "I have nobody to unburthen myself to. In silence are all of my sorrows and in the solitude of night indulged . . .

I am stupefied. Judy is tolerably well, but complains of a sore throat. Nancy has exerted her fortitude in such a manner as engages my highest esteem. So far from disturbing her sister by giving way to her grief, she indulges it only out of her presence and pays her every soothing attention in her power."

Jane visited her sisters at Bizarre for two weeks. She was, Judith told Mary Harrison, "The only rag of comfort I've had since you left me. Nothing to wish for, no flattering prospect to cheat my senses with, the cup of my afflictions has overflowed."

And Alexander Campbell, who may have been the last friend Dick saw before he returned to Bizarre, committed suicide. The "eccentric and celebrated Mr. Campbell," who had defended Dick in his trial, died by an overdose of laudanum.

There were rumors that Dick died of medication administered by a woman's hand and that Judith had murdered her husband. Jessie Ball Thompson Krusen wrote in her book, *Tuckahoe Plantation,* that Judith killed Dick. No charges were brought and no investigation took place. Two decades later, Judith, when questioned by Jack about his brother's death, told him that Nancy had poisoned Dick.

"I was told that an emetic (tartar) was used. Did she mix or hand him the medicine . . . ? Had she the opportunity for doing the deed that caused his dissolution?"

Tartar emetic is a poison, corroding the mucous lining of the stomach, eventually inhibiting the vomit reflex that protects the stomach. If the body does not quickly reject the poison, the victim can succumb within one or two days.

What motive would Nancy have had for poisoning Dick, and if Judith suspected her, why wouldn't she have also feared being poisoned? Was there another reason that Mrs. Dudley, a close observer of the household routine, moved out, other than having lost her benefactor?

⤚⊱⤙

In the 1950 novel about Judith and Nancy, *The Bizarre Sisters,* by Audrey and Jay Walz, the ingredients for a dose of tartar emetic consisted of ten grains of calomel, one-half grain of jalop, one and a half grains of opium, a drop of oil of aniseed, and a pinch of tartar emetic. Judith changed the recipe to read ten grains of tartar and instructed Nancy, who was unfamiliar with the precise amounts used, to mix the dose. The recipe disappeared and when Judith "found" it, the amount of tartar emetic was shown again as a pinch. Through Judith's alteration of the recipe, Nancy was blamed as preparer of the fatal dose.

In addition to the tartar, ten grains of calomel, a purgative, would be enormously excessive, the normal dose being two grains given at specified intervals.

≫

St. George Tucker lost another child that summer, Elizabeth, his and Frances's youngest child. In four years, he had lost two stepsons and two children by Frances and one by Lelia. Judith's condolences to Tucker seemed apathetic, almost indifferent.

"Sympathies on loss of Elizabeth. Tudor walks at ten-and-one-half months."

≫

Benjamin Latrobe was still in Virginia and his work took him to Tuckahoe in July 1796. His purpose was to ascertain the navigation of Tuckahoe Creek, but he visited with Colonel Randolph's widow, Gabriella, and "much time was spent in amusement and indeed the party was so agreeable, we were all sorry to return to Richmond."

The widow Randolph retained her enthusiasm for entertaining and in August Latrobe returned. According to neighbors, "The whirl of gaieties added little to the fame and prestige of the mansion." Gabriella frequently visited Richmond, where her parents lived. A banker, Dr. John Brockenbrough, began a courtship.

Jefferson continued his remodeling of Monticello in early 1796, enlarging the house to accommodate Martha's growing family while Tom was building his and Martha's home, Edgehill, near Monticello.

≫

George Washington announced that when his term as president ended in 1797, he intended to retire to Mount Vernon and would not consider running for a third term. Jefferson suggested that Madison run for the presidency; instead, Madison, without Jefferson's knowledge, had begun campaigning for Jefferson's nomination. Jefferson learned of Madison's intent and refused to campaign.

Martha, happy to be back home with her children, father, and sister Maria, had another child in October. Ellen Wayles Randolph was named for her sister who had died the year before.

In November the electoral voting gave seventy-one votes to Adams, sixty-eight to Jefferson, and fifty-nine to Pinckney. Under the Constitution, the candidate receiving the most votes became president and the one with the second highest number became vice president. Jefferson, a Republican (later the Democratic party), would become vice president under a Federalist president. He would have to return to Philadelphia, and Martha, anxious for him to remain at home, and whose "every sentiment of tenderness" was centered in him, "interwoven with my very existence," would again be separated from the person she loved most.

1797

udith felt truly adventurous in sending Mary a letter from Williamsburg by "post," rather than through friends, in early 1797. She had been there two weeks, and her "health and spirits are somewhat recruited by the change of scene . . . yet amidst the society which I unwillingly engage in here, there is a void . . . for an instant I seem lost in the gaiety of those around me, but I return as rapidly to those corroding reflections which in secret prey on my mind."

On April 18, 1797, she, as executrix, filed Dick's will for probate at Prince Edward Courthouse.

In the will, he liberated his slaves to "exculpate myself . . . from the black crime . . ." of ownership.

If the slaves were sold to pay off the British debt, Judith was to raise money from the estate, free them, and use four hundred acres of his land to resettle them.

By May, Judith had forgotten her February "state of wretchedness, continuing to fatten," and made "a flying trip to Petersburg" to visit a good friend for a week, leaving both children with Nancy. St. George Tucker and Lelia planned a trip to Bizarre, so Judith sent Nancy away. She needed Nancy's help on the plantation, yet avoided including her in social events.

Instead, Tucker canceled his visit due to Lelia's illness, "her malady a common one with lasting consequences." Lelia's pregnancy ended in miscarriage.

Nancy wrote Mary Johnston of her latest ejection from Bizarre.

"I was turned out of the house . . . it became necessary to assign a reason for my going . . . Judy conceived an idea that Mrs. Sally Taylor espoused my cause . . . nothing cou'd have been more erroneous . . . also, it will never be forgotten."

Jack was a disruptive presence at Bizarre. Mrs. Dudley and her children returned, and she described Jack's "bizarre" behavior. His room was directly below hers, and at night she heard him striding back and forth, feet booted, crying out:

"Macbeth hath murdered sleep, Macbeth hath murdered sleep."

Then, strapping on his pistols, he would order his horse saddled and ride wildly across the plantation in the darkness.

Dick's estate inventory, filed in July 1797, listed slaves and their value, left after disposition of a number "in part satisfaction of the Cape and Osgood Hanbury mortgage." Excepted slaves to the mortgage were Syphax the elder and four of his offspring. Judith had to work those that were left at Bizarre to generate money to pay off the mortgage and to purchase their freedom.

The highest valued item in the personal inventory was a mahogany secretary with glass doors, at fifty pounds, which had held Dick's large collection of books. Among these were Plutarch, Bollingbrook, Hume's *Essays,* Rousseau, and Cicero's *Orations.*

With Jack's indifference to Bizarre's operations, Judith learned the harsh realities of being the head of a plantation, including its production. Her neighbors, Creed and Sally Taylor, provided assistance and advice when they could but seldom visited.

"Why do we not see you at Bizarre? Tell Mrs. Taylor I shall never return from Williamsburg, if she goes on thus, we are really moped to death," she wrote before she left to visit the Tuckers.

Nancy had written to her brother William without Judith's knowledge because she "considered it unjust to be ordered by one party respecting conduct to the other." Although earlier she had repulsed William's efforts to reconcile after the trial, she and William met secretly at the Taylors'.

Excited, Nancy wrote, "It is scarcely possible to wield my pen."

⁂

When Jefferson arrived in Philadelphia for the inauguration, he was greeted by artillery of sixteen rounds from two twelve-pounders. He was inaugurated early in the morning in the Senate, then entered the House Chamber of Congress on March 4, 1797, with George Washington and awaited John Adams' appearance. Adams gave the inaugural address and then took the oath of office as president.

Adams and Jefferson had different points of view, and the two men were never again able to enjoy the camaraderie that they had in Paris. Jefferson was in Philadelphia only eleven days before he returned to Monticello, bitter. Adams wrote of Jefferson, "He is as he was."

⁂

In June 1797, the *Lidderdale v. Randolph* debt case was heard, in which Colonel Thomas Mann Randolph's estate was sued by the British merchants. John Marshall was one of the defense attorneys. They lost the case. William and Tom were ordered to pay $64,000, and the decision brought financial ruin to the Tuckahoe Randolphs.

Life changed at Tuckahoe. Gabriella, the Colonel's widow, remarried at age twenty-five. The bridegroom was Dr. John Brockenbrough, the man who had courted Gabriella for months. The wedding was held at Tuckahoe, and she, with her son, Thomas Mann II, moved to Richmond.

Tom's sister Jane had married a cousin, Thomas Eston Randolph, from Dungeness. Harriet and John were still single, as was Virginia, who lived with Tom and Martha.

Tom entered the race for the General Assembly. The children were inoculated against smallpox, but Martha was unable to go to Richmond for their injections. On election day, Tom did not go to the polls because the children were so ill. He was roundly criticized by those whom he had solicited for votes, but Martha wrote Jefferson that the children's father was a tender and more skillful nurse than she. Tom lost the election.

Maria Jefferson, dark and petite, was the beauty of the family, being "remarkably handsome." Shy and retiring, she turned away the many compliments that she received, attributing them to kindness. A number of eligible men courted her, including Congressman William Branch Giles, but she refused them all and waited for her cousin, John Eppes, to propose. He was considered a handsome man although described as having a harelip. When he proposed, Maria hesitated to ask her father's permission; Martha asked for her. He acquiesced readily, viewing Eppes as the joining link in the family circle.

At the wedding on October 13, Maria wore her mother's white satin wedding gown. Her father's gift was a carriage with a matched set of horses, twenty-six slaves, and eight hundred acres of land at Pantops, very close to Monticello and Edgehill. However, she and her husband never built at Pantops. Instead, the newlyweds went back to Eppington in Chesterfield County and then to Mont Blanco, near Petersburg.

That summer of 1797, Tom moved from Varina to Belmont, John Harvie's plantation in Albemarle, and continued to build Edgehill. The family spent summers at Monticello but were nearby throughout the year.

✂

After James Monroe replaced him as minister to France, Gouverneur Morris stayed on in Europe. He assisted Lafayette and his family, using both his influence and personal funds. Lafayette had returned to military service and was captured and imprisoned at Armutz in Austria, unable to intervene as executions wiped out his wife's family. Her mother, grandmother, and sister were beheaded. She sent their son, George Washington Lafayette, to safety in America for asylum, but her daughters, Virginia and Anastacia, stayed in Paris with her. She and her daughters were seized and imprisoned in the Bastille.

Morris arranged for the Lafayette family's release and provided, with a large loan, the money they needed to flee France, saving them, the Marquise wrote, "from the frenzy of a monster." They fled France only to be imprisoned in Austria.

1798

*I*n February, from Williamsburg, Judith sent Mary Harrison a charming account of the social activities there. St. George and Lelia Tucker had generously provided new party clothes for the sisters.

"I have not been to a ball yet, but I had a narrow escape about ten days ago, when my father laid his positive commands on me to prepare for a very brilliant one at Mr. Bassett's and nothing but a violent cold could have reprieved me . . .

" . . . as to Nancy, had you seen, in the elegant Book muslin, with balloon sleeves, little pearl colored Tiffin hat stuck on one side of the head, the old woman you knew at Glentivar in October last, with a cambric mob on, I know not what you would have thought. She would not credit her own eyes when she viewed herself thus adorned."

Judith had not been metamorphosed into a lady yet, she was still the "laughing stock of the fair damsells who wore hats with a brim one inch deep, over one eye, to turbans." Her dress was always a plain black, and she wore a "large double bordered blowze cap . . . or a neat, plain, satin bonnet dressed with ribbons."

"Your acquaintance, Mr. Bassett, is paying his devoirs to Miss Polly Champs Carter (Lelia's daughter, Mary) whose fame no doubt has reached your ears; she is, beyond anything you ever beheld or I could form any idea of, the most angelic being. . . . You know what an enthusiast

I am on female loveliness, and I do not believe that even Mr. Bassett gazes at this divinity with more rapture than I do. It is said she is cruel as fair and that he is most certainly refused. . . . ”

Nicknames were often used, such as Polly for Mary, Patsy for Martha, or Nancy for Ann.

❧

Nancy's letter to Tucker painted a different picture of the visit and of Judith's animosity. An agreement was made between Judith and Fanny Tucker that the children should never visit Bizarre except when Nancy was absent.

"I promise to keep my room constantly unless it be in my power to leave Bizarre this summer."

Jack and Judith reconciled their differences, excluding Nancy. "I have witnessed the mutual animosities of the two members who compose the family at present – since they became friendly to each other they appear to condemn me for enduring odium so unjustly bestowed. . . .”

She noted how often Tucker had "mitigated my pangs with the soothing voice of affection. . . . I can only include you and yours when I implore protection from that being who has never yet forsaken me."

In November, Nancy was sent to the Harrisons at Glentivar, where "the obligation to seek asylum among averred enemies must indicate atonement." When, finally, Nancy was allowed to return to Bizarre, Judith punctually sought Sally Taylor's company:

"Nancy has at length reached Bizarre and I hope that her company will be a sufficient inducement to bring you hither. The carriage awaits your command and be assured that I shall always be singularly grateful in having the pleasure of seeing you.

In haste, Judy Randolph.”

❧

Creed Taylor, now a member of the House of Delegates, learned that Abraham Venable intended resigning from Congress and urged Jack to run for the House of Representatives in the April 1799 election. Jack, intrigued, visited around the district, then confirmed his candidacy. Thus was his congressional career launched.

Another interest was a romantic one with Maria Ward of The Hermitage in Amelia County. She was younger than Jack but had matured

early, and was a beautiful young woman at age fourteen. Her attachment to Jack deepened as his plans for Congress piqued her interest.
Few women had evinced an attachment to Jack, and for the first time
since his Philadelphia days, he became genuinely involved. His trips to
Amelia became more frequent, and Maria began visiting Bizarre. She
and Judith formed a warm attachment, excluding Nancy.

From a distance, Jefferson advised another Maria, his daughter, on
matters such as her dress and her relations with her husband. If her
opinion differed from her husband's, "Leave him in quiet possession of
his views.

"What was the use of rectifying, if it was unimportant, otherwise,
let it pass and wait for a softer moment and more conciliatory occasion."

He reminded her that time makes inroads on one's person, to pay
close attention to her articles of dress. Cultivate the affection of a circle of acquaintances. "Think every sacrifice a gain which shall tend to
attach them to you."

Maria related fascinating details of her recent visit to Petersburg,
where she had met Mr. and Mrs. John Walker, former friends of
Jefferson. Mrs. Walker had invited her for a visit, but since Mr.
Walker did not think it proper to invite Maria, she was not forced
to make excuses. Maria referred to the gossip that had spread some
years earlier that Jefferson had made improper advances to Mrs.
Walker, who had told of his having written her notes condoning
promiscuous love and of attempting to sneak into her bedroom
while her husband was away.

Martha's letters to her father were far different. From Belmont she
wrote him of the rapture with which she looked forward to being reunited with him, her "dearest and adored father."

"The heart swelling with which I address you . . . convinces me of
the folly or want of feeling of those who dare to think that any new ties
can weaken the first and best of nature."

Jefferson urged her to move to Monticello. "The south pavilion,
parlor and study will accommodate you. The extra riding for Tom
would be less inconvenient than the loss of his family's health."

Maria inherited her mother's childbearing problems. After a

miscarriage, she was too ill to travel to Monticello as planned. When she came later, she traveled in slow stages.

In the spring of 1798, President Adams sent John Marshall and Elbridge Gerry to join Minister to France Charles Cotesworth Pinkney in Paris to meet with Foreign Minister Charles de Tallyrand. Meantime, Jefferson was convinced that the best course was for France to defeat England. Tallyrand highhandedly refused to deal directly with the Americans, relegating them to three of his agents who attempted to obtain bribe money for Tallyrand's assistance and money and loans for France. Outraged, Marshall refused to consider such terms and returned to America.

John Adams informed Congress of the unsuccessful mission, but Jefferson demanded full disclosure. Adams gave details of Marshall's report, designating the agents as X, Y, and Z. The French conspiracy to demand unlawful compromises, now known as the "XYZ Affair," sent the country into a frenzy against France. Marshall returned a hero while Jefferson was maligned.

Congress began crafting the Alien and Sedition Acts. The Alien Acts tightened naturalization and citizen requirements. The president was given power to arrest, imprison, or banish foreigners without a trial. Under the Sedition Acts, any citizen who criticized the president or Congress—either verbally, in writing, or by publication—could be tried, fined, and/or imprisoned. As presiding officer in the Senate, Jefferson was so opposed to the passage of these acts that he found his position untenable, and he left Philadelphia, remaining at Monticello until December 1798.

Virginia Republicans felt the laws infringed on individual rights, and some states rightists even suggested that Virginia withdraw from the Union. To express disapproval of the despised laws, Jefferson and Madison wrote the Kentucky and Virginia Resolutions and the two state assemblies adopted them.

George Washington learned of the country's increasing opposition to the central government and urged Patrick Henry, formerly the most vehement states rights advocate, to run for the General Assembly as a Federalist candidate. Henry had moved to Red Hill in Charlotte County, was in poor physical condition, and longed for retirement. But he had become convinced that the nation would succeed only in having a strong central government, so he reluctantly agreed to become a candidate.

Washington then persuaded John Marshall to run for the House of Representatives. At his urging, Marshall repudiated the despised Alien and Sedition Acts, leading many Federalists to consider him a traitor, but in Richmond it enhanced his candidacy.

⤛

Gouverneur Morris returned to America in the winter of 1798 after ten years overseas. His ship was forced to Newport, Rhode Island, because of ice in the New York harbor. On December 23, his nephew and two friends, John Church and Alexander Hamilton, welcomed him home after his long absence. His properties needed immediate attention, and he began by refurbishing his home, Morrisania, in what is now the Bronx, New York.

Edgehill, Albemarle County, VA, 1800,
Library of Virginia

1799

During the 1799 election campaign, Patrick Henry spoke from a tavern porch near Charlotte Courthouse on March court day. Hampden-Sydney College, in nearby Farmville, suspended classes to allow the students and professors to hear Henry. Even the grand jury left deliberations and members ran outside to listen, and the size of the crowd overwhelmed Henry.

He contended that "the state had quitted the sphere in which she had been placed by the Constitution . . . opposition to the acts of the General government must beget the enforcement by military power." Opposition would probably produce civil war and foreign alliances, ending "in subjugation to the powers."

"United we stand, divided we fall."

Henry referred to himself as "but a poor worm of the dust, as fleeting and unsubstantial as the shadow of the cloud that flies over your fields, and is remembered no more."

He collapsed, and a voice in his audience rang out, "The sun has set in all its glory."

❧

Henry's last speech set the stage for Jack Randolph's first, from the same porch. Jack's admiration for Henry was as great as ever, but he spoke as a states rightist, in opposition to Henry. Smartly attired in a blue coat, buff trousers, and white boots, Jack appealed to constituents' pride of community and fear of federal encroachment. Powhatan Bolling, flamboyant in a scarlet coat, opposed him. Creed Taylor accompanied Jack, and knowing well his fluency, did not concern himself about the speech. Instead, he and Jack's supporters heckled Bolling about his red coat.

While Jack campaigned for the April 1799 election, Nancy and Judith pursued their usual erratic course while Jack's relationship with Maria Ward flourished. Jack, the awkward, skinny loner, was flattered by her admiration.

"Maria has completely riveted Jack's chains," Judith wrote Tucker. "He is attentive, this is serious."

Both General Meade, Maria's stepfather, and his wife were fond of Jack and consented to his engagement to Maria, but no wedding date was set.

Bizarre did not hold the enchantment for Fanny Tucker, Jack's half-sister, as it did for Nancy. Visiting Bizarre while Nancy was at Monticello, Fanny found the place boring and depressing compared with the active social life in Williamsburg. She gave a capsule description of a summer with Judith to Tucker and Lelia, who were at Sweet Springs.

"Low spirits, the most terrible of all complaints, is raging here. I have gained a thicker skin tho' I cannot boast of flesh. One quarter of a sheet of paper would easily contain the news of Cumberland and Prince Edward."

Fanny was now twenty years old and lived in the same household with her beautiful and wealthy stepsister, Mary Carter. While Mary turned aside suitors' proposals, none came forward to ask for Fanny's hand.

John Thompson, Dick's friend, died, leaving a younger brother, William. The year before, Jack and William had taken a trip through the Blue Ridge Mountains before William left for Europe to study medicine. His affinity for women and alcohol weakened his resolve for any profession, and he returned to Virginia. The death of William's brother served to forge a relationship between the two young men. Jack brought William to Bizarre, hoping that its isolation would remove him from the temptation of the taverns and brothels of Petersburg.

Both Patrick Henry and Jack Randolph were elected to their respective offices in April, thereby ending Jack's fear that he would "dwell in an obscurity from which he would never emerge."

John Marshall was also elected, although only by a few votes. Colonel Henry died at Red Hill before he could assume office.

Jack left for the Sixth Congress in Philadelphia in December 1799. He had been under the legal age to serve on the election date, but his twenty-sixth birthday in June qualified him.

⚬⚬

At Edgehill, Tom completed the two-storied house with a gallery, and the family moved into their new home. Gradual acquisitions of furniture and accessories made the home comfortable. Even so Martha always preferred Monticello. She bore another daughter, Cornelia Jefferson, at Edgehill in July.

Summer brought its influx of visitors to Monticello. Nancy Randolph, during her stay there, wrote Tucker of her admiration for Jefferson, confiding that "Mr. J's presence imposes upon me the reserve which I should feel in yours."

Maria Eppes was once again "in the straw," and a daughter was born on December 31, 1799. She lived less than a month.

⚬⚬

Molly Randolph, Judith's and Nancy's older sister, and her husband, David Meade Randolph, now lived in Richmond, where he served as Federal Marshal, a position that Jefferson had obtained for him. They had sold Presqu'ile, where the boggy land was conducive to malaria. Molly claimed never to have enjoyed one month of good health while living on the plantation.

Moldavia, the large home they built in Richmond, was on property covering a square block at Fifth and Main Streets. It was a city plantation with a carriage house, outdoor kitchen, necessary (outhouse), and slave quarters on several acres. The home had an octagonal ballroom on the second floor. Molly became well known for her hospitality and sumptuous entertaining, customs learned at Tuckahoe. The dishes she served were well seasoned with herbs, a departure from the bland English method, and her recipes were highly prized.

On December 13, 1799, George Washington returned, wet and cold, from a ride over his lands. He sat in front of the fireplace, disheartened, after learning that Madison, a strong states rightist and Republican, had been elected governor of Virginia. The next day he was ill, with a high fever. Within a few days, weakened even more by being bled, he died.

When word of his death reached Philadelphia, John Marshall made the announcement in the House of Representatives, and offering a resolution of mourning, delivered the ringing commendation written by his cousin, Light Horse Harry Lee: "First in war, first in peace, first in the hearts of his countrymen." Members of Congress requested that Gouverneur Morris deliver Washington's funeral oration in New York. Morris was bitterly disappointed in his performance, sure that he had not given Washington the tribute that the great leader deserved.

Congress passed a resolution to build a monument to honor Washington. Citizens in mourning wore black crepe on the left arm for thirty days. Jefferson, not included in the funeral ceremonies, did not leave Monticello until December 29, arriving after their conclusion. He had been away from Philadelphia for ten months.

Maria Ward 1784-1826,
Library of Virginia

1800

*J*udith felt hopeless, both for her children's education and for the future prosperity of Tudor, which was "damped" by the conviction that Saint, "with a genius otherwise capable of any improvement," was "disbarred from almost every requirement, as well as enjoyment. It continually haunts me and shuts every avenue to hope... there are times when I sicken at the prospect before me."

She sold part of the Bizarre plantation to a group that included Creed Taylor and Jack. They divided the parcel into over fifty lots for the village of Farmville. The half-acre lots sold for fifty pounds each.

Beset by plantation problems, she sought Creed Taylor's help before he left for Richmond regarding the overseer.

"I forgot yesterday to say something of Mr. Wray and of his proportion of the crops, which he has so ill earned. He is entitled to a thirteenth part but I wish to know whether some deduction must be made for the keeping of his horse which he had been feeding these two months. Can you tell me how much pork I must furnish my overseer?" He had a wife and two children.

"Believe me, my dear sir, I have no other friend to whom I can apply, in the numerous difficulties which continually assail me, and which are often too great for me to bear up against."

But Judith softened with William Thompson at Bizarre, postponing her visit to Williamsburg. Instead, William escorted her to social functions around Prince Edward, Cumberland, and Amelia counties. Nancy's usual banishment was postponed because her services were required at Bizarre. She was pleased at first, enjoying Judith's improved disposition, but after a while she resented the exclusion.

"On Sunday, William Thompson and Judy left me amid the gloom allied to solitude and misfortune. I shall soon become a paragon of resignation."

William's letters to Jack in Philadelphia painted a blissful portrait of Bizarre's serenity.

"Our sister is now asleep; she would have written but for her being busy in finishing the children's clothes and being obliged to write to Mrs. Harrison. When I came in last evening, I found her in the passage, a candle on the chair, sewing. I could hardly help exclaiming what a pattern for her sex.

"Farewell, dearest brother, hasten to join us."

⁂

Unfortunately, William fell from grace and succumbed once more to temptation. He visited Petersburg, indulging his former diversions, and attempted to justify his amorous dalliance with a married woman.

"The lady's husband is a beast, she married him only for his money."

Jack's thinly veiled annoyance reminded William that the marital choice had been the lady's and implied that other men besides William may have been clasped to her ample bosom.

⁂

Then, another problem surfaced.

Neighborhood gossip about Bizarre rekindled. Rumors flew that William Thompson's stay at Bizarre was to ingratiate himself with its mistress to establish a marital relationship. Mary Harrison heard it and asked for an explanation.

"The report which you have heard is as false as it is ridiculous," Judith responded. "My friend, I beseech you, I am content with my situation, providence has assigned it and I submit. I shall never change it for a worse and cannot for a better."

Nonetheless, she refused to leave Bizarre. "Necessity has compelled me to postpone my jaunt." Judith would not visit Mary while William was at Bizarre.

There was more trouble. William wrote Jack of a report being circulated concerning Jack's activities when he studied law in Philadelphia. He related his conversations with Maria and her mother, Mrs. Meade.

"Heed not the shafts that are thrown against you. . . . Mrs. M. assured me that in your honor she placed the most implicit confidence. When you communicate with M as probably you have already done, she will declare herself unaffected by this tale which has disturbed your peace."

When Jack arrived home at the end of the session, he went to the Meade home. The slaves at the Hermitage passed down their account of Jack and Maria's confrontation, following the "bright lights and music" period of their engagement. Jack galloped up, it was said, threw the reins to a slave, telling him to hold the horse, and sent Maria a note. If Maria went into the garden, the boy was to let him know. The boy returned with the news that Maria was in the garden, and Jack dashed behind the house. Shortly afterward, he returned, mounted his horse, and galloped wildly away. Maria ran into the house, her hands covering her face.

The engagement was broken, and county people expected General Meade to challenge Jack to a duel, the usual course when a man broke off an engagement to a lady. Apparently the General received a satisfactory explanation, for no challenge was issued and Maria continued to exert a strong influence on affairs at Bizarre.

Judith and William's relationship ended, too. He left Bizarre and moved into Ryland Randolph's home.

"Would you suppose, my dearest brother, that the world would have dared to insinuate that my object in remaining at Bizarre is to solicit the affections of our friend? View the subject with impartiality . . . tell me whether I am not bound to leave the abode of innocence and friendship?"

William proposed a trip to Canada. Jack suggested that he make his journey, then return to Bizarre.

"Consult your own heart," he told his friend, "it alone is capable of advising you."

With William's departure, Judith resumed her customary role in the household at Bizarre, furious at the consequences of the gossip, and Nancy was the closest at hand upon whom she could vent her rage.

"Judy bestows all the displeasure excited by others upon me.," Nancy wrote. "I have had to struggle against all the storms of life . . . and eventually sacrificed to appease the animosities of others."

Gouverneur Morris was appointed to serve out the unexpired term of New York Senator James Watson and was confirmed on May 3, 1800. He went to Philadelphia for the last congressional term to be held in the "city of brotherly love."

After Congress adjourned, Morris traveled along the Niagara River to Fort Erie, near Buffalo, and envisioned a canal from the Great Lakes, the Erie Canal.

"Waters of the great inland sea that would mingle with those of the Hudson's," he wrote.

"Hundreds of large ships will in no distant period bound on the billows of these inland seas . . . a navigation of more than a thousand miles."

In late January, Martha wrote Jefferson of the death of yet another baby born to Maria. Martha had been bitterly disappointed in not having gone to her sister's lying in, where Maria had suffered dreadfully from an abscessed breast.

In 1800, Monticello became the headquarters for Jefferson's presidential campaign. He composed a biography, printing 5,000 copies. Both his daughters, unable to understand his interest in politics, were opposed to his continuing in public office. They felt that he had already made significant contributions to his country, and they wanted him to retire to Monticello.

The Federalist Party had been weakened by the country's opposition to the Alien and Sedition Acts. Under the sedition law, one congressman had been fined and sentenced to jail for protesting President Adams's behavior. One case affected Jefferson personally. He had befriended James Callendar, a newspaper reporter. Callendar's articles in the *Richmond Examiner* infuriated Federalists, and he was arrested on charges of sedition for criticizing the president. He was brought to trial in June 1800. Supreme Court Justice Samuel Chase came to Richmond to hear the case. His behavior from the bench so angered defense attorneys George Hay and William Wirt that they withdrew from the case and the trial lasted only one day. Callendar was found guilty only two hours after the jury began deliberating.

Virginians were furious, both with Chase's unfair rulings and at the Alien and Sedition Acts under which he had acted.

⸗

The upcoming session of Congress was scheduled to be in Philadelphia, then the government would be moved to Washington, which would become the Federal City, the District of Columbia. The city was actually a quagmire, and the President's House was unfinished. President Adams came to Washington while Abigail returned to Quincy. He stayed ten days and, after appointing John Marshall as secretary of state, left for home. Jefferson was with his family in Albemarle.

In the fall general election, Jefferson and Aaron Burr were the Republican candidates for president and vice president. Adams and Charles Cotesworth Pinckney were the Federalist candidates. Jefferson left Monticello at the end of November and was in Washington when the electoral voting results were announced. He received seventy-three votes, as did Burr, while Adams received sixty-five, Pinckney sixty-four. The Constitution had no provision for a tie, since the candidate with the most votes became president and the one with the second highest became vice president. The vote went to the House of Representatives to be decided. Senator Gouverneur Morris would be there to observe and Jack Randolph would be there to vote.

⸗

Maria Eppes graciously congratulated her father on the election. "I shall endeavor to be satisfied in the happiness it will give so many." Martha took an unusual stance for her, so bitterly disappointed that she did not write her father for three months. Jefferson was so hurt by her silence that he finally suggested that three words would have been enough. When she did write, she spoke vaguely of the many problems that beset her as a mother and in educating her children.

1801

At first, Jefferson believed that Burr would withdraw gracefully. Then he learned that Burr intended to accept the position of president, if the House members voted him in. Shocked, Jefferson called on Adams to help resolve the dilemma. Although Adams secretly believed Jefferson to be the better choice, he felt there was nothing he could do. John Marshall, appointed by Adams to serve both as chief justice of the United States and as secretary of state, refused to support either Burr or Jefferson, saying, "I cannot bring myself to aid Mr. Jefferson, I can take no part in this business."

When a report of a threatened Federalist coup reached Virginia, members of the General Assembly made plans to reconvene immediately if such an action were taken. Jefferson informed Governor James Monroe that the day such an action passed, the middle states would arm and "no such usurpation . . . should be submitted to." Monroe arranged for express riders, traveling day and night, to bring any news.

Then Alexander Hamilton, who aspired to being a king maker and who hated John Adams, stepped in. He contacted the undecided Federalists, urging them to vote for Jefferson, openly accusing Burr of being "the most dangerous man of the community."

"His elevation can only promote the purpose of the desperate and profligate. If there is a man in the world I ought to hate, it is Jefferson,"

Hamilton proclaimed. "With Burr I have always been personally well. But the public good must be paramount to every private consideration."

❧

Senator Gouverneur Morris, Hamilton's friend, thought the two men were about equal in qualifications but cast a jaundiced eye at the machinations and took no part.

❧

Jack Randolph was in the House when the balloting began on February 11, as a heavy snow fell. The president and Senate members were allowed on the floor, and visitors were in the galleries until the doors were closed and the voting began. The House remained in session throughout the first night, then recesses were called and five more ballots were cast in short sessions.

Jack sent a report on February 12 by Governor Monroe's special messenger.

"Past 5 o'clock p.m.

"We have balloted ten times, the result, with some variety in the majorities of the respective states uniformly the same. 8 states for Jefferson – 6 states for Burr. Two (Maryland and Vermont divided."

Each state was allowed one vote. The representatives from each state voted on a candidate for their state's vote.

"General vote of Virginia has been 14 to 5, never more than 5 against. Mr. Joseph Nicholson at the hazard of his life left his sickbed and presented the vote of Maryland being given to Mr. J." Joseph Nicholson was Jack's friend.

❧

After thirty-five ballots and the outcome still undecided, James Bayard, the sole Delaware representative, acceded to Hamilton's pressure that "disgrace abroad, ruin at home, are the probable fruits of Burr's elevation." To avoid the appearance of making a deal, he cast a blank.

On the thirty-sixth ballot, Jack reported, "Ten states for Jefferson, four for Burr. Delaware and South Carolina voted with blanks."

At 2 p.m. on February 17, Jefferson was officially elected president of the United states. Most Virginians were elated with the election results. Students from the College of William and Mary, Jefferson's alma mater, mounted a jubilant procession through Williamsburg and, as they passed Tucker House, St. George and Lelia Tucker invited them in for a glass of wine to toast the president-elect.

To leaders from both parties Jefferson threatened to "reorganize the government."

To his daughter Maria he wrote that he "panted to be away. . . from the circle of cabal, intrigue and hatred."

⚹

Before the inauguration, the lame-duck Congress, complying with Adams's requests, expanded the 1789 Judiciary Act, creating new federal court districts, adding twenty-three additional judges, and reducing the Supreme Court by one justice, which the Republicans said was to impede a Jeffersonian appointment.

Adams proceeded to fill the positions, appointing mostly Federalists. There was no rush to appoint "midnight judges," as has been reputed. He made final plans to return to Massachusetts and ended his official entertaining with a dinner for an Indian delegation. Adams left at 4 a.m. on March 4, the day of Jefferson's inauguration. An early departure was necessary to reach Baltimore in time to take the stage north.

Senator Gouverneur Morris was appointed to reply to Jefferson's Farewell to the Senate. In his address, he regretted the "loss of that intelligent attention and impartiality" and assured the president-elect of "our Constitution's support of your administration."

On March 4, Jefferson rode to the Capitol, "escorted by a body of militia and a procession of citizens," tethered his horse, went to the Senate chamber, and was inaugurated as the third president of the United States. He wore a plain suit with frayed cuffs. One enemy in sartorial splendor, Aaron Burr, became vice president, while another, his distant cousin, John Marshall, administered the oath of office.

His address was delivered in a voice so low that only Burr and Marshall heard him. His audience applauded politely, not knowing what he had said until they read the speech later.

⚹

On March 11, Jefferson removed David Meade Randolph, husband of Tom's sister Molly, as Federal Marshal in Richmond. He believed that Randolph, an ardent Federalist, had been involved in slandering him. Not only did the firing cause more animosity among the Randolphs, but it also dealt a severe blow to Molly and David's financial situation. David sold his favorite horse, Desdemona, hardly making a dent in his indebtedness. Later, they were forced to put their home, Moldavia, up for sale.

⤝✂⤞

Those in Washington who professed dismay at Jefferson's frayed cuffs and practice of wearing carpet slippers during meetings applauded his fine continental cuisine and superior wines at official functions. In addition to the best food and wine, he had the best hostess, Dolley Madison. Attractive and vivacious, she was an ideal choice, exciting many congressmen in town without spouses but with an appreciation for high bosoms in low-cut gowns and well-turned ankles. Senator Gouverneur Morris was among those who cast an approving eye, until he learned that she dipped snuff, a habit that he abhorred.

⤝✂⤞

Back at Monticello, Jefferson continued the building and rebuilding of his home. Some of the rooms had no floors, other rooms had no doors. It was cold in the winter and hot in the summer, at times 98 degrees inside. Even his personal suite—a bedroom, study, and library—was often unsheltered from the weather during the process of construction., But there was always a stream of visitors, with Martha as the hostess. Jefferson became a grandfather twice that summer. Martha's sixth child, Virginia, was born. In August, Maria returned from Bermuda Hundred for her lying-in. Her second child, Francis, was born on September 20.

Jefferson was back in Washington when the children developed whooping cough. Unlike in the past at the time of the smallpox vaccinations when Tom had been the strong parent, now it was Martha. The children were delirious, laughing and singing and Tom was tormented, "his mind calling forth every energy of mine." Martha acted both as nurse to the children and comforter to the father.

⤝✂⤞

When Jack returned to Bizarre, he found Judith ill and despondent after William Thompson's departure for Canada.

"Judy is so thin and looks so badly I shall take her to the Warm Springs this summer," he wrote Tucker, and continued to Nicholson, "The health of my family compels me to try the benefits of the mountain air and water – we will pass six to eight weeks at the Warm and

Sweet Springs." He extended the invitation to Fanny to accompany them. With a high ratio of men to women at the springs, there was a possibility of a suitable attachment.

Before they left, Fanny received a letter from her friend Lelia Ann Byrd, who had recently returned to Riveredge, on the James, after a visit to cosmopolitan Williamsburg. From a more rural community, Lelia Ann described a wedding she had attended. The bride had wished the bridegroom might "brake" his neck while going for the license and had cried throughout the event. One of the bridesmen was so affected he could scarcely perform his duties.

"Don't you think it rather in the romantic way?" she asked Fanny, adding her hope that an upcoming race and ball at the courthouse would enliven her.

"Give my love to Brother Henry," she ended her epistle, perhaps wishing for an attachment there.

In June, Judith roused from her apathy to impart a little excitement when she told Mary of her plans.

"Since you left us, I have consented to accompany my brother to the springs and about the middle of July we commence our journey over the mountains. When I tell you that I leave both my boys at home it is useless to elaborate on the agreeable anticipation which I entertain on the subject. With Nancy's care and attention, however, I am entirely content."

She would not complain of her health but knew that "the real evils of life preclude the approach of Chimera. . . . "

On the way to the springs, Jack, Judith, and Fanny visited John Coalter, now a judge, at his home, Elm Grove, outside of Staunton. He had lost two wives who died in childbirth. Before they left, he extracted a promise that they would stop by again on their return home.

Judith's health improved at the springs, but her critical tongue found a target with the dinner guests, "sitting down to dinner with one hundred people, literally alone in a crowd, all pulling and snatching like a parcel of school boys, to see who can get the goodies."

They returned home in mid-September, without a male attachment, and stopped again at Judge Coalter's, where the widower viewed Judith and Fanny with renewed interest.

Nancy had taken good care of the boys at Bizarre but the slaves were more unhappy than usual. The payments on the old debt continued to haunt the family, overwhelming Judith with the complexity of the situation.

"The slaves are entitled to their freedom," she wrote Tucker, "which is delayed by the mortgage on them. The labor of the slaves is the only means of discharging the debts of my husband. Last winter while I was in Williamsburg and Creed Taylor was in Richmond, the negroes were quarrelsome with the overseer and demanded their freedom."

By December, she was ill again, with Nancy once again in charge.

Jack returned to Washington for the next congressional session, leaving Judith ill and brooding, Nancy busy with household responsibilities, and the slaves and overseer uneasy. With the Republicans now in control of the House, he became chairman of the powerful Committee on Ways and Means, as well as Republican majority leader. These were tremendous political accomplishments for a twenty-eight-year old congressman entering his third year in the House. His knowledge and eloquence on the House floor impressed legislators, but his waspish temper and thin skin won him few friends.

1802–1804

*I*n January 1802, Jack Randolph left the "temple of confusion," the House, and strolled over to hear the Senate debates on the repeal of the 1801 Judiciary Act. He predicted that it would be repealed, but only by a bare majority. Senator Gouverneur Morris's oratory impressed him.

"Breckenridge and Stone . . . Morris and Tracy have been the Achilles and Ajax, the Hector and Sarpedon of their respective parties. Of Morris I will state an opinion . . . a fine gentleman has destroyed a good orator."

Jack was right. The Judiciary Act of 1801 was repealed by one vote.

❧

John Wickham, a Richmond Tory attorney serving as agent for Hanbury's of London, contacted Jack, offering to mediate more favorable terms for payment on Jack and Richard's debts to the commission merchants. With Tucker's encouragement, Jack and Wickham negotiated an arrangement to extend the payments to 1810.

❧

Diminished crop production and a drop in tobacco prices adversely affected Judith's resources and her mobility in visiting expeditions. Instead, she brought Maria Ward, Jack's former fiancée, to Bizarre while Nancy was away attending her sister Jane during yet another confinement.

Nancy's choices were even more limited than Judith's. Judith's sisterhood, at times benign and other times malign, governed Nancy's life at Bizarre. She returned to Bizarre from Jane's but was sent away again when Mary Harrison came to visit.

⸎

John Coalter began courting Fanny and when he proposed, she accepted. Both Tucker and Lelia were overjoyed at Fanny's good fortune, but Jack did not share their enthusiasm.

"The object of her choice, amiable and most estimable, yet my fears have no relation to the individual," Jack wrote. He felt that Tucker was giving up "the richest treasure that man ever possessed."

After Jack's return to Bizarre and a visit to Roanoke plantation, he took Judith down to Williamsburg for the festivities.

⸎

Jack planned lessons for Tudor while he was away. Tudor displayed brilliance equal to that of his father and uncle. Everyone worked with Saint, a difficult undertaking considering his hearing and speech impediment. Saint deplored his inability to write without help.

At Edgehill, Martha had become a proficient overseer of her children's education. Jeff walked two miles to a small school, leaving about dawn. At ten years of age, he was already reading Latin. Martha worked with the girls at home; Ann was translating and Ellen had begun to read.

⸎

In the summer of 1802, James Callendar began a campaign from Richmond to blacken Jefferson's reputation after Jefferson severed their relationship, which had been primarily to discredit President Adams. In July, the *Portfolio,* a Philadelphia newspaper, published an anonymous poem about Jefferson's supposed preference for black women. In the *Richmond Recorder,* Callendar dredged up the story of Jefferson's attempted seduction of John Walker's wife. On September 1, 1802, the *Recorder* published the rumors of the Jefferson/Hemings liaison, referring to her as a "black Venus." A rash of articles appeared in newspapers, and when John Marshall praised the *Recorder,* the *Richmond Examiner* suggested that his character in this respect "is not invulnerable."

The gossip reached Monticello, leaving Martha "wrathful and venomous at the attacks," while Maria remained silent. The affair ended with Callendar's death by drowning, either by accident or by suicide. Jefferson never publicly addressed the matter, admitting to a correspondent only that "when young and single, offering love to a handsome lady . . . the only truth among their allegations."

In September 1802, Anna Maria and William Thornton, two of Jefferson's Washington friends, came to Monticello with Dolley and James Madison. Mrs. Thornton left an account in her diary of their visit that provides some insight into the physical state of Monticello and of family routine.

The house was in its almost perpetual state of being torn down and rebuilt. When their party entered, they crossed wobbly planks in the front hall to get to the tea room. Here they found Jefferson with his two daughters and their husbands, the grandchildren, Tom's sister Virginia, and other guests. Martha Randolph, the six-foot "not so handsome" daughter, presided at tea. Mrs. Thornton thought that Maria, the younger daughter, was "very beautiful, but reserved."

During her stay, Mrs. Thornton observed the difficulties Martha encountered as hostess at Monticello. A constant stream of visitors came and went whenever Jefferson was in residence. While he appeared comfortable entertaining visitors under such circumstances, it was Martha's responsibility to arrange for sleeping accommodations, plan meals, make the provisions available to the cooks, and to entertain. She established a housekeeping and menu routine and developed many of her own recipes. One that has been passed down was for a "Sunday pudding," where the mixture was boiled for four hours in a cloth bag.

Breakfast was served at eight o'clock, and dinner between three-thirty and four. Tea and coffee were served later. Upstairs, the bedrooms were reached by a narrow, winding, inside stairway, treads barely twenty-four inches with high risers. The beds were in alcoves.

Mrs. Thornton described the house as being "in a state of commencement and decay."

In the past, Martha and Maria had declined their father's invitations to visit him in Washington, but, surprisingly, they planned a trip for late 1802. Martha asked her father to send locks of hair that she enclosed with her letter to Dolley Madison in Philadelphia. Jefferson was to ask Dolley to use her own judgment in selecting two fashionable wigs for his daughters, as neither Martha nor Maria was adept in dressing hair.

Jefferson sent them an itinerary and arranged for fresh horses to meet them en route. John Eppes accompanied them to Strodes where Captain Meriwether Lewis met them with the fresh horses and carriage. It took four days to travel the 120 miles from Monticello to Washington.

Jefferson entertained on New Year's Day 1803, inviting senators, congressmen, and diplomats to the President's House to meet his daughters. They were charmed by Maria's beauty. A Virginian later described her complexion as "exquisite, features all good. . . . I never beheld such a countenance."

Margaret Bayard Smith, a social leader and wife of the editor of the *National Intelligencer,* described Maria as "beautiful, simplicity and timidity personified when in company, but when alone with you of communicative and winning manners."

Of Martha, Mrs. Smith wrote, "Rather homely, a delicate likeness of her father, but still more interesting than her sister. She is really one of the most lovely women I ever met. . . . Her manners, so frank and affectionate, that you know her at once, and feel perfectly at your ease with her."

Martha and Maria returned to Virginia in mid-January. Jefferson rode alongside the carriage over the ferry, then turned back. He did not hear until ten days later that they had reached home safely. They had a disastrous return journey, the horses becoming so fatigued that they had to stop for an entire day to rest them.

Jefferson sent James Monroe and Robert Livingston to France as emissaries to negotiate the purchase of Louisiana. Jack opposed the acquisition, in his opinion, it was a "subject of embarrassment. . . . To buy it is to buy off a war with France. . . . To conquer it is to depart from our character."

Fortunately, for $15 million, the French sold the land that ranged from the Mississippi River to the Rocky Mountains, from the Gulf of Mexico to British North America.

Judith found a means of travel for her social visits—a "giggy," an open, two-wheeled carriage. Dissension increased as her trips to Amelia became more frequent. Her mood, when she returned, caused another flare-up. Nancy, whose "employment consists of some species of drudgery or needlework," was sent away again.

According to Judith, "Poor Nancy cannot be less satisfied with any of her friends . . . than with me. She is unfortunate and she is my sister . . . perhaps at a distance she will think more kindly of me."

In the years since William Thompson's departure and Jack and Maria's broken engagement, Judith and Maria appeared to have forged a bond that, during the period, was referred to as "romantic friendship."

Lillian Faderman, in *Surpassing the Love of Men – Romantic Friendship and Love Between Women from the Renaissance to the Present*, discussed "passionate commitments." Faderman found these friendships "often involved a mature woman and a younger woman." Two women, widows and unmarried women especially, often preferred each other to men. Men found romantic friendship between women charming and quite unthreatening. In such a situation, the women were fiercely jealous of other women. They often hugged, kissed, met secretly, and sometimes slept together.

Judith, who had expressed her admiration of Mary Carter—"You know what an enthusiast I am on female loveliness . . ."—found a similar object to admire in Maria, who was described as one of the most "celebrated" women of her time. Maria surely reciprocated Judith's feelings.

⁂

Tom, well aware of his wife's preference for her father and burdened with his and William's responsibility for paying the British debts, fell into ever deepening despair. He told his father-in-law that, when with the father, daughters, and Eppes, he felt like "a silly bird . . . among swans."

Professor Tucker, who knew Tom both socially and as a university friend, wrote of his friend:

"One of the most generous, disinterested and high-minded men on earth . . . gradually transformed into a gloomy, unsocial misanthrope—his proud spirit suffering intensely, but suffering in silence, seeking solace of no one, but was showing too plainly the discontent which secretly preyed on his mind, by the harshness or coldness with which he treated all around him."

Both John Eppes and Tom ran for Congress, and Eppes won easily from Chesterfield County. Tom ran against Samuel Cabell, an experienced politician in Albemarle County, and won by only a few votes. Cabell challenged the election, but the vote was upheld and Tom was seated in the Eighth Congress. Both he and Eppes lived in the President's House with Jefferson, providing them with opportunities to meet with cabinet members and foreign diplomats.

Even though Jefferson acted without constitutional authority in the Louisiana Purchase, the Senate ratified the treaty and Congress approved the payment. Secretary of the Treasury Albert Gallatin arranged to pay for the purchase without levying additional taxes. The U.S. flag was raised over New Orleans on December 20, 1803.

From Edgehill, Jeff missed Tom and wrote Jefferson, asking him to "give my love to papa." Maria came from Eppington to Edgehill for her next lying-in and was with her sister when Martha's baby, another girl whom they named Mary Jefferson, was born. Unlike her robust sister, Maria already had such serious problems that she could be neither cheerful nor comfortable in her pregnancy. She wanted her husband with her, but they were "doing as well as can be expected," Martha assured her father.

Jack had easily won reelection, and at the beginning of the 1804 congressional session he addressed the House on Supreme Court Justice Samuel Chase's reported misconduct in hearing cases, including Callendar's trial in Richmond. Jack prepared preliminary measures to bring him into impeachment, but the discussion was deferred, at Chase's request, to enable him to obtain legal counsel and prepare his defense.

Jack opposed the Jefferson administration's plan to include the Georgia claimants in the Yazoo frauds in a compromise settlement on land east of the Mississippi River. He proposed resolutions to exclude these claimants from the settlement. The debate, with lengthy and emotional interjections by Jack, was steamy when Tom Randolph rose to speak.

Tom, too, opposed the administration's position, blaming the Georgia legislators who had authorized the original sales. Moreover, Tom proposed that an examination be made to differentiate between the purchasers in good faith and the "band of sharpers" who had sold the land. He referred to the Yazoo incident as "a fraud of unprecedented enormity. . . ."

Both of Jefferson's sons-in-law voted with Jack and against Jefferson in postponing the bill until the next congressional session. Jack reported to James Monroe in England that "our political adversaries . . . foment every discontent which breaks forth . . . every machine is at work to infuse jealousy among us."

Senator William Plumer wrote disdainfully that Jack "had swaggered back into Congress . . . booted and spurred, with his whip in his hand. He appears youthful, but upon a near approach, you perceive his wrinkles and grey hairs.

"The Federalists ridicule and affect to despise him but a despised foe often proves a dangerous enemy."

Jack complained of "almost incessant employment of my pen. . . . We have no committee clerks and it is the practice for all propositions to come thro the chairman, who drafts all the reports, bills, etc. To me, pen and ink are odious."

⤝

At Christmas, Judith left again for Amelia, not returning until late January 1804.

⤝

From Edgehill, Maria wrote her husband in Washington that her health was steadily growing worse as her pregnancy advanced but begged him not to worry about her.

"Adieu once more, best beloved of my soul."

At Jefferson's urging, Eppes left Washington before the House adjourned and hurried to Edgehill for the birth. Bad weather prevented him from getting to the mountain before Maria's baby, a girl, was born on February 15. They named her Martha. Maria's breast abscess prevented her nursing the baby, and so Martha, who was nursing three month-old Mary, nursed her small namesake, too.

When Eppes arrived, Maria asked to go to Monticello to recuperate. Her husband arranged to have her taken there by litter, as she was too weak to travel by carriage. Tom wrote a friend that "the fairest flower which my eyes ever beheld has already lost her enchanting appearance." Jefferson found her at Monticello when he returned, and she died on April 17. Jefferson sat all evening holding her handkerchief in his hand.

After a five-year silence, Abigail Adams wrote to Jefferson when she learned of Maria's death. She recalled how Maria had clung to her and wept when they were separated in London in 1787. Her affection for him still lingered, she informed him, although esteem had taken flight.

"The powerful feelings of my heart burst through the restraint."

Nancy had been sent to Tom and wrote of "a gloom in unison with my feeling . . . indeed the surrounding scenery here assumes a melancholy aspect.

"I am here for the summer . . . unless Judy expresses a wish for my return . . . to dear Bizarre. Oh God, if only I could be allowed to remain there in peace – My whole soul is devoted to the spot."

Aaron Burr and Alexander Hamilton were, on the surface, personally congenial, but political situations arose whereby notes were exchanged between the two. When Burr heard rumors that Hamilton had accused him of having been his own daughter Theodosia's lover, he challenged Hamilton to a duel. On July 11, having put his personal affairs in order, Hamilton wrote Betsy, "Adieu, my darling, darling wife," and crossed the river to Weehauken, New Jersey. With their seconds in place, both men fired simultaneously. Hamilton missed but Burr, although considered a poor marksman, did not. Hamilton, mortally wounded, was taken back to New York. When Morris was told of his friend's condition, he rushed to Hamilton, staying until he died, then witnessed the autopsy.

Asked to deliver Hamilton's funeral oration, Morris, in his melodious voice, honored his friend without stirring up further violence. He appealed, "I charge you to protect his fame." As he left the building, the editor of the *New York Post* stopped him. He had been so moved by

Morris's oration that he was unable to take notes and asked for Morris's copy.

Hearing the news of the duel and death, Jack's "incredulity refused to credit" it. He thought it would be contradicted by the next mail.

❧

When Jefferson returned to Monticello, he found Nancy still there and invited her to stay the entire season.

"His gentle manner made me quite easy," she wrote Tucker.

The family of "wild children" around her were too fond of her to be repulsed, but "what would I give to be at Bizarre with my darling boys and be able to walk to the graveyard. . . ."

❧

Many considered and referred to Aaron Burr as a murderer. He was not on the ballot as Jefferson's running mate in the November 1804 election. Jefferson and George Clinton, the new nominee, won handily.

❧

Jack and Judith checked into appropriate schools in England and France for Saint. He continued as Tudor's mentor and tutor. Not yet eleven years old, Tudor had already finished Roman history and had begun Erasmus.

❧

Judith's need for help overcame her animosity and she sent for Nancy. She wanted her sister at Bizarre while she joined the Tuckers in Williamsburg. But Nancy found Maria Ward with Judith when she returned.

❧

A contemporary of Maria Ward left a vivid account of why men admired her.

John Briggs, from Dinwiddie County, maintained a detailed diary. In "A Trip to the Sweet Springs, from July 23 to September 29, 1804," he recounted how after "taking the waters," they returned through Amelia County, stopping at The Wigwam, the home of Senator William Giles. When first introduced to Miss Ward, Briggs felt "disappointed and secretly wondered at her being so frequently celebrated." He soon changed his mind.

"The elegance and fascination of her manner attaches a person, and makes it impossible for the male sex to withhold their admiration and few of the females their envy." Her singing and polished conversation rendered her irresistible, he thought.

Nancy's feelings about Maria were very different. She felt that Maria had been trained in artifice since birth.

"I hope my sister will become free from the influence of the insidious Maria, see the enclosed note." The contents of the note, sent to Tucker, are unknown, but apparently were such that Lelia and Tucker refused to allow Mary to visit Maria. Fanny wrote them that their reasons for not allowing the visit were "unanswerable."

Judith was well. "Although quite thin, her time is engrossed by domestic management that appears to be her ruling passion . . . .

"You may conceive the state of my feelings when I tell you I have passed ten days since my return hither, witnessing the lover like attentions between Judy and Maria Ward without one word addressed to me, except an offer of something to eat at table. . . . Full well do I know what a suspicious temper would have proved to me."

Mary Harrison wrote of Judith's strange behavior. She ate nothing but lettuce and was still up and around at 2 a.m.

Fawn Brodie, in *Thomas Jefferson: An Intimate History,* wrote that Judith had become addicted to laudanum after the death of her child. Plantation mistresses, including Judith, had access to all drugs that were administered, and her brooding nature made her especially prone. She may have been troubled in her relationship with Maria Ward, perhaps now more sexual than sisterly. During a period when sexual fulfillment with the opposite sex was not possible, both men and women sought pleasure with members of their own sex. The name for such a relationship, homosexual, would not emerge for several generations.

1805

I n early 1805, Jack, as chairman of the Committee for Ways and Means, had a full agenda, implementing House action on the Louisiana Purchase, the resolutions on the Mississippi Yazoo land claims, and Judge Chase's impeachment. Mental pressure mounted in tandem with his physical ailments.

"The Yazoo claims – Louisiana and the impeachment are all at this time on my shoulders and crush me to the earth."

He spoke three times opposing the Georgia claimants in the Yazoo land settlement. He launched a violent tirade denouncing Postmaster Gideon Granger, who had inappropriately solicited votes on the House floor. His "emotions were excited to the point of frenzy, literally beside himself with anger."

Jefferson was publicly silent. Jack's friend from Georgia, Joseph Bryan, Tom Randolph, and John Eppes voted with Jack and against the president. The resolutions were voted down, 63—58, thereby preventing passage of the compromise bill.

❦

Ill, Jack returned to his boarding house and sent Congressman Joseph Nicholson a message; he was suffering "the torments of the damned," with pain from his digestive disorders and "stupefied with opium and lack of rest." Being heavily addicted to opium, he required large quantities to ease his suffering.

He was chief manager, with no time to adequately prepare to try the impeachment case against Chase.

Vice President Aaron Burr was still in office, and, dapperly attired, he presided over the impeachment and had the Senate chamber arranged in a regal setting. Jack, Nicholson, Caesar Rodney, and three other managers were seated on the right, while Chase and his attorneys, Luther Martin, Charles Lee, and Robert Harper, sat on the left. Seating was also provided for House members, the military, and foreign dignitaries.

Burr's earlier indictments for Alexander Hamilton's murder caused Senator William Plumer to exclaim:

"We are indeed fallen on evil times, the high office of President is filled by an infidel, that of Vice President by a murderer."

Jack had no real knowledge of law, and, although his managers were good attorneys, they were no match for Chase's defense, particularly Luther Martin. Many observers believed that Chase richly deserved conviction, while others viewed the entire matter as another fight between the Republicans and the Federalists. Still others were convinced that this was actually a secret battle between Jefferson and Marshall for control of the judiciary.

John Marshall was vague in his testimony, and it was said that the "Chief Justice appeared to be frightened."

Plumer felt that Marshall "discovered too much caution, too much fear, too much cunning – He ought to have been more bold, more explicit.

"That dignified frankness which his high office required did not appear."

⤜⤏

Jack was too ill to participate for part of the trial but was pleased when Harry Tucker called on him.

"Today, I crawl out to the Senate, where I have not been for three days. Harry tells me that many false reports are in circulation . . . they are most of them utterly untrue and the others grossly exaggerated. I am on terms of the greatest intimacy with Mr. Jefferson and Secretary Gallatin – but I am not therefore less independent in my votes."

As the trial continued, Luther Martin spoke without food or drink, except for two glasses of wine, until five in the afternoon. Joseph Nicholson made a fatal blunder in his summation. Jack closed for the managers, and, although he asked for a two-hour delay, lost his notes, and writhed in pain, his summation made the best argument for impeachment. Federalists, however, called his speeches "spiteful, feeble, outrageous, devoid of argument or consistency, deranged. The fellow cried like a baby with clear, sheer madness."

His words were, at times, both poetic and passionate.

"Follow the respondent, then, with the steady and untired step of justice, from Philadelphia to Annapolis to Richmond, and back again to Newcastle. You see a succession of crimes each treading on the heel, galling the gibe of the other, so connected in time and place of circumstances, and so illustrated by his own confession, as to leave no shadow of doubt as to his guilt."

But the Senate failed to find Chase guilty by the required two thirds vote, and he was acquitted, with the blame falling on Jack as chief manager. He, burning with fever and with rage at his failures, with "Yazoo and Judge Chase making a devilish noise," dashed home. Tudor was very ill again, and Jack was anxious to be at the bedside of "the last hope of a declining family."

⸎

In Jefferson's second inaugural message in March 1805, he proudly listed the first term's accomplishments: the peaceful acquisition of Louisiana, curtailment of public expenses, a prosperous state of finances with increasing surplus, the vast extension of American trade, and an increase in the number of banks and insurance companies formed.

⸎

Nancy, unaware of a firestorm brewing, was at Bizarre "without fire, my feet under me for the purpose of warming them," as she wrote Mary Johnston.

She soared "above the language of reproach – and make indefatigable efforts to heal those wounds so mercilessly inflicted. My mind cannot be shackled – Yet my person has willingly resigned itself to various species of read drudgery. Months . . . have been devoted to the needle, for Judy who cherishes not a latent spark of affection toward me.

"Since my return from Albemarle, I have been deprived of all conversation – there I was obliged to be social."

Nancy wanted to borrow, again, *Caleb Williams* and the poems of Collins to make transcripts. *Caleb Williams* was written by William

Godwin and has been described as the first real detective novel and a precursor of the twentieth-century novel of guilt and pursuit. Godwin was the husband of Mary Wollstonecraft, who in 1796 had published *A Vindication of the Rights of Women,* demonstrating her contempt "of men corrupted by their power over women."

⸱⸱

Tudor improved, but after Judith left for Amelia, he had a relapse. Jack sat at his bedside for fifty-six hours while he was given antimonials, a dose of salts, and was bled.

"He never closed an eye but lay patiently mute . . . baring his little arm for the lancet."

Then Jack left, going to the "low country."

⸱⸱

In May, Nancy cared for Tudor until he was taken to Staunton to convalesce with Fanny. One evening, after Jack returned, he talked with Judith and apparently angered, confronted Nancy. Years later Nancy described his attack.

"Nancy, when do you leave this house, the sooner the better for you take as many liberties as if you were in a tavern."

"My course was silent submission. I was poor, I was dependent. I could not appeal to my sister. I replied with the humility suitable to my forlorn condition, 'I will go as soon as I can.'"

He stalked out and she fled, crying, to her room. She packed her few belongings, had Billy Ellis, a slave, put her trunk into a wagon, and she left Bizarre, "to which my whole soul is devoted." She found refuge with Mary and Peter Johnston, then went to the Dillons at Sandy Ford. When Tucker received her letter telling of her banishment, he wrote Jack, asking about the circumstances. In his reply, Jack accused his stepfather of "want of confidence."

While Tudor was in Staunton, Jack enrolled him and Theodore Dudley, his cousin, for the winter term at Dr. Haller's Academy in Richmond. Jack also scheduled Saint's trip to Europe to study at schools for the hearing and speech impaired. Saint, now thirteen, was a sensitive and dutiful boy who enjoyed hunting and trapping, and he visited the Roanoke plantation frequently. Jack enrolled him first in Braidwood School near Harkney in England and then at the Secord School in Paris. He planned to have the slave Essex accompany Saint to

England to James and Elizabeth Monroe, who had agreed to serve as his surrogate parents there, and later arrange for his trip to Paris as Essex would then return to Bizarre. They left Bizarre in mid-November for Norfolk and boarded the *Intrepid.* Saint became seasick merely crossing the Chesapeake Bay to the ship.

⤜⤛

Nancy wandered, homeless, always grateful for a haven. She visited the Harrisons, her former "avowed" enemies, in Cumberland where Tom picked her up and took her to Monticello. He brought her mail from Richmond and she answered Mary Harrison's letter.

"Every member of your family is remembered with grateful affection," she wrote. She had never heard as much noise as at Monticello, with, as always, so many people visiting.

⤜⤛

Virginia became engaged to a cousin, Wilson Jefferson Cary, who lived in Williamsburg, and Martha was pleased and excited. Virginia had lived with them for so long that Martha cherished her as a daughter. She ordered a trunk of "wedding cloaths" from Washington because they were so important to the family. Also, so many teacups had been broken in entertaining that she needed more. Jefferson rescheduled his trip to Poplar Forest to be there for the August wedding. The ceremony was private, and only family members attended.

Tom's sister Harriet, who had stayed at Tuckahoe with Gabriella, also married that year. Her husband was Richard Hackley of New York, and their wedding took place at her brother William's home, Chilhowee. Jefferson later appointed Hackley to serve as consul at Cadiz, Spain.

Nancy was now the only sister who was unmarried.

⤜⤛

When he returned to the President's House, Jefferson was lonely, particularly so when he learned that Dolley Madison, in Philadelphia recovering from surgery on her leg, would be unable to serve as his hostess. He invited Martha to visit him with the younger children. Both Tom and John Eppes would be with them at the President's House. She was reluctant, being more than six months pregnant; she would surely have the baby while in Washington. As usual, she acquiesced to her father's wishes, provided that Dolley would select a fashionable wig to match her sample, a set of combs, and bonnet, shawl, and white lace veil for paying morning visits.

Jefferson confirmed that Mrs. Madison had made the necessary purchases, and he sent her $100 for expenses on the road. He arranged for a carriage to meet her halfway, noting the distances between various points, 26 miles to Orange Courthouse, 38 miles to Elkrun Church, 37 miles to Fairfax Courthouse, then 15 miles to the President's House and dinner. Martha did not look forward to the trip and having the baby away from home.

"My courage shrinks from the horrors of a trial so severe even under the most favorable circumstances."

The delivery would be even more difficult in Washington from not knowing whether she would have her usual medical assistance. She also would not have a trusted friend with her there.

⁂

Judith found hostility without leaving Bizarre. Rumors and speculation arose about her frequent trips with Maria Ward in Amelia, and her unusual habits. Mary Harrison asked questions and gave pointed advice. Judith answered with a lengthy letter, thanking her for the "censure" and advice.

If she could share with Mary the record of sufferings and afflictions that had consigned her to premature old age, then Mary would seek no "trifling cause" for her habits. She had made many trips to Amelia, which she could not explain, but they had been happy. She had tried to "rescue an exemplary young female from . . . evil counselors" and to "screen her from calumny."

⁂

Judith suffered from rheumatism and other ailments. Saint and Tudor were away at schools, and she was unable to eat alone. She abstained from vegetables, living almost entirely on mutton. As to her late hours, she could not sleep because of anxiety. She had the responsibility for forty-five grown slaves and as many children, unsupervised by an overseer. She had large financial obligations with Saint in England and Tudor in school in Richmond.

She wrote Fanny of Bizarre's physical condition.

"This old house is not habitable in cold weather."

Plaster crumbled, snow and rain came in and the chimney, now a

John Randolph of Roanoke 1773-1833,
Library of Virginia

foot away from the house, threatened to fall. The court of appeals had ruled that she had to keep the slaves, still without an overseer, for another year.

She did not know where she would spend the winter.

❧

In mid-December, Jack traveled to Baltimore, where he visited Saint before the *Intrepid* sailed for Europe. The next day, Saint, who had never been more than a hundred miles away from home, began the journey with Essex across the ocean to foreign countries where he would stay for almost three years.

Thomas Mann Randolph 1768-1828,
Library of Virginia

1806

Martha had the option to make and receive social calls either as President Jefferson's daughter or as Congressman Randolph's wife. Her popularity with Washington society soared when she elected the less prestigious role of Tom's wife. On January 16, 1806, she gave birth to her eighth child, second son, and the first child born in the nation's Executive Mansion. She named her son James Madison Randolph.

On the same day, Jack strongly opposed the passage of a bill allowing the president to negotiate for the purchase of Florida, considering it "an unconstitutional suggestion of the private wishes of the President." He voted against Jefferson and the bill, while Tom and Eppes supported the measure.

Jack's first public criticism of Jefferson's foreign policy in the House included Secretary of State Madison, saying he conducted "the foreign business . . . from first to last . . . in the most imbecile manner."

Joseph Bryan, retired from Congress, wrote Jack, "You have passed the Rubicon and Madison or your self must come down."

Two headstrong Randolphs were soon on a collision course to destroy their collaboration in the Yazoo fraud claims. On April 7, Jack announced that he could no longer cooperate with the Jefferson administration. Tom Randolph, appalled, was convinced that his cousin faced political doom.

Later, Jack presented a bill to repeal the salt tax needed to pay for
Florida. Pennsylvania Congressman William Findley, fortified by alcohol consumption, accused Randolph of trying to thwart administrative
policy. David Williams of South Carolina rebutted, and Tom Randolph
called him to order.

Jack, unusually mild, responded.

"What has thrown us into this heat? Is it the dinner we have just
eaten. . . . I did hope that, whatever, contumely or hostility may have
been manifested during the earlier period of the season . . . we should
have parted like men not ashamed of what we had done. . . . "

Although Jack's reference was to Findley, Tom, misunderstanding,
took it as applying to himself. Enraged, he made a few hostile comments. Jack had injured and humiliated his sister, Nancy, by evicting
her from Bizarre, and then publicly declared his opposition to Tom's
father-in-law and benefactor.

Tom noted Jack's caution in comments elsewhere than when behind the shield of the House. Also, John Randolph "made more noise
than had been useful. . . ."

"That lead and even steel make very proper ingredients in serious
quarrels."

Unable to restrain his temper further, Tom strode from the House
chamber.

Jack, equally enraged, demanded an apology. Their seconds conferred and a duel seemed imminent.

⚯

Jefferson appealed to his son-in-law.

"On his side . . . a single life, of no value to himself or to others, on
yours, yourself, a wife and family of children. Is it possible that your duties
to these dear objects can weigh more lightly than those of a gladiator?"

With associates prodding him to apologize "with honor," Tom rose
in the House chamber, while Jack was away, and in a low voice apologized for his "severe and harsh language." After Jack's acceptance the
matter ended, but the *Richmond Enquirer,* the pro-Jefferson *National
Intelligencer,* and the anti-Jefferson *Aurora* rehashed the episode.

⚯

While bitter winter weather persisted, Nancy was in Williamsburg,
Tudor was at Dr. Haller's Academy in Richmond, Saint was in England,

and Judith found a refuge with Fanny and John Coalter at Elm Grove in Staunton. Mary Harrison heard important news about Maria Ward. She had chosen a husband.

"Maria Ward is to be married on March 20 to Peyton Randolph. I have received pressing solicitations to the ceremony but it is impossible to comply," Judith wrote.

Peyton, an attorney, was the handsome son of Edmund Randolph. The father was also unable to attend the wedding, and he apologized to Maria.

"I fear that I ought not to hazard my health by a journey to the Hermitage tomorrow. A cold has been very troublesome. . . [and so] accept my most cordial wishes that the union may be a source of uninterrupted bliss. . . . "

Beverley Tucker represented the Randolphs, enjoying festivities that for four days "all was cards and dancing and merriment."

Judith was heartsick, and Fanny sadly related to her father that "Maria's marriage has taken sister's last comfort." More happily, Fanny repeated Judith's good news that Saint and Essex had arrived safely in London.

When Jack reached Bizarre, he found an admonition from Bryan: "Leave the President alone – unless self-defence is necessary to use his name."

⊰⊱

Essex returned to Bizarre from abroad after a six-month roundtrip to England, reporting that Saint was as happy to be there as Essex was to leave it. He had left Saint with James Monroe. To Saint, Jack expressed his appreciation of James Monroe's kindness "for relieving the infirmity with which providence has been pleased to afflict you. . . . "

⊰⊱

Nancy, at Tom's insistence, went to Richmond to visit her sister Molly. Then the Randolphs at Wilton sent a carriage to take her to Curles Neck, southward on the James River. About the time that Nancy left Richmond, tragedy and scandal erupted at Fifth and Grace Streets in a gambrel-roofed house with tall windows.

George Wythe, chancellor of Virginia, freed his slaves when he moved to Richmond, but three came with him. One, Michael Brown, was a well-educated freedman. Gossips said that he was the son of

Wythe and his mulatto housekeeper, Lydia Broadnax. In Richmond society, having "a yellow woman" as a mistress was not unusual. Wythe's 1803 will provided for support of his freed slaves but left his estate to a grandnephew, George Wythe Sweney. However, while living with Wythe, young Sweney stole and sold valuable books belonging to his uncle.

Wythe added codicils to his will in 1806 that caused his agonizing death. He asked Thomas Jefferson to rear Michael Brown, using Wythe's income from investments. The estate would be divided equally between Michael and Sweney; if Michael died first, all would go to Sweney. Sweney learned of the changes, and on May 25 he struck, lacing the morning coffee with arsenic. Michael died, Lydia survived, and Wythe lay mortally ill. Sweney was arrested for forging his uncle's name on checks, arsenic was found in his room, and a packet of the poison appeared under his jail window.

Wythe, in agony, summoned Edmund Randolph to his bedside and added another codicil to his will, disinheriting Sweney. Wythe refused to prosecute on the forgery charges. He authorized Randolph to defend Sweney, as he could not leave a blemish on his sister's name. After lapsing into a coma, Wythe died and an autopsy confirmed arsenic poisoning. His body lay in state in the Capitol; his former student, William Munford, delivered the funeral eulogy, and Wythe was interred in the "Old Church" yard.

William Wirt and Edmund Randolph defended Sweney, whom a jury refused to convict due to "lack of evidence of poisoning." He disappeared and later perished in the West.

⤜⤛

Customs and traditions were changing. Harry Tucker practiced law in Winchester, and Lelia's son Charles was studying medicine in Paris. Her daughter Mary attended Mrs. Fitzhugh's School in Alexandria and Jack sometimes stopped off to visit her. She was as independent as she was lovely, and traveled alone, insisting that the trip from Alexandria to Williamsburg did not fatigue her.

Jack and Judith received good reports of Saint's progress and conduct. Jack wrote Saint of his expectations and to give advice.

"I would have you taught to dance and fence . . . exert such faculties as you may possess to procure an independent maintenance. . . . Should your misfortune preclude you from the science of medicine or the art of surgery . . . mechanics and agriculture are open to your pursuit.

"I desire that you . . . inure yourself to hardship, to venerate truth and to despise and abhor effeminacy, cowardice, cruelty and injustice. . . . "

Jack gave Saint the current news. His Uncle Henry and a Winchester lady, Miss Hunter, were engaged. Joseph Bryan could become governor of Georgia, if he desired.

"His lady has brought him a little son named John Randolph Bryan."

Nathaniel Macon had been reelected speaker of the House and often inquired about Saint. Jack's and Saint's friend Joseph Nicholson had been appointed to a judgeship in Baltimore.

⚬⚬

Visiting yet another relative, Nancy saw her welcome wore thin, and she sought Tucker's help in escaping.

"I have spent two miserable months at Ben Lomond. Could you send a hack up to the little town of Jefferson in Powhatan?"

Then she canceled the request a few days later from Tuckahoe because Brother John had sent to Ben Lomond for her.

"I expect my brother (Tom) here tomorrow. I intend going to Monticello and trust the carriage returns safely."

⚬⚬

Jack's political popularity was fading. Senator William Giles of Amelia County considered Jack's behavior in Congress an embarrassment. He proposed that Creed Taylor oppose Jack in the election. Area constituents, however, were loyal and returned Jack to Washington for another term.

Judith, isolated at Bizarre with the boys away at school, ignored Sally Taylor's coolness and invited her for a visit. She was all alone, except for the slaves.

1807

Excitement filled Tucker House. The "cruel and beautiful" Mary Carter had finally said yes and was engaged to Joseph Cabell, the brother of Governor William Cabell. He had recently returned to America from Europe.

Jack declined Tucker's invitation to the wedding. "I cannot think of leaving my seat even for one day . . . . Assure my friend Cabell that my best wishes for his welfare constantly attend him." Judith also declined to attend.

There were detailed financial arrangements for Tucker's stepdaughter's marriage, with precise instructions from Cabell for the placement of guests and family members at the January 1, 1807, wedding to be held at Tucker House.

The groom-to-be insisted that his brother, Governor Cabell, be seated appropriately.

∽⸰∾

Molly had skillfully planted a suggestion to Nancy that she leave Virginia.

"During the horrible visit my brother caused me (to make to) Mrs. D. R., she was perpetually telling me how cheaply I could live in Newport, Rhode Island – and how friendly her acquaintances would be."

Tom promised Nancy $300 annually to rent or board, and she moved to Richmond. In February, Nancy rented a small apartment above Major and Mrs. Pryor's living quarters at Haymarket Gardens. David Meade Randolph proposed that she rent larger quarters, and he would share the space and cost. Whatever his motive, she wisely declined the offer.

Public gardens provided recreation and entertainment. The Falling Gardens, near Sixteenth and Franklin, built by Joseph Lownes, boasted public baths. The Haymarket Gardens were large, extending from Sixth to Eighth Streets. From Arch Street they descended down toward the river, the slope being adjusted by terraces with walks. The owner, Major John Pryor, offered rides, music, and theatrical presentations.

The major's wife, Ann Pryor, was an interesting and strong-minded young woman who would empathize with Nancy's situation. Major Pryor engaged Jean Charles Frémon, from Haller's Academy, to teach his wife dancing. Ann Pryor and Frémon later eloped and became the parents of the nineteenth-century explorer John Charles Fremont.

At first, Nancy enjoyed her independence.

"Ryland Randolph will convey my affection to you," she wrote Tucker. "I am now situated in a beautiful part of town. I visit nearly every house on the hill except the governor's.

"Tell Virginia our brother is better but is still unable to leave Washington."

⚬

Apparently, Tom and John Eppes had a disagreement, and Tom left the Executive Mansion, going to a boarding house. After a raw day out without a greatcoat, he was taken with chills and fever, so weakened that he was unable to return to Virginia. After he refused to return to the mansion, Jefferson engaged a physician to care for him. Tom's personal servant, Joseph, and Captain Meriwether Lewis were also with him. Jefferson reported Tom's progress to Martha; by mid-March he returned to the Executive Mansion but was too weak to travel. In early April, they left Washington and traveled for five days before reaching Monticello. Thus ended Tom's congressional career.

⚬

"I am absolutely enchanted with Richmond, and like it more and more each day. The society is polished, sociable and extremely hospitable,"

Mary Randolph Randolph 1762-1828,
Library of Virginia

wrote Washington Irving, the creator of Ichabod Crane. He had "set out for Richmond then to Williamsburg to see his friend Joseph Cabell who has lately married one of the fairest girls in Virginia."

∞

A large, ugly brick building housed Dr. Haller's Academy where Tudor Randolph and his cousin Theodore Dudley were taught. Students were enrolled because Haller engaged excellent teachers.

The largest residencies were clustered within a few blocks of Capitol Square. John Wickham's faced the capitol from the west and Edmund Randolph's elegant home was north of the capitol. Unlike most of the homes, which were frame, John Marshall's was a handsome brick structure.

The city had progressed from the sleepy state capital to a commercial hub. A new theater had been completed on Academy Square, where Academy Hall, site of the 1788 ratification debates, had stood. Easterly was the old church, later named St. John's, where Patrick Henry had electrified his people in 1775.

∞

After Burr's term as vice president ended, he headed west and joined General James Wilkinson, governor of the Louisiana Territory. They planned to invade Mexico and add the land to the U.S. territories; they obtained financial assistance from one Harmon Blennerhasset. Rumors spread that they planned to separate from the Union, invade Washington, and assassinate the president.

Wilkinson, Spain's secret agent #13 for years, demanded $100,000 for thwarting Burr's plan. He sent Jefferson false information and an altered copy of a cipher letter, supposedly from Burr. To avoid disclosure, he imprisoned several officials and sent a military party to find and kill Burr.

Orders were issued for Burr's arrest and a reward was offered. Burr learned of Wilkinson's betrayal and fled to the Mississippi Territory. Although in disguise, he was recognized and arrested and six armed civilians and two military officers brought him east.

Southerners recorded Burr's progress. In Virginia, Beverley Tucker saw them pass Charlotte Courthouse, then Jack reported seeing them near Bizarre. Burr was still in disguise, "accoutred in a shabby suit of homespun and an old white hat."

Since the island where the plans were hatched was in Virginia, Burr came to Richmond. He arrived at the Eagle Tavern on March 28, 1807, and Marshall interrogated him two days later. This set up another battle between Marshall and Jefferson as to whether the executive or judiciary branch would control the Supreme Court.

Marshall had made an important ruling on February 21. He established the doctrine of "constructive treason," saying a defendant need not have been present at a treasonous assemblage, if he had performed any part "however remote" in the enterprise. The prosecution hoped to hang Burr using this doctrine, since Burr had not actually been present at the time of the "treasonous assemblage."

Some Richmond residents extended courtesies to former Vice President Burr. Colonel Robert Gamble and Robert Taylor loaned Burr $1000 to buy new clothes for his court appearance. After the hearing was moved to the Hall of Delegates in the Capitol, bail was set at $5,000 and Gamble and Taylor signed the bail bond.

Burr explained that he was attempting to escape from General Wilkinson, who planned to kill him. United States District Attorney George Hay introduced evidence of the "cipher letter" in which Burr allegedly used a combination of hieroglyphics, Arabic numerals, and other code elements to pass information to Wilkinson. According to Marshall, "exclude this letter and nothing remains which can affect Colonel Burr." He ruled that Burr could be charged with high misdemeanor but that a grand jury must decide on the charge for treason.

Marshall appointed Jack to serve as grand jury foreman to decide on Aaron Burr's indictment. Riding Brunette, he came down from Farmville with his personal servant, John, and Theodore Dudley. Tudor accompanied them in the "chair," a small open carriage.

Lieutenant-Governor Alexander MacRae and attorney/orator William Wirt assisted George Hay in the prosecution. Burr's attorneys, John Wickham, Edmund Randolph, Charles Lee, Benjamin Botts, and the shrewd, coarse alcoholic Luther Martin defended him without fee. Burr selected Martin because of his legal skills in saving Justice Samuel Chase from impeachment earlier.

Richmond enjoyed a high social season while Burr awaited trial. When Wickham invited Burr to a dinner party, Marshall was also a guest, infuriating many Virginians who called the affair "the treason rejoicing dinner."

"Let me inform the conscience of the Chief Justice," wrote "A Stranger from the Country" in the *Richmond Enquirer,* "that the public do not find his dining with Burr as a circumstance so trivial as he himself may claim to consider it. We regard it as a wanton insult he might have spared his country."

As the grand jury convened, Burr objected to Senator Giles and W. C. Nicholas serving and Marshall removed them. Luther Martin dramatically shook up spectators, who were lethargic in the summer heat, when he accused the president of unleashing "the dogs of war, the hell hounds of persecution."

Burr requested that Marshall subpoena President Jefferson to come with papers necessary to his defense. The chief justice agreed, ruling that only a king was exempt from court summons. However, if the papers were sent, the president need not personally attend. Jefferson, enraged, sent his reply. Papers of his choice would be sent, but he would not come and "leave the nation without an executive branch, whose agency is constantly necessary."

The grand jury, dismissed while awaiting Wilkinson's arrival, allowed the jurors, according to Washington Irving, "to see their wives, get their clothes washed, and flog their negroes."

Grand jury foreman Jack Randolph demanded that General Wilkinson, now en route to Richmond to testify for the prosecution, be indicted for treason as well. When Wilkinson finally arrived on June 13, according to Washington Irving, now covering the trial for a northern paper, the beefy, pompous general strutted into court "swelling like a turkey cock." Burr glanced momentarily and contemptuously at his former friend, then resumed his conversation. The general was with the grand jury for four days, finally admitting that he had altered the "cipher letter," placing in doubt a key piece of prosecution evidence. Both Burr and Blennerhassett were indicted and their lawyers prepared for the trial.

On June 25, Jack Randolph wrote, "Yesterday the grand jury found bills for treason and misdemeanor against Burr una voce but the master of iniquity escaped." The grand jury had voted nine to seven against charging Wilkinson with treason.

Burr pleaded not guilty to the charges and was taken to the new penitentiary until the August 3 trial date. Here he had three rooms on the top floor and received visitors who brought various delicacies. When Washington Irving went to the penitentiary, he was allowed only a few minutes with Burr.

"The keeper had orders to admit only his counsel and his witnesses, strange measures, these."

Harmon Blennerhasset was particularly irked when Burr, always popular with women, entertained them in his rooms. "Jupiter might invisibly elude the guards of Danae," Blennerhasset wrote his wife, "but the bonne amie of the Col. does not pass the keepers with the same address."

In Richmond's unusual social season, which was rapidly becoming pro-Burr, Blennerhasset found that Molly Randolph, whose criticism of Jefferson he considered "better founded than others," "ridiculed the experiment of a republic in this country." She hoped that if anything else were attempted, "the Atlantic States would be comprised in the plan." Blennerhassett considered Gabriella Brockenbrough "the nearest approach in this town to a savant and bel esprit."

When Theodosia Burr Alston arrived with her husband, Thomas, and their son from South Carolina, rumors soon flew about Theodosia and men. Martin regarded her in "idolatrous admiration." Her name was connected with Washington Irving. Meriwether Lewis came to Richmond to observe, and gossip spread that the two had revived an earlier love affair. The lovely Theodosia, however, appeared devoted only to her family.

After jury selection began, Burr realized that he could be convicted. Relying only on Marshall's interpretation of the law, he agreed to jurors being selected at random. Most Virginians felt that too many Federalists were empanelled, including the jury foreman, Edward Carrington, who was Marshall's brother-in-law, and whose wife sent the men soups and jellies.

George Hay was chief prosecutor but Jefferson followed every detail of the trial and they exchanged numerous letters. Soon realizing that his witnesses' testimony would not convict Burr, he told the president, "I shan't be able to hang Burr." Later, Hay was convinced that "the Chief Justice is prejudiced against the prosecution." Prosecutor Wirt spoke of Burr's cool, courteous manner in the courtroom. His "seductive and fascinating power" made many doubt the prosecution's case.

Winfield Scott, a handsome young Virginia attorney, who was a spectator, remarked that "Burr stood . . . on the brink of danger . . . composed . . . immovable as one of Canova's living marbles." He felt President Jefferson "directed and animated the proceedings" but Marshall was the "master spirit."

On August 20, Wickham moved that the court suspend all further testimony. Although Hay was livid at the suggestion, Marshall consented to hear arguments from both sides.

The arguments, pro and con whether additional witnesses should testify, continued for days.

Martin delivered the defense summation. Warmed both by his sipping whiskey and the soaring temperature, he spoke for fourteen hours.

⚬⚬

Marshall ruled in favor of the defense motion. In three hours of instructions, Marshall backed out of his previous "treasonous assemblage" doctrine. The prosecution should have charged Burr with procurement and then proved it with witnesses.

"The jury have now heard the opinion of the court on the law of the case. They will apply that law to the facts and will find a verdict."

In twenty-five minutes, the jury returned with the verdict.

"We of the jury say that Aaron Burr is not proved to be guilty under this indictment by any evidence submitted to us. We therefore find him not guilty."

Defense attorneys objected to the wording and Foreman Edward Carrington offered to change it, but a Jeffersonian on the jury refused "to allow one syllable to be altered." Marshall ruled that the verdict should remain as found by the jury, and an entry of "not guilty" should be made on the record.

Marshall knew that abuse and criticism would follow, but he had won another round in the battle with his cousin from Monticello. Jefferson sent the depositions of the witnesses who had not been allowed to testify to Congress, "that it might judge whether the deficit was in the testimony, in the law, or in the administration of the law."

"I have learned that judicial opinions are like changeable silks, which vary their colors as they are held up in political sunshine," Senator Giles observed.

After misdemeanor charges were nol prossed, the accused men left Richmond. Burr and Martin took a stage to Philadelphia, but Blennerhasset watched from cover in Baltimore as marchers pulled two carts, with four effigies "habited for execution." The effigies were dressed to resemble Marshall, Burr, Martin, and Blennerhasset.

Both Dr. John Brockenbrough and Joseph Cabell had served on the Burr grand jury with Jack, and afterward Jack became close friends with John and Gabriella Brockenbrough, but his friendship with Joseph Cabell ruptured. Sometime during this period, Brockenbrough apparently informed Jack that Nancy, who lived at Haymarket, "associated with the players" and had become a prostitute.

Judith sent Nancy $100 by Tudor, but Nancy was so deeply hurt by the eviction from Bizarre that she refused to take the money.

While in Richmond Jack visited Nancy once. Her pleasure in seeing him was short-lived, although she was encouraged by his long visit and his profession of regard. She later learned that Jack had written letters accusing her of immodest conduct and joined his friends in spreading rumors that she had become a prostitute.

"None laid so profound a plot as Ryland Randolph, when his 'friendly visits' were made at Haymarket; my situation was such as might have softened the worst of hearts."

Jack later wrote that he found her and her quarters "fastidiously neat . . . but the bait did not take," implying that she had solicited him for sexual services.

In her January 2, 1815, letter to Jack, Nancy reminded him that her chamber at Haymarket Gardens was directly over that of Mrs. Pryor, the owner's wife. Their dwelling was separate from the gardens and enclosed by a fence. On his visit, he sat on her bedstead with a blanket over the sacking.

His professions of regard during his long visit led her to believe that he had acted only as her sister's agent in turning her out of Bizarre. Regardless of where the money came, she had refused it because her "feelings were too indignant" to accept it.

Then Nancy made a bad mistake. She wrote to Jack, admitting a birth had taken place at Glentivar in 1792. With her letter was a packet of letters, with certain passages removed, that Dick had written her years before.

Her 1815 letter contained more about the events of 1807. "You will perhaps mention a letter which I wrote on leaving Virginia, but ... permit me to tell you that the very mention of it destroys your credibility. . . . "

After learning of the accusations of immodest conduct, Nancy decided to "brave all dangers rather than remain the victim of persecution." Taking Molly's advice, she left Virginia and went to Newport, Rhode Island., where several of Lelia Tucker's relatives lived.

Newport, a small town on Newport Bay, was linked by bridges to the mainland. During colonial times, it had been as popular a cultural center as Boston or New York, but it later declined. When Nancy went there, Newport was visited mostly for its salubrious quality. Here she expected a welcome refuge. Instead, she found animosity and hatred. Her sister Molly had betrayed her.

In December Nancy wrote Jack in Washington, asking to borrow $50, saying she was "emaciated and suffering, was turned unsheltered on the world." He did not reply.

"I united them all for awhile against me," Jack recalled to Kidder Randolph in 1816. "They espoused the cause of their dear sister, aunt or cousin Nancy, whom they pursued to the foot of the gibbet and to whom they would not give a mouthful of bread before she left Virginia to keep her from starving."

Jefferson disavowed the terms of the Monroe-Pinkney treaty with England and negotiators Livingston and Monroe returned home, almost disgraced. The Monroes, leaving Saint in the custody of Frank Skipwith, Lelia's kin, came to Williamsburg, bringing their two daughters with them. Tucker, always alert for ideas for Lelia and his granddaughters Frances and Elizabeth, made special note of the new European fashion. Under a mid-calf length dress, Maria Monroe wore full-length pantaloons. The "new look" later became high fashion in America.

Mary Carter Cabell and her husband visited her parents in Williamsburg. She was now pleasingly plump and disappointed with her lack of success with the cabbage diet, a current fad in Virginia. Lelia reported, however, that she "is not in the way."

Braidwood teachers wrote of Saint's great proficiency in drawing and sent some of his work to Jack, who was delighted. Judith's greatest interest and concern, however, was with her younger son.

"Tudor has seen his mother's difficulties and never was there a nobler child."

Saint sent word that he and Charles Carter, Lelia's son studying medicine in Paris, planned a reunion.

But Judith's petulance with Jack increased, and she questioned whether they could continue living together under one roof.

Jack Randolph caustically referred to the Nonimportation Act as "a milk and water bill, a dose of chicken broth to be taken nine months hence." The Embargo Act, passed December 21, 1807, along with the Nonimportation Act, prohibited the import of certain goods. Neither act was successful.

Ellen Randolph was her grandfather's social editor, relaying news from home, Albemarle, and the state.

"The embargo seriously afflicted the dissipated citizens of Williamsburg," she wrote. "The ladies were unable to do without their tea and coffee and the men were unable to give up their wine."

Her sister Ann, Jefferson's gardening advisor, offered suggestions on bedding plants, care of tuberoses and amaryllis, and on planting everlasting peas.

1808–1809

Martha's son, Benjamin Franklin Randolph, was born on July 16, 1808. Immediately afterward, she planned her eldest daughter's wedding. Ann was now seventeen years old and engaged to Charles Lewis Bankhead from King William County. With her grandfather present, they were married in the Monticello parlor in September. The couple lived in Front Royal, northwest of Monticello, and Ann's separation from her family left her depressed. The move also deprived Jefferson of his gardening expert.

Jefferson supervised Maria's son, Francis Eppes, in his studies in Washington and arranged for Jeff to enter the University of Pennsylvania. Martha feared Jeff's inherited traits; she found him lazy and resentful when criticized. Although she considered this part of his Randolph character, she hoped that society and acquired habits would equalize them.

Having lived beyond his means, Jefferson was concerned about leaving the presidential office burdened with debt. Tom was in even worse financial circumstances, and Martha felt he was not realistic about finances, refusing to sell any of his Edgehill slaves because of the emotional attachment, having "raised many of them." Also, he considered payment of the stipend to Nancy a "sacred obligation." Jefferson urged Martha and Tom to live with him at Monticello, and suggested that Tom use Edgehill for producing income to pay off his debts.

Nancy Randolph Morris 1774-1837,
Library of Virginia

James Madison was Jefferson's choice to succeed him as president, while a splinter group of Republicans, the Tirtium Quids, sought James Monroe's nomination. When Madison emerged as the overwhelming favorite, Jefferson attempted to portray neutrality between his two friends, writing Monroe that he viewed them both as "pillars of my happiness." Jack Randolph, an active leader of the Quids, had worked against Madison and Jefferson and for Monroe's nomination, but Monroe's long friendship with Jefferson was too strong. He declined becoming a candidate, citing others' maturity and experience, and the decision ended his friendship with Jack. Madison and Vice President George Clinton were elected in November 1808. Beginning in early 1809, Jefferson packed to leave Washington, ready to return to his "scenes of rural retirement."

Dolley Madison prepared for her most important role, that of first lady. At the inaugural ceremony, she wore an imported, champagne-colored, cambric dress with a long train and a purple velvet bonnet. Madison wore an American-made black woolen suit. He trembled, perspiring, during the inaugural ceremony, while Jefferson was cool and composed. Jefferson was so elated that he attended a ball and danced for the first time in forty years.

When Jefferson left Washington, a blinding snowstorm and the muddy, rutted roads stopped his carriage again and again. Finally, unable to bear the delay, the former president, almost sixty-eight years old, traveled for eight hours on horseback to reach Monticello. Although happy with his family there, his mind was already on Poplar Forest, his retreat in Bedford County. Tom had sold, for $10 an acre, the thousand acres that Jefferson had given Martha as a wedding gift, but her father had kept his land there and planned to build another home. They had made bricks for its construction and began laying the foundation. Building this home offered Jefferson the rewards that he had experienced in his early years at Monticello, and he relished the opportunity to bring it to completion.

He came to Richmond on October 19, 1809, on personal business but his popularity with Richmonders turned the visit into a celebration. The governor and James Monroe accompanied him to Capitol Square where they viewed drill muster. Later, he was guest of honor for a dinner at the Eagle Tavern. He was never to return to the capital city.

In Richmond, Molly and David Randolph, in financial difficulty too, had sold Moldavia and moved to the street later named Cary after her mother's family. Her husband sailed for England about the time that she opened a boarding house, and Tom helped her in the venture. Richmonders, who had enjoyed Molly's bounty earlier at Moldavia, now attested to her "festive boards" after the announcement appeared in the *Richmond Gazette* and *General Advertiser.* Word spread quickly of the "Queen's new realm," and her business soon boomed.

Cool drinks and ice creams enhanced Molly's dinners through the use of a "refrigerant" that she invented for her own use. Historian Samuel Mordecai reported that a shrewd Yankee, a guest, took the plans of the invention, and it soon became commonly used. Molly later published a cookbook, *The Virginia Housewife.* The recipes used over forty vegetables and at least fifteen herbs but did not require the long cooking times used by most Southern cooks. Her recipe for "Southern fried chicken" was simple: "Cut up the chicken into pieces, dredge in salted and peppered flour and cook in hot fat."

During the severe winter of 1808—1809, ice on the pond at Bizarre was three inches thick; Theodore Dudley and Tudor skated for days. Judith received flattering reports about Saint from Paris, where he now attended the Secord School, and she believed his drawings and his "engravings on stone" were "specimens of genius."

Jack wrote frequently, but not to Judith. He had not as yet withdrawn his affection from Tucker, and letters to his stepfather castigated Jefferson and Madison, yet betrayed Jack's loneliness and isolation in Washington. He saw scarcely anyone, except in the "human desert the H. of R." He even ate alone. Jack considered Madison's presidency the "government of a single man with regal powers." In Jack's loneliness, were there awakened memories of his years in Philadelphia and thoughts of Hester Hargrave? Did he wonder what had become of the young woman that Edmund Randolph and Joseph Bryan had sent to England because she was socially inferior?

Jack continued to attack those whom he regarded with contempt and scorn and spoke for five straight days on the House floor attacking General James Wilkinson. Although Wilkinson was considered by many to be a felon and was referred to by Winfield Scott as "an unprincipled imbecile," he retained his army command, with Jefferson's and Madison's support, through the War of 1812.

Saint returned to America, arriving in Philadelphia tired and ill from the long crossing but happy to be reunited with his family. The ten-year-old brother that he had left was now fourteen, tall and heavy, and studied with the Reverend John Rice in Farmville. Theodore Dudley had entered medical school in Philadelphia.

Saint, now able to better communicate, described to his Grandfather Tucker the pleasures of the "play house and the animals" in London, and reported that Charles Carter had grown taller than Tucker. In author Marion Harland's book, *Marion Harland's Autobiography*, she gave her mother's description of Saint, whom she met at Reverend Rice's, shortly after his return to the United States.

"One of the handsomest young men I ever saw, with flashing black eyes and dark, beautiful curls."

He frightened her when he offered to teach her the finger alphabet, but "seemed gay in spite of his affliction."

His gaiety gradually diminished when he returned to the isolation of Bizarre and Roanoke after the excitement of his years abroad. There was no money for art materials or instruction, and the strained relationship between his mother and his uncle made him uneasy.

The debt to Hanbury's, dating from John Randolph of Matoax's loan guarantee of 1773, was due to be discharged. Dick's remaining slaves were to be freed and resettled, and Theo's property would be divided between Jack and Judith, Dick's widow. Jack offered her several proposals for division. Knowing that she often consulted Tucker for legal advice, in early November Jack hurriedly laid out for Tucker his proposals for the division, as Judith vacillated. There were four options, including leases, purchase, or an exchange of Dick's and Theo's properties. He was upset because she had spoken of selling Bizarre, against which his "judgment and feeling equally revolt." Tucker believed the propositions were deserving of serious consideration, but they needed clarification.

He hoped that Saint's "European education had been of service to him."

Saint had returned a good patriot but was idle, and thus dissatisfied, Jack reported. Time hung heavily, Judith was a confirmed hypochondriac, and Saint was "little calculated to enliven us." Saint sank into despair.

⤚⊱⤙

The haven that Nancy Randolph sought was not in Newport. A few people, including Peyton Skipwith and his wife, were friendly; others were cruel. They accused her of crimes and cheated her out of money, saying that she had "fled from justice." Among the stories spread were those that Dick had died just before she left Virginia, and that Jack and Judith immediately turned her out of Bizarre, having been prevented from doing so earlier by Dick.

Some of the townspeople refused to believe such gossip and blamed Molly for spreading the accusations. One, a Mrs. Pollok, befriended the lonely and humiliated Southerner and Nancy moved with her to Fairfield, Connecticut. Here, Nancy finally broke her self-imposed silence with several Virginians. One of the first was to her friend Tucker, telling of the past year's events and of living in a house of "deceit and abuse."

She had found a "cheap retreat" where she could again breathe easily enough. She had no personal servant and was pleased and surprised that the people in Fairfield did their own errands.

"The simple privilege of walking abroad with kind greetings is inconceivable."

⤚⊱⤙

Nancy heard news about Gouverneur Morris, the wealthy aristocrat who had visited her family at Tuckahoe long ago when she was a young teenager. She wrote him to say that she and her friend, Mrs. Pollok, were coming to New York in October. He replied, suggesting a meeting, and called on Nancy at a boarding house in Greenwich Village, finding a handsome woman in her mid-thirties. With his worldly background and a sharp eye for attractive women, he appreciated her good looks and vivacious personality, as well as her intelligence. During their visit he mentioned problems with retaining good housekeepers and his search for a reduced gentlewoman to take charge. When they parted, he went to settle property matters in upper New York State and Nancy returned to Fairfield.

Tucker, gratified to finally hear from his ward, eagerly sought details, and she complied. Her apartment was without shutters or a fireplace; a gentleman had told her recently that he had met Saint in England; she was seeking a lady going there who needed a companion.

Shortly before Christmas, she wrote Tucker of her winter hibernation in cold New England. Her "refrigerator" had not yet reached the freezing point, but she would "bid him adieu" until "with other frogs" she could announce warmer weather. She went with Mrs. Pollok to visit a niece in Stratford, but memories of her past were still with her, she said. She wanted justice done to Dick's memory and to guard Tudor against future insult, concluding that she did indeed love Tucker with the "fondest gratitude."

Then Nancy wrote to Morris again, asking for advice on her situation and expressing appreciation for his interest. He told her that he had heard of certain "events, which brought distress." A letter exchange followed; the correspondence became more intimate. He sent a poem, then promised that, if they were ever alone, "You shall tell your tale of sorrow when the tears from your cheek may fall in my bosom."

Nancy accepted his offer of the housekeeper position at Morrisania. He would pay her the salary he was presently paying and it, along with the pension that Tom provided, would make "provision for future storms."

Addressing their intimate association, he assured her that he had never approached previous housekeepers with "anything like desire," but revealed his feeling toward her and of the folly of basing happiness on "sensual gratification."

"Time in taking away the ardor has not quelled the rashness of youth. I will love you as little as I can."

She left Stratford for New York, and on April 23, 1809, he picked her up at Armstrong's Tavern and took her to Morrisania. Nancy had finally found a home. She refused, "tho perishing from want," to enter his house without first telling him the story of her life at Bizarre and Hay Market.

❧

Morris had spent over $50,000 on extensive improvements to Morrisania, even adding an indoor bathroom. Nancy found the two-story, white, frame house impressive, with a portico, upstairs porch, English basement, and 130-foot-long terrace overlooking Manhattan Island, where the East River ran into the Harlem River. The land approach was from Union Avenue in what is now the South Bronx, although most visitors came by boat. The manor house held the treasures that he had collected abroad. Glass door bookcases displayed his extensive collection. Dark paneled walls enhanced the rich imported tapestries and the Marie Antoinette mirror.

$\sim$

The summer and early autumn of 1809 passed pleasantly. Even with Nancy's inexperience, Morris was pleased with her efforts. Nancy, happily, did not have to worry about food and shelter, and Morris was a true friend. Then his friends and extended family began to talk. In November, David Parish visited from Philadelphia and said the relationship with Nancy hurt Morris's friends. Parish's rude meddling angered Morris. He wrote John Marshall, inquiring about Nancy's reputation in Virginia. He described her "good sense, good temper" and her beauty, in which he personally disclaimed any interest. He had heard gossip and sundry reports based on happenings in the past while he was in Europe but wanted more information.

Marshall's response noted the "comparison of the situation" in which Morris had found Nancy in Connecticut and when she had lived a life of luxury at Tuckahoe. There were those who had believed the accusations against her, while others "attached no criminality to her conduct." Marshall felt that the rumors were "spread and magnified . . . probably invented by the malignant." He said that Nancy was welcome in homes of those who did not condemn her because of the pronouncement "of an unfavorable sentence."

His letter reached Morrisania two days before Christmas and reassured Morris, who wrote a short contract and Release of Dower and presented it to Nancy on Christmas Eve morning, "the first declaration." He felt that her "Good Will and Amusing conversations" had made him feel in a way "which ought not to be expected by people of my age." She accepted his proposal of marriage, and they planned a Christmas wedding. This took place on a Sunday, and with the next day being Christmas Day, there was no time to shop for wedding clothes. There were nine guests at the festive Christmas Day dinner and the highlight of the evening was the host's and housekeeper's wedding. The bride wore a "brown gown patched at the elbows, being one of only two that I owned."

On his wedding night, Morris, the suave and worldly bachelor who had eluded marriage with women on two continents, noted in his diary, "I marry this day Ann Cary Randolph. No small surprise to my guests."

Nancy's first letter as Mrs. Gouverneur Morris of Morrisania, New York, was to her benefactor, St. George Tucker of Williamsburg, Virginia.

"Yesterday I became the wife of Gouverneur Morris, who personifies every generous and truly noble quality."

1810

"Married on Christmas Day, 1809, Gouverneur Morris, Esquire of Morrisania and Ann Cary Randolph."

*M*any eyes bulged as they read page two of the *Virginia Advertiser.* Disbelief was erased by the confirming announcement found on page twenty-two of the *Visitor.* Gossips had a field day discussing the marriage of Nancy Randolph to the northern aristocrat.

Morris's marriage shocked and angered his relatives. Their fifty-six year-old uncle, whose generosity had been taken for granted and whose fortune they had expected to inherit, had taken a much younger wife, with heirs a possibility. From Philadelphia, his niece, Gertrude Meredith, chastised him for not consulting her. His reply was like a rapier thrust, couched in polite language.

He asked pardon for "violating an obligation . . . of which I was not apprized." He had found no cause to repent.

"If I had married a rich woman of seventy the world might think it wiser than to take one half that age without a farthing. . . . If the world were to live with my wife, I should certainly have consulted its taste. I thought I might, without offending others, suit myself, and look into the head and heart rather than into the pocket."

Mrs. Meredith's husband hurriedly replied with a congratulatory letter, inviting the bride and groom for a visit.

Morris was appointed president of the Erie Canal Commission and decided he would take his bride with him to inspect the proposed route through upstate New York. Before leaving, the couple had wedding portraits painted by the Sharples, husband and wife artists who came to Morrisania in early June. Morris's portrait, with white hair and a pleasant, benign expression, presented an aristocratic bearing. Nancy's dark curls crept from her cap, a smile hovered on her lips, and a décolleté gown emphasized a voluptuous bosom.

The Morrises left Morrisania on June 21, traveling the proposed route, 363 miles long between Albany and Buffalo. Accommodations were at times primitive, and they vied with others for the private rooms at inns. They visited the "Falls of Niagara," awing Nancy, before returning home in early September.

Jack began 1810 at Bizarre by venting his animosity in his diary. He scrawled "Tantrums of Mrs. R" over and over, up and down, boxing in other notations with the words.

On a "fine January day," Dr. Dillon and Kidder Randolph appraised Dick's slaves before the final division, emancipation, and resettlement. Later, the commissioners began the division of Theo's estate between Jack and Judith.

Jack assumed responsibility for the balance due British creditors, with the slaves at Roanoke plantation pledged as security. Disagreements arose on the division and on the interpretation of Dick's will. Jack planned to discuss the problem with Tucker, but when he stopped in Richmond to meet with him, they missed each other and instead he continued on to the House of Representatives, "which I can compare to nothing but the famous Dog Hole near Naples."

The interpretation hinged on Dick's freeing "every slave of which I die possessed or to which I have any claim through inheritance."

Judith, confused and uneasy about the legal aspects of the division, turned to Creed Taylor for clarification on March 17.

"My dear Sir:

"I have had much reflection upon the subject of our conversation the other day, and I have determined to apply to you once more, as the friend in whom my husband had the highest confidence, and from whom I have received numerous acts of kindness, to solve some of my difficulties, which are in great measure the offspring of my ignorance."

Judith was concerned that she or Creed Taylor might be held liable if the slaves were taken to Roanoke instead of being freed. She felt that they had discharged their proportion of the debt by the sacrifices she had made.

"Without ruin to all parties the negroes cannot be discharged till autumn. I deplore the delay of a measure, which their just rights, my interests, and I firmly believe, my safety, imperiously demand."

Settling the complicated legal and financial details of the Randolphs' estates ensued for the rest of the year. The final surveyed property at Israel Hill, the land set aside as directed in Dick's will, comprised three hundred and fifty acres. More than ninety slaves were freed and given plots of land of between twenty-five and fifty acres per family. Freed slaves not wishing to settle at Israel Hill went to Farmville and Petersburg.

Jack and Judith's enmity finally became so heated that he and Theodore Dudley moved to the isolated Roanoke plantation. In explaining the move to Theodore, Jack spoke more temperately rather than openly expressing his hearty dislike of his sister-in-law.

He had made the move to place himself as far as possible "from as many headaches as I have been made to feel (by feminine caprice and affection)."

Two seals burned by Saint while in Paris arrived in Richmond, along with his books, desk, and "burning machine" used in his art work. They were too heavy to send by post. Saint had asked Tucker to have them sent and wished Tucker could have come as well, because he "used to explain everything."

Judith was excited, for Maria Ward Randolph had promised to send a carriage to bring her to Maria's new home, Moilena, for a visit.

Instead, word arrived that Tudor was seriously ill with typhus and she had gone to Farmville to nurse him.

Judith left the Episcopal Church, joining the Rices as a Presbyterian. Jack attended the service when she joined, outwardly approving. Afterward, on a visit to her at the Rices', he accused them of being "wolves in sheep's clothing" to get to her money.

"In his piercing falsetto," heard throughout the house, "the irate Congressman berated her, in the coarsest terms 'for the disgrace she had brought upon an honorable name in uniting with the Dissenters.'"

When Martha's next son was born in 1810, she named him Meriwether Lewis in honor of her father's deceased friend, whom he believed had committed suicide in the Louisiana Territory.

Tom's land was planted in income-producing crops when a heavy rain fell throughout Albemarle, three inches in one hour. His and his father-in-law's crops were the only ones to survive the deluge, their good fortune being due to Tom's controversial horizontal method of plowing. Jefferson had authorized his overseer to employ this method and had unsuccessfully urged his neighbors to do likewise. Instead, they had used the traditional method and watched as a season's labor washed by.

Jefferson later wrote that Tom's method had "changed and renovated . . . our country. Previously the rain had carried away the soil. In the horizontal method, none of the soil is lost, rain not absorbed is retained in the hollows between the beds until it is absorbed."

Tom's modest accomplishment was dwarfed by the news of his friend, John Leslie, in Scotland. Leslie had frozen water using an air pump, thereby making ice.

1811

When Jack was in Bizarre's neighborhood, he passed the door without stopping to speak, and Saint was mortified.

Judith had received several of the Matoax slaves as part of the estate distribution, but they did not live up to her strict standards: "They are useless." Her younger sister Harriet Hackley came to Bizarre to live; she and her husband, Richard Hackley, back from Cadiz, Spain, became estranged. He had brought his Spanish mistress with him. Harriet's presence gave Judith more freedom in visiting with Mary Harrison, Fanny Coalter, and Maria Ward Randolph.

In contrast to his mother's jaunts, Saint, constrained by near poverty, was forced to decline his Aunt Fanny's invitation to visit in Staunton. He had no transportation, he wrote, because Tudor rode one horse to school and the work horses had to be used for ploughing.

Before Jack returned home, he had a public altercation with Congressman Willis Alston.

While the House was in session, Alston's remarks provoked the short-tempered Randolph, who responded with a sarcastic tongue-lashing, referring to Alston as "that thing."

After the session, Alston persevered in his derisive comments as he preceded Jack down the stairs and "took care to throw himself in my way," said Jack. Unable to resist the temptation, Jack beat him over the head with his cane. Alston resisted, Jack persisted, and, before fellow members could restrain Jack, Alston received severe bloody cuts. A grand jury indicted Jack for breach of peace, and the judge fined him $20, a modest penalty for Jack's pleasure in obtaining retribution and in observing Alston's bandaged head.

Another display of Jack's temper occurred during a heated argument in Congress between Jack and John Eppes. It appeared that the two were headed for a duel, before their seconds resolved the dispute. Eppes had moved into Jack's congressional district when he purchased Millbrooke in Buckingham County. In the next election, he challenged Jack for the district seat in Congress. Jack blamed everything on Jefferson, but on April 11, 1811, an article appeared in the *Richmond Inquirer* regarding the contest.

"We understand a poll will be taken for Eppes by some of his friends in every county lately represented, or rather misrepresented, by John Randolph. . . . Mr. Eppes is as much an ornament to Congress as Mr. Randolph is a nuisance and a curse. . . ."

Jack's constituents obviously felt differently; he won easily. Eppes had 199 votes to 198 for Jack in Buckingham County, but in Prince Edward, Eppes received only 98 to Jack's 250 votes.

❧

Saint's responsibilities at Bizarre occupied most of his time, sidetracking his artistic projects, while his mother visited first Warm Springs and then the Coalters in Staunton. In mid-summer, Saint wrote his uncle, asking permission to visit at Roanoke. Jack welcomed him warmly, in writing from Halifax.

❧

"My dear boy,

"I dined here yesterday and the rain prevented me from returning. I have barely time to tell you to come and stay with me as long as you please – the longer the more agreeable to me. . . .

"Yours affectionately,

"JR of R"

Saint's pleasures there included fishing for perch in the Staunton River, practicing his marksmanship, and working with his burning machine. Jack considered his ivory chessman (a castle) superior to the European model.

Jack found another letter from him when he arrived back in the House of Representatives. Sensing Saint's need for reassurances of affection and his diminishing self-esteem, Jack answered immediately.

Nov. 4, 1811

"My dearest boy,

" I received your very kind letter. . . . I shall continue to love you and your dear brother better than all the world as long as you deserve it and are dutiful & good & humane & kind . . . but not prodigal & rash & cruel & perverse. I do want to see you very much indeed. I gave your friend Mr. Macon the shaving brush in Richmond. He was much pleased.

"He will not be speaker. The friends of Mr. Madison hate him and will elect Mr. Henry Clay of Kentucky who is a young man never before in the House. Show this letter to your dear brother whom I love as if he was my own son.

"My love to Sally [Dudley, Theodore's sister].

"Your fond uncle,
"JR of Roanoke."

Nathaniel Macon of North Carolina had entered Congress in 1799, the same year as Jack. As Speaker of the House, Macon had successfully fought Jack's removal as chairman of the Ways and Means Committee in 1806. In *John Randolph of Roanoke,* Randolph's biographer, William Cabell Bruce, portrayed Macon's and Randolph's feelings toward each other as being "more like the love of a woman for a man or a woman, than of a man for a man."

Henry Clay had come to Richmond in 1793 at age sixteen to serve as secretary to Chancellor of Virginia George Wythe. He later moved to Kentucky and, as Aaron Burr's attorney there in 1806, successfully defended his client against indictment on conspiracy charges. Clay entered the House of Representatives in 1811, having already served as senator from Kentucky.

Other new Southerners entered Congress whose philosophy differed from Jack's and Macon's. Richard Johnson of Kentucky, Felix Grundy of Tennessee, and William Lowndes and John Calhoun of South Carolina wanted to expand the country's frontiers—in Canada by war with England and in taking the Floridas from Spain. Through Henry Clay, they soon had Secretary of State James Monroe on their side. Nominees for the 1812 presidential election were being discussed, and these men would be influential in deciding whether Madison would be the Republican choice.

❦

Gouverneur Morris's relatives never became reconciled to his marriage. When he traveled to Philadelphia in July to visit his niece and David Parish, Nancy stayed at Morrisania. Her Virginia relatives were coming to visit.

The Morrises left for Washington on December 12, where Morris was scheduled to meet with President Madison and congressional members regarding support for the Erie Canal project. They traveled in their own carriage, accompanied by baggage wagons, and arrived in Washington on December 15, staying at Tomlinson's Boarding House.

While Morris called on the president, Nancy went to the House of Representatives. She sat in the gallery where "Jack's public speaking delighted" her. In his speech on foreign relations, he attacked the plan put forth by Henry Clay and John Calhoun to conquer Canada.

Nancy's feeling of being "so happy [because] Jack came to see me today," was far different from his later version of the visit.

"When Mr. Morris brought you to Washington, he knew that I held aloof from you." He "asked me if I intended to mortify his wife by not visiting her. I went. I repeated my visit. I was led to hope you had seen your errors and was [sic] smoothing his passage through life."

Nancy mistakenly believed that, over six years after she had been sent from Bizarre, there had actually been a renewal of family ties.

❦

Thomas Jefferson was torn between relief at not being in office and depression from being out of the arena of public life. He expressed delight in his 1811 crops, gardens, and orchards to artist Charles Willson Peale, saying, "I am an old man, but a new gardener."

Jefferson and John Adams had never ended their estrangement after the bitter 1800—1801 election. During a summer visit to Adams, Jefferson's friend Edward Coles spoke to Adams of Jefferson's respect and affection. Jefferson had said that Adams was "an honest man, an able man with his pen." He retained the "same good opinion of Mr. Adams which I ever had."

Adams responded, "I have always loved Jefferson and still love him."

∽✗∽

As 1811 ended, Nancy became ill in Washington, while the War Hawks gathered momentum in Congress, determined to force the United States into combat with England.

1812

*J*efferson's correspondence with Abigail Adams was secret, and John Adams had no personal contact with him until New Year's Day 1812, when he wrote. Jefferson responded promptly, describing his vigor in old age, with sometimes eight hours on horseback, his quarterly visits to Poplar Forest, and his pleasure that Ann had recently made him a great-grandfather.

⁂

In Congress, the War Hawks continued to push for a declaration of conflict with England. Henry Clay and Peter B. Porter lobbied hard for a bill, which became law, to increase the standing militia force, in paper numbers only, since the ranks were never filled. The navy was also seriously undermanned, with only four thousand enlisted men, fifteen hundred marines, and 234 officers. Bitterness between the two countries escalated. Madison was a "master of words, not of men" and was unable to control the clamor in Congress. The war became more certain as he endured Jack's vehemence in the House. Jack refused to accept naval crises as the reason for the War Hawks' demand for war.

"Agrarian cupidity, not maritime rights, urges the war. We have heard but one word – like the whippoorwill [sic] but one eternal monotonous tone – Canada, Canada, Canada."

After William Henry Harrison reported that the British were supplying weapons to the Indians in the Northwest Territory, the War

Hawks became more insistent. Finally, on June 1, President Madison, ashen and shaken, asked for a declaration of war. At Speaker Henry Clay's urging, the House passed a bill within three days. Jack's vote was with the Federalist minority of 49 against, but a vote of 79 came in for the declaration. The Senate deliberated longer, and its vote of 19 for and 13 against, was not passed until June 18.

∽

Nancy and her husband returned to Morrisania from Washington in early February, disappointed in not obtaining funding for the canal's construction. Morris turned to New York for help and left for Albany to negotiate. On June 17, the day before the declaration of war, New York passed the Canal Bill, authorizing $5 million for the construction of the Erie Canal.

Morris's elation with the funding was eclipsed by Nancy's exciting news that she was pregnant . . . " expecting to be confined in February."

Morris wrote John Parish in Bath, England, inviting him to Morrisania.

"Perhaps some wind may yet waft you over the bosom of the Atlantic and then you shall become acquainted with my wife and you shall see that fortune – fortune? No the word befits not a sacred theme – let me say the bounty of Him, who has been to me unsparingly kind, gilds with a celestial beam the tranquil evening of my day."

∽

If Saint had inherited Dick's good looks and compassion, then Tudor had inherited his father's superior intellect and Judith's dark vindictiveness. Surprisingly, Jack encouraged in Tudor traits that he deplored in Judith. Tudor attended a school in Farmville operated by Dr. John Rice, a Presbyterian minister, who encouraged Tudor to enter the ministry, but Jack balked. Instead, he enrolled his nephew at Harvard University, ruling out William and Mary as well as Princeton, where he had studied.

Jack took Tudor as far as Washington where he met Josiah Quincy, who escorted him to Cambridge. En route they stopped at Morrisania, where Nancy was reunited with the nephew whom she had not seen for five years.

At Cambridge, Tudor lived with Harvard's president, John T. Kirkland. Quincy oversaw Tudor's financial affairs, a task that proved greater than expected. Tudor was an extravagant spender with a small stipend and had inherited his Uncle Jack's attraction to the "smack of the whip." He was described as being tall and swarthy, with Pocahontas and Powhatan features, "a very peculiar character, never very friendly."

Saint's situation at Bizarre was as far flung from his brother's as the distance that separated them. He farmed the plantation and oversaw various aspects of both the Bizarre and Roanoke operations. His letters confirmed Jack's prediction of the necessity "of following the plough." His recreation was hunting and he had "killed two woodcock and was almost ashamed to say he had wounded another." He also killed partridges and a very large hawk. With other members of his family away visiting, "I am lonesome by myself. I am very glad to tell you that my horse became very gentle as to draw the old buggy."

Jack's slave Jupiter brought Saint a letter from Jack and helped him sow the wheat.

"I have not been shooting for nearly a fortnight. I am always so busy and the days are so short. If you write to Theodore, give my love to him . . . I expect to hear from you and Brother also. I write this with a crow quill and I have no knife to mend more."

Jack answered from Georgetown. He had heard from Tudor and enclosed the letter with his to Saint.

"I think you do not write your English so plainly and intelligibly as you used to do which I suppose it for the want of practice . . . write frequently and endeavour to express your thoughts as plainly as possible."

Jack suggested that Saint keep a journal of the weather and daily occurrences and send him the sheet weekly to be corrected and returned. Theodore, he wrote, had been seriously ill in Philadelphia, where he had been bled and blistered.

As a forerunner to a disastrous year to come, Jack lost the friend of his early manhood. Joseph Bryan died of dropsy at Wilmington Island, Georgia, leaving his wife, Delia, and five children.

United States single ship victories elated Americans and humiliated the British, but had little effect on the war. As Jack had predicted, the American war effort was concentrated on taking parts of Canada. In the presidential election, Madison was the incumbent nominee, running against Democrat DeWitt Clinton. Madison was an unpopular choice with the Federalists, and First Secretary of the Navy Benjamin Stoddert predicted, "If Virginia should persist in fastening upon the middle and eastern states the obnoxious and fatal administration of Mr. Madison, we may bid adieu to the Union, and prepare for the horrors of intestine commotion."

Madison carried every state south and west of the Delaware River and lost every one north, except Vermont. The December Electoral College votes were 128 for Madison and 89 for Clinton for president, and 131 for Elbridge Gerry to 86 for Charles Ingersoll for vice president.

1813

What would be a calamitous year for the Randolphs of Bizarre began quietly enough. Saint flooded his uncle with minutiae of his solitary life. Sally made new shirts for Jupiter, the slave. Saint's dog, Capitan, was hunting well, since he had given him a scolding. In the deep snow, it was impossible to catch hares; only the starving partridges could be found. He had ordered oats for both Roanoke and Bizarre. Unfortunately, he had no time for his art and burning machine. But he expressed his love for his uncle, his brother, and his cousin Theodore. He rarely mentioned his mother.

Jack's friendship with Joseph Nicholson ended after a contentious disagreement over the war, but he became friends with Francis Scott Key, Nicholson's brother-in-law. Key was a deeply religious man of integrity, and he sought to become an uplifting influence on Jack.

❧

On February 9, Gouverneur Morris handled business affairs at home, and late that evening Nancy gave birth to a son, Gouverneur Morris, Jr. The next day, Morris made the announcement to Tucker.

"My wife was delivered of a son last evening. He is fat and strong. The mother is exhausted, feeble and feverish."

A few days later, Jack heard the news and sent Morris congratulations on the birth of a son with "cordial wishes for Mrs. Morris' speedy recovery."

Jack had defeated Creed Taylor, John Baker (John Eppes's brother-in-law), and Eppes himself when they had opposed him for his congressional seat. This year Eppes announced his candidacy again, from Buckingham County. With Jefferson quietly campaigning for him, he was a formidable foe. Eppes accused Jack of being against the war, which Jack admitted, speaking eloquently of his reasons. Eppes persisted, dragging volumes of materials around the district, boring his audiences, until his opponent remarked that Eppes was a "good reader." Jack accused Eppes of being prodded by "Sir Thomas of Cantingbury."

❧

Shortly before the election, Judith's black cloud covered Jack. On March 31, while she was away on one of her frequent jaunts, sparks from the chimney set fire to the roof at Bizarre. The dwelling was a "heap of ruins." Trees Dick had planted when Saint was born were destroyed; Judith lost twenty years' work in homespun fabric and a cream pot that she was "preserving for a relic." Jack lost many of his books that he had not moved to Roanoke. A few pieces of furniture and some books were saved, but the yard was "strewn with burnt papers."

Tucker quickly sent Judith $500 to help with immediate expenses, and she moved to a few rooms in a home on Main Street in Farmville. She was concerned about Saint's safety with the freed slaves and transients there, so he returned to the plantation, where he moved into a small building that had escaped the fire.

When the congressional poll was taken in April, Eppes received 206 votes to Jack's 147. Randolph Harrison voted for Eppes, and Saint voted for his Uncle Jack. Jack blamed his first defeat since his initial election in 1799 to the time spent on handling matters relating to the fire, rather than campaigning. But he assured Francis Scott Key that the "grapes were not sour," he had fought the good fight. Jack asked Key to retrieve his belongings from Crawford's Boarding House, but Key had already collected everything, including Jack's gun.

❧

Fanny Tucker Coalter developed severe back problems after the births of her three children. She had the burden of the slaves she had inherited who were so elderly and ill that she was forced to care for them.

"Agga is not even able to bring us water in the morning," John Coalter wrote Tucker.

After Coalter's appointment to the Virginia Court of Appeals, he moved his family to Bush Hill near Richmond. Fanny's condition worsened and Jack took her to his home at Roanoke where Judith nursed her. She failed to improve, and her husband took her to Red Sulphur Springs, then to Sweet Springs.

⚮

Jack, thin-skinned as always, refused to write to Saint for weeks after an unfortunate comment he made in a letter. Poor Saint, anxious to hear from his uncle, wrote, asking that Jack "accordingly accept my pardon."

"I did not mean to speak so plainly. Mother talks of going to see you soon with me, I hope on Wednesday."

He reported that the Prince Edward troops had left for Hampton and his Uncle Beverley had gone with them. British forces attacked fortifications on Craney Island, near Norfolk, on June 22, but the Americans repulsed them, with heavy British losses.

"The people are frightened about British and have taken all their furniture away for fear being attacked or burnt by them."

⚮

Saint was disappointed in gaining the affection of a very amiable, exemplary girl, Jane Hackley, possibly related to his aunt, Harriet Hackley.

"I am afraid it will give you grief to hear that I was declined to be married . . . my pride has kept me from having a regard for one which I was not uncaring about. . . ."

"I wish to lead a single life. I hope you will not mention it to anybody . . . . I wish I could live with you with all my heart."

His life continued its mundane course. In mid-August, Saint's workhorse had a nail puncture in his heel, and he needed him to thresh the wheat. Saint feared that "the rats would love the corn in one or two months."

Incessant rain forced Saint to put off threshing his wheat and when he did, he worked all day and still more, with no time to go to Farmville to dine with his mother. Once again, Jack took offense at his comments, forcing Saint to apologize, "I am more mortified than you should think

. . . . I am afraid you think me a mean man. . . . I beg your pardon all."

Quasha, Jack's servant, came from Richmond and stopped during the heavy rains, but Saint was afraid to allow him to stay longer "without orders."

He wrote his grandfather Tucker of being all alone at Bizarre, except when his Uncle Jack and Theodore stopped by for a few days on their way to Roanoke.

Tucker received word from Fanny's husband that her condition was hopeless. His last letter to his only daughter comforted her as he prepared her for a final separation.

"And you, my darling, my most beloved child . . . look up to the Father in the hope that we shall meet again . . . never more to separate."

Tucker and Jack lost the "richest treasure that man possessed" when Fanny died on September 7.

Naturally, the birth of Nancy's child stirred up even more animosity among Morris's relatives. Instead of their receiving a generous inheritance, they understood Morris's money would now go to his son. Privately, they referred to the baby as Cutusoff, a pun on the name of Russian General Kutusov in the 1812 campaign when Napoleon invaded that country. They accelerated their demands on Morris's largesse while he lived.

For the second year, Tudor came to Morrisania and spent the Christmas holiday with his aunt and her family. While there, he received an unusual letter from his Uncle Jack and the lengthy and biased epistle recounted his entire life. He wrote that his brother Dick had died in a "strange and Neptunian manner."

Jefferson spent part of each year at Poplar Forest, the octagonally shaped brick home that he had built in Bedford County. The focal point inside was a central dining room, twenty by twenty feet, with a long, narrow skylight and two fireplaces. The salon was enclosed and overlooked formal gardens. Jefferson made the ninety-three-mile, three-day journey four times a year. His grandson Francis Eppes, who attended a school in nearby Lynchburg, came often to see his grandfather and eventually inherited the estate.

Now seventy years old, Jefferson relinquished more and more of Monticello's operation to Martha and her family. They, in turn, relied more and more on Jefferson's dwindling financial resources.

Tom was a lieutenant-colonel in the Virginia militia, and in March 1813 President Madison commissioned him a full colonel in the Army. Although Jefferson desperately needed his assistance at home, under the circumstances of friendship and war he had no alternative except to delegate Tom's responsibilities to young Jeff. In command of the Twentieth Regiment of Infantry, Tom received orders to march to Lake Ontario and meet General James Wilkinson, where the army would launch an attack on Montreal from the St. Lawrence River. Tom's orders placed him directly under Wilkinson's command, the man whom he had attacked while in Congress. Tom's command was only one-fourth of the needed numbers. His men considered him a sympathetic, no-frills leader, sharing their rations and sleeping arrangements. Surprisingly, Wilkinson promoted him to command an elite corps.

Under Wilkinson's deplorable lack of leadership and with untrained troops, the Americans retreated. Tom, convinced that the campaign would fail, requested a leave. He was anxious to see his mountain and his wife. Martha, now past forty years old and a grandmother, was herself expecting yet another baby. Septemia, their eleventh child, was born a few weeks before her parents observed their twenty-fourth wedding anniversary.

1814

*A*fter the Duke of Wellington defeated Napoleon at
Leipzig, Napoleon abdicated as emperor. With Europe
again open to British trade, England, anxious to "chastise
the savages," turned from Europe to America, intensifying efforts
to bring its former upstart colony to its knees.

The entire United States suffered because of the British block-
ade. In the South, grain and cotton spoiled in warehouses, its currency
declined. In New England, manufacturers were unable to move their
stock. Federalists, disgusted, met to consider setting up a separate New
England States of America and making a separate peace.

In Virginia waters, the British fleet moved up the Chesapeake Bay,
pillaging at Windmill Point and burning Corotoman, taking seventy-
five slaves with them. Lelia's son, Dr. Charles Carter, had inherited
the property.

Harry and Beverley Tucker were on active military duty. Beverley
was a captain of a light infantry company, and Harry was with Winchester forces.

Jack, without congressional duties, developed more and more twist-
ed reasoning. He refused to shake hands with Tucker and then wrote
him an insulting letter, accusing him of ill treatment during his childhood. Tucker was deeply hurt, denying that he had ever done anything
to injure his stepsons, and the Tucker family was outraged.

It was said of Jack that "the arrows from his quiver, if not dipped in poison, were pointed and barbed . . . (and) "seldom failed to make a wrankling sound. . . . "

❧

Jack sometimes recorded his "conversations" with Saint in his journal. Saint seemingly was unable to understand, finding it more and more difficult to express his concerns. He had worried about his uncle.

"I am so easy of it but the people in Cumberland want to put you in prison, uncle, like Uncle William."

"No, you are mistaken, who told you that?"

"My brother, he loves me. He has a large ring I ever knew."

"This county has none of the gold rings. I wish you to get one for me in Richmond."

"You have misunderstood your brother. Nobody can put me in prison."

"I have only a small house . . . . Since winter I have suffered . . . ."

Later, acting as his mother's emissary, Saint asked Jack to send him a deed.

"My mother says if you please. . . . She wishes me to go to Cumberland Court, I am not very anxious."

It was not lawful, having delayed recording the deed from the summer and was of great consequence. "Your unchangeably and firmly affectionate nephew."

❧

One matter weighed heavily on Saint's mind, and he could not explain it. He bore the responsibility for Bizarre's farming operation, without adequate slave help. The fire at Bizarre had sent his mother to Farmville and him to an isolated cabin. All of these adversities may have precipitated the loss of reason.

On May 10, Jack received Judith's letter advising him of Saint's insanity. She could not keep him in Farmville: "The high road, the taverns opposite . . . visited by strangers . . . the excessive sun and heat in this house would destroy him."

Theodore Dudley took Saint to Roanoke to care for him. Jack explained his sudden departure from Richmond by saying his nephew had become "unsettled in his intellect, due to an unsuccessful attachment to his mother's neighbor." Also, Saint appeared to be "incurably alienated from his mother." At Roanoke, "a friend and treasure to me above all price" helped Saint.

When Nancy heard the news of her "darling Saint," Morris suggested to Jack that Saint's problem arose from his lack of "amorous dalliance." Jack acknowledged this possible cause of Saint's malady, for it had "not escaped our attention. It occurred to me on the very first view of his situation. . . . My best wishes to Mrs. Morris."

Tucker urged Judith to take Saint to Philadelphia for treatment and sent her $500 for expenses.

Tudor asked Nancy for money. Then writing of his "earnest wish to come home," he left Harvard by carriage with a friend and arrived at Morrisania on August 4, too ill to continue to Virginia. With maternal affection, Nancy put him to bed and informed Judith of his illness.

Leaving Virginia, the British continued up to Havre de Grace, Maryland. In Washington, President Madison had the Declaration of Independence and the Constitution dispatched to Leesburg, bade Dolley goodbye, and left with Secretary of State Monroe to join his troops. On August 24, General John Armstrong declared that the British had no interest in Washington; that afternoon Admiral Cockburn and Major-General Robert Ross began their march.

At the President's House, Dolley had her staff preparing for a dinner party for forty guests, roasting meat on spits and pouring wine into coolers. One of the guests, Mrs. William Jones, sent her regrets, saying, "It will be more convenient to dispense with . . . your hospitality today."

When Dolley heard cannon firing, she ordered a wagon filled with silver, books, and the red velvet drawing room curtains. Madison's messenger arrived, urging her to flee. Before leaving, she oversaw the removal of Washington's portrait. The huge frame was nailed to the wall. The gardener climbed a ladder and, with an axe, removed the canvas. Dolley gave the portrait, East Room eagle ornaments, and presidential papers to two men who left quickly.

Dolley left in her carriage, "flying at full speed accompanied by an officer carrying a drawn sword."

More than 4,500 British troops entered the city, uncontested by 7500 untrained militia. Even with little opposition, they fired over

100,000 rounds of ball cartridges. They invaded the President's House in a hilarious mood, sitting in the dining room, feasting on Dolley's dinner, and drinking Madison's Madeira wine. One officer appropriated a clean shirt. Admiral Cockburn took Madison's hat as a souvenir, another officer stuffed Madison's love letters to Dolley in his pocket. Before leaving, they torched the house, then burned the Capitol and other government offices. They even wrecked the printing presses.

❧

Thomas Tudor Tucker, the treasurer of the United States, wrote his brother of the calamitous situation.

"In a few hours I became a wanderer without a resting place. The city was in the hands of the enemy and the public buildings were in flames. . . . I have no longer a country or a government . . . I can speak of with pride."

British troops departed on August 25, leaving the President's House so blackened by fire and smoke that, after repairs and repainting, it became known as the White House. When news of the British troops in Washington reached England, a member of Parliament called the action abhorrent and a newspaper questioned whether such destruction was a legitimate method of warfare.

The Madisons returned to the capital and moved into Octagon House. Washington residents were highly critical of Madison, almost insolent. Many considered him a coward for abandoning them to invaders.

❧

Lieutenant-Colonel Thomas Randolph was called to active duty at Camp Fairfield near Richmond. Private Jefferson Randolph accompanied his father to camp on the York River near West Point. Tom, commanding more than six hundred men and sleeping on the ground with them, was a popular officer.

Even Jack, in a fervor of patriotism, offered his services. He too was assigned to Camp Fairfield and sent to reconnoiter the "lower country between the York and James Rivers, from the confluence of Mattapony and Pamunkey to the mouth of Chickahominy."

❧

After the danger was past, the bands of patriots returned to civilian pursuits. Jack resumed his social life in Richmond, with one nephew temporarily insane at his plantation and another critically ill at Morrisania. Because Jack had an abundance of free time, his preoccupation with Dudley's affairs produced three letters to him in a day.

"In truth, I can think of nothing but you, for of poor dear Tudor and his unfortunate brother I try to think of not at all."

✄

Tudor suffered a hemorrhage on September 22 so severe that Morris summoned two New York physicians. Nancy noticed that Tudor rarely looked anyone in the face, but she thought that "his gloomy, guilty look came from bashfulness . . . of uncommon modesty."

Morris was also in bed ill by the end of September, and Nancy had two patients and her son to care for. She sent for Judith to come at once. With funds provided by Tucker and traveling with a woman servant, Judith arrived on October 20.

Quashee brought letters to Jack in Richmond from both Judith and Nancy describing Tudor's serious condition. Jack could no longer delay going to Morrisania. He advised Dudley of his hasty departure in "the fourth letter that I have addressed to you within 12—18 hours."

He had a disastrous accident. While walking down a passageway in the dark, he misjudged the steps and fell, injuring his shoulder and ankle. He recuperated in Baltimore, not reaching Morrisania until October 22.

By then, Morris was well enough to take Judith out for carriage rides.

After a long and private visit at Tudor's bedside, Jack left, having stayed only one night. He later said that someone had tried to smother him by stopping up his keyhole.

Nancy and Morris were amazed when Jack left so hastily. He handed his host a note giving permission for Judith and Tudor to spend the winter at Morrisania. On the return to New York, Jack's carriage overturned, injuring him again.

"The narrow street was shaded and a pile of rubbish lay in the shade. I am a cripple for life. I am at Mrs. Bradishche's behind Trinity Church . . . . I am like one broken on the wheel."

Judith and Tudor left Morrisania the following day.

✄

Nancy and Morris visited Jack after the accident, and she returned later for another visit. She and Judith dined with David Ogden, Morris's nephew. Tudor was unable to go to dinner, but he was well enough to connive against his Aunt Nancy. David Ogden visited Jack, and they found fertile ground for plotting against Nancy. Ogden wanted her out of the will but also had a more urgent need. He had obtained money fraudulently and needed his uncle as guarantor on a note renewal.

Ogden and Jack conferred with Tudor, in whom Jack had already created an inclination for accusation. Tudor told his uncle that he had seen love letters that Nancy had written to a slave, Billy Ellis. To both Jack and Tudor, discrediting and dishonoring Nancy were justifiable revenge. On November 2, Jack wrote to Morris, warning him that his life was in danger. He enclosed a damaging letter to Nancy for her husband to read before giving it to his wife.

Greenwich St., Oct. 31, 1814
Madam:
When at my departure from Morrisania, I bade you remember the past, I was not apprised of the whole extent of your guilty machinations. I had nevertheless seen and heard enough in the course of my short visit to satisfy me that your own dear experience had availed nothing toward the amendment of your life. . . .

Unhappy woman, why will you tempt the forbearance of that maker who has, perhaps, permitted you to run your course of vice and sin . . . a life of wretchedness, alarm and suspicion? You now live in the daily and nightly dread of discovery. . . .

Some of the proofs of your guilt, those which in despair you sent me . . . on your leaving Virginia. . . . You told Mr. Morris that I had offered you marriage subsequent to your arraignment for the most horrible of crimes . . . you have, therefore, released me from any implied obligation . . . to withhold the papers from the inspection of all except my family. I laid them before Tudor (then eleven years old) soon after they came into my hands with the whole story of his father's wrongs and your crime. . . .

Her apprehension for her child, he wrote, brought to his mind the one that her hands had deprived of life in 1792. She had told Dick that the baby was Theodorick's, who was unable to walk, with his bones worn through his skin at the time she went to his bed.

Her confiding in Dick put his life and fame in jeopardy; he passed his word and the pledge was redeemed.

It was only by means of Randolph Harrison's caution that the two escaped hanging on the same gibbet.

Tudor, Jack said, told him that Nancy had poisoned Dick. She later tried to get Judith to turn her out of Bizarre, but her intimacy with a slave, her "dear Billy Ellis," attracted notice and she left. She went to Richmond where she had declined into a very drab. Jack visited her, noting that her apartment was fastidiously neat, "But the bait did not take."

He was not surprised that she went to live with Mr. Morris but was surprised that he had married her.

He quoted Tudor as saying, "How shocking she looks. I have not met her eyes three times." Tudor's first impression of her was that she was an unchaste woman.

"I have done. Before this reaches your eye, it will have been perused by him, to whom, next to my brother, you are most deeply indebted, and whom, next to him, you have most deeply wronged. If he be not both blind and deaf, he must sooner or later unmask you unless he too die of cramps in his stomach. You understand me. If I were persuaded that his life is safe in your custody, I might forbear from making this communication to him. Repent before it is too late. May I hear of that repentance and never see you more.

"John Randolph of Roanoke"

The letter was sent to Morris's friends and associates in New York, then dispatched to Morrisania. The conspirators waited eagerly for Nancy's expected expulsion.

Morris read both letters and shared them with his wife. They were confounded that her family would repay her hard work and Morris's generosity in such a manner. Already knowing the sad story of her past, Morris's heart ached for the unhappiness of the "houseless girl" whom he loved.

Tucker wrote her of his regret of the "wound that has been inflicted."

"May the father of mercies comfort you under such heavy afflictions as you are again exposed to."

After a wait, Ogden, with unbridled curiosity and audacity, came to Morrisania and obtained Morris's endorsement of a loan again.

The stream of visitors to Morrisania diminished and few dinner invitations arrived. Rumors of ugly gossip floated in from the city. Anonymous letters were received. Numerous people, both in New York and Virginia, had now been made acquainted with Jack's masterpiece.

&

After Judith and Tudor arrived home, she decided not to take Saint to Philadelphia, one reason being that she had used the money sent her to care for Tudor. She took Tudor to Dr. Rice's home in Richmond. When Tucker visited there, Judith spoke with pleasure of Nancy and her family. Tudor spent the last of Judith's money on salt, tea, and sugar, compelling her to borrow $50 from John Coalter.

&

Jack, still recuperating in New York, made a statement of the circumstances surrounding his letter to Nancy, clearly implicating Morris's relatives in its instigation. Meanwhile, the Morrises sent Tucker a packet containing anonymous letters.

"Can you account for all the unheard of hypocrisy of Judy and Tudor, with her belief of my guilt that she allowed him to remain here twelve weeks on my charity," asked Nancy.

Judith had reproached Nancy at Bizarre for her "great fondness for Dick." When Nancy left Virginia, information sent to Jack proved that Nancy was not the "blasterer of your happiness." Dick's letters proved otherwise.

&

Judith had "embittered every crumb I swallowed but her misfortunes touched" Nancy's heart. Before Bizarre burned, Nancy had sent her "goods to pay for every mouthful I ate because I could not bear to be under obligation to her."

"In mercy, in pity," she implored Tucker, "please write as soon as you can."

Tucker expressed dismay at the fabrications "not only with those emotions which I have expressed before, but . . . sympathy for yourself and not less to Mr. Morris. . . ."

~~

Finally well enough to travel, Jack left for Virginia, stopping in Philadelphia. His friend Joseph Clay, who had helped him in Congress years earlier, had died. Jack took his son, John Randolph Clay, with him to Roanoke to rear.

~~

A disastrous year ended at Morrisania, with only family for Christmas. The next day Morris answered Tucker's letter.

"Your goodness cannot persuade me that Mr. Randolph has not originated the calumnies of the anonymous letters you have returned. . . . At a distant day there will be transmitted to Virginia a copy of his letter to her, sent open to me after having been exhibited to other persons in New York. . . . Her candor had screened her against his assault. She would not, tho perishing from want in Connecticut, enter my house, even as a servant, without telling me her story. I took her to my bosom from the knowledge of her virtue and the only [feeling] . . . in me was disgust."

~~

Nancy, with her husband's help, began preparing a response to Jack, former suitor, friend, foe, and now character assassin.

~~

On December 15, Federalists met in Hartford to discuss secession. Jack wrote to friends there, exhorting them to abandon the idea of a separate peace. Although Americans did not know yet, the war had already ended. John Quincy Adams, Henry Clay, and others were in Belgium negotiating, and the Treaty of Ghent was signed on Christmas Eve.

In Louisiana, combined British army and naval forces pushed toward New Orleans, but American troops, led by their dynamic commander, Major-General Andrew Jackson, and heartened by the lively strains of "Yankee Doodle Dandy," achieved the only decisive American victory of the war, but after its end!

1815

*N*ancy fought back by publicly rebutting Jack's accusations in a letter, saying she had just learned of his accusations of October 31, 1814. Jack's letter to her and her January 16, 1815, reply are in a pamphlet, dated 1888, at the Lipscomb Library of Randolph College, formerly Randolph-Macon Women's College in Lynchburg, Virginia, entitled *A Spicy Correspondence Between John Randolph of Roanoke and His Cousin Nancy.* It notes that "as a literary performance this letter of Mrs. Morris' is entitled to rank as one of the finest specimens of English composition anywhere to be found, equaling if not exceeding in vigor and point, as well as elegance in form of expression, the celebrated letters of Junius."

Junius was the pseudonym of an English political writer who, in letters to the London Public Audience from 1769 to 1772, attacked George III and his ministers.

Nancy's letter to Jack brought the facts into the open and settled a few scores with others. She did not, however, break her promise to Dick, exacted by him before his death, to not speak publicly of his seduction of her.

Morrisania, January 16, 1815

Sir:

My husband yesterday communicated to me for the first time your letter of the last of October, together with that which accompanied it, directed to him.

In your letter to my husband, you say, 'I wish I could withhold the blow but I must in your case do what under a change of circumstances I would have you do unto me.' This, Sir, seems fair and friendly. It seems, Sir, as if you wished to apprize Mr. Morris and him only of circumstances important to his happiness and honor, though fatal to my reputation, leaving it in his power to cover them in oblivion or display them to the world as the means of freeing him from a monster unfit to live. But this was mere seeming. Your real object was widely different.

You have professed a sense of gratitude for obligations you suppose my husband to have laid you under. . . . Why did you permit your nephew to be fed from my bounty and nursed by my care during nearly three months? Could you suppose him safe in the power of a wretch who had murdered his father? Does it consist with the dignified pride of family you affect to have him, whom you announce as your heir . . . dependent on the charity of a negro's concubine?

You say I confine my husband a prisoner in his house that there may be no witnesses of my lewd amours, and have driven away his friends and old domestics that there may be no witnesses of his death. If I wished to indulge in amours, the natural course would be to mingle in the pleasures and amusements of the city, or at least to induce my husband to go abroad and leave me a clear stage for such misdeeds. . . .

You say your brother 'passed his word and the pledge was redeemed at the hazard of all that man can hold dear'! Pray, Sir, admitting (tho it is not true) that I had exacted from your brother a promise of secrecy, how could you have known it unless he betrayed it? And, if he betrayed it, how was the pledge redeemed?

People of proper feelings require that the evidence of accusation be strong in proportion as the guilt is enormous; but those, who feel themselves capable of committing the blackest crimes, will readily suspect others, and condemn without proof on a mere hearsay, on . . . instigations of a malevolent heart.

Those who possess a clear conscience and sound mind, will look through your letter for some proof of my guilt. They will look in vain. You have thought proper to found suspicions on suspicions of your nephew, and . . . you have the insolence to impute crime at which nature revolts.

You . . . say that you mention a piece of evidence in your possession – a letter which I wrote on leaving Virginia . . . the very mention of it destroys your credibility with honorable minds.

If you had the feelings of a man of honor, you would have known that there are things the communication of which involves that injunction. You have heard of principle and pretend to justify the breach of confidence by my want of respect for your name.

Formerly Jack Randolph – now 'John Randolph of Roanoke.' It was then a want of respect to the great John Randolph of Roanoke to say he had done the honor of offering his hand to his poor cousin Nancy.

While on the chapter of self-contradiction, (which, with all due respect to 'John Randolph of Roanoke,' make up the history of his life) I must notice a piece of evidence not contained in your letter. I have already hinted at the indelicacy of leaving your nephew so long in my care. . . . You pretend to have discovered, all at once in this house, the confirmation of your suspicions, but surely the suspicion was sufficient to prevent a person having a pretense to delicacy from subjecting himself to such obligation. One word, however, as to this sudden discovery made by your great sagacity.

Recollect, Sir, when you rose from table to leave Morrisania, you put in my husband's hand a note to my sister expressing your willingness that she and her son should pass the winter in his house. Surely, the discovery must have been made at that time. You will recollect, too, some other marks of confidence and affection, let me add of respect also, which I forbear to mention because you would no doubt deny them, and it would be invidious to ask the testimony of those who were present. One act, however, must not be unnoticed. . . . When you entered this house, and when you left it, you took me in your arms, you pressed me to your bosom, you impressed upon my lips a kiss which I received as a token of friendship from a near relation. Did you then believe that you held in your arms, that you pressed to your bosom, that you kissed the lips of a common prostitute, the murderess of her own child and of your brother?

As to the fact communicated shortly before I left Virginia. That your brother Theodoric paid his addresses to me, you knew and attempted to supplant him by calumny. Be pleased to remember that, in my sister Mary's house, you led me to the portico, and, leaning against one of the pillars, expressed your surprise at having heard from your brother Richard that I was engaged to marry his brother, Theodoric. That you hoped it was not true, for he was unworthy of me. To establish this opinion, you made many assertions derogatory to his reputation—some of which I knew to be false. . . . The defamation of your brother whom I loved, your stormy passions, your mean selfishness, your wretched appearance, rendered your attentions disagreeable.

Your brother, Richard, a model of truth and honor knew how much I was annoyed by them. . . . It was your troublesome attentions which induced Richard to inform you of my engagement. At that time, my father had other views. Your property . . . was hampered by a British debt. My father, therefore, preferred for my husband a person of clear and considerable estate. The sentiment of my heart did not accord with his intentions. Under these circumstances, I was left at Bizarre, a girl, not seventeen, with the man she loved. I was betrothed to him, and considered him as my husband in the presence of that God whose name you presume to invoke on occasions the most trivial and for purposes the most malevolent.

Your brother, Richard, knew every circumstance, but you are mistaken in supposing I exacted from him a promise of secrecy. He was a man of honor. Neither the foul imputations against us both, circulated by that kind of friendship which you have shown to my husband, nor the awful scene, with which you attempt to blacken his memory, could induce him to betray the sister of his wife, the wife of his brother; I repeat it, Sir, the crime with which you now attempt to blacken his memory. You say that, to screen the character of such a creature as I am, the life and the fame of that most generous and gallant of men was put in jeopardy. His life alas! is now beyond the reach of your malice, but his fame, which should be dear to a brother's heart, is stabbed by the hand of his brother. You not only charge me with the heinous crime of infanticide, placing him in the condition of an accomplice, but you proceed to say that 'had it not been for the prudence of Mr. Harrison, or the mismanagement of not putting me first on my trial! we should both have swung on the same gibbet and the foul stain of incest and murder been stamped on his memory. . . .

This, Sir, is the language you presume to address to me, enclosed to my husband for his inspection, after having been already communicated to other people. . . . What must be the indignation . . . to behold a wretch rake up the ashes of his deceased brother to blast his fame? Who is there of nerve so strong as not to shudder at your savage regret that we did not swing on the same gibbet?

On the melancholy occasion you have thought proper to bring forward there was the strictest examination. Neither your brother or myself had done anything to excite enmity, yet we were subjected to an unpitying persecution. The severest scrutiny took place; you know it. He was acquitted to the joy of numerous spectators, expressed in shouts of exultation. This, Sir, passed in a remote county of Virginia more than twenty years ago. You have revived the slanderous tale in the most populous city in the United States.

For what? To repay my kindness to your nephew by tearing me from the arms of my husband and blasting the prospects of my child!

You acknowledge that every fact ... every circumstance you had either heard or dreamt of in the long period of more than twenty years, had never imparted to you a belief, which nevertheless you expect to imprint on the minds of others. You thus pay to the rest of mankind the wretched compliment of supposing them more ready to believe the greatest crimes than 'John Randolph of Roanoke.' Doubtless there may be some who are worthy of this odious distinction; I hope not many.

No respectable person can overlook the baseness of leaving your nephew so long, or even permitting him to come under the roof of the wretch you describe me to be, you acknowledge that you did not believe in the enormities you charge, until yourself had paid a visit to Morrisania.

You have, Sir, on this subject presumed to use my sister's name. Permit me to tell you, I do not believe one word of what you say. Were it true, it is wholly immaterial. But that it is not true, I have perfect conviction.

The assertion rests only on your testimony, the weight and value of which has been already examined. The contradiction is contained in her last letter to me, dated December 17th, of which I enclose a copy. You will observe she cautions me against believing anything inconsistent with her gratitude for my kindness, and assures that, altho' prevented from spending the winter with us, she is proud of the honor done her by the invitation. . . . No one can think so meanly of a woman who moves in the sphere of a lady as to suppose she could be proud of the honor of being invited to spend a winter with the concubine of one of her slaves. Nevertheless . . . I am determined they shall appear in the neighborhood under your hand; so that your character may be fully known and your signature forever hereafter be not only what it has hitherto been, the appendage of vainglorious boasting, but the designation of malicious baseness.

You speak with affected sensibility of my sister's domestic bliss, and you assume an air of indignation at the violence of my temper. Be pleased to recollect that, returning from a morning ride with your brother, you told me you found it would not do to interfere between man and wife; that you had recommended to him a journey to Connecticut to obtain a divorce; that he made no reply, nor spoke a single word afterwards. Recollect, too, how often, and before how many persons, and in how many ways, you have declared your detestation of her conduct as a wife and her angry passions. One form of expression occurs which is remarkable: 'I have heard,' said you, 'that Mrs. Randolph was handsome, and perhaps, had I ever seen her in a good humor, I might have thought so; but her features are so distorted by constant wrath that she has to me the air of a fury.'

And now, as to my disposition and conduct, be pleased not to forget . . . that, during full five years after your brother's death . . . I was the constant theme of your praise and, tho you wearied everyone else, you seemed on that subject to be yourself indefatigable. I should not say these things, if they rested merely on my own knowledge, for you would not hesitate to deny them, and I should be very sorry that my credibility were placed on the same level with yours.

You have denied the fact of turning me out of doors. This also shall be made known in the neighbourhood where it must be well remembered. I take the liberty again to refresh your memory. Shortly after your nephew had left home to take the benefit of a change of air, you came into the room one evening, after you had been a long time in your chamber with my sister, and said, addressing yourself to me, 'Nancy, when do you leave this house? The sooner the better for you take as many liberties as if you were in a tavern.' On this occasion, as on others, my course was silent submission. I was poor, I was dependent. I knew the house was kept in part at your expense. I could not therefore appeal to my sister. I replied with the humility, suitable to my forlorn condition, 'I will go as soon as I can.'

You stalked haughtily about the room, and poor, unprotected 'Nancy' retired to seek the relief of tears.

Two years after when I saw you at Richmond . . . I refresh your memory on this subject. I notice another malicious falsehood respecting my residence, while in Richmond. You say I took lodgings at Prior's a public garden. It is true Mr. Prior owned a large lot in Richmond, and that there was a public building on it, in which public balls and entertainments were given, and this lot a public garden, but it is equally true that Mr. Prior's dwelling and the enclosure round it were wholly distinct from that garden. In that house, I lodged. My chamber was directly over Mrs. Prior's, a lady of as good birth as Mr. John Randolph and of far more correct principles. All this, Sir, you perfectly well know. From that chamber, I wrote you a note complaining that your nephew, then a school boy in Richmond, was not permitted to see me. You sent (it) back, after writing on the same sheet, 'I return your note that you may compare it with my answer, and ask yourself, if you are not unjust to one who through life has been your friend.' This, with the recital of your professions of regard . . . led me to suppose you had, in the last scene at Bizarre, acted only as my sister's agent. I, therefore, wrote to you, remonstrating against the reason you assigned for turning me out of doors, which you yourself knew to be unfounded, for you had often observed that I was 'Epicene, the Silent Woman.'

You knew that I was continually occupied at my needle or other work for the house, obeying, to the best of my knowledge, the orders I received, differing from any other servant only in this: I received no wages, but was permitted to sit at table, where I did not presume to enter into conversation or taste of wine, and very seldom of tea or coffee. I pause here, Sir, to ask whether you pretended to deny having turned me out of doors? You dare not say so. You shortly after paid me a visit, the only one during your stay. You sat on my bedstead, I cannot say my bed, for I had none, I was too poor. When weary, my limbs were rested on a blanket, spread over the sacking. Your visit was long, and I never saw you from that day until we met in Washington.

It is true that, afterwards, when in Newport, suffering from want, and borne down by a severe ague and fever, I was so far humbled as to request not the gift (I would sooner have perished) but the loan of that sum. My petition struck on a cold heart that emitted no sound. You did not deign to reply. You even made a boast of your silence. I was then so far off my groans could not be heard in Virginia. You no longer apprehended the (reproaches) which prompted your ostentatious offer at Richmond. Yes, Sir, you were silent. You then possessed the letter on which you grounded your calumnies. You supposed me so much in your power that I should not dare to complain of your unkindness.

Yes, Sir, you were silent, and you left your nephew nearly three months dependent on the charity of her, to whom in the extreme of wretchedness, you had refused the loan of fifty dollars.

Yes, Sir, you were silent. Perhaps, you hoped that the poor forlorn creature you had turned out of doors would, under the pressure of want, and far removed from every friend, be driven to a vicious course, and enable you to justify your barbarity by charges such as you have now invented.

I defy you Mr. Randolph to substantiate by the testimony of any credible witness a single fact injurious to my reputation from the time you turned me out of doors until the present hour; and God knows that, if suffering could have driven me to vice, there was no want of suffering. My husband, in permitting me to write this letter, has enjoined me not to mention his kindness, otherwise I could give a detail of circumstances which, as they would not involve any pecuniary claim, might touch even your heart. You speak of him as an infirm old man, into whom I have struck the fangs of a harpy, and having acted in your family the part of a vampire. I pray you, Mr. 'John Randolph of Roanoke' to be persuaded that such idle declamation . . . is misplaced on the present occasion. You know as little of the manner in which my present connection began as of other things with which you pretend to be acquainted. I loved my husband before he made me mother of one of the finest boys I ever saw; now that his kindness soothes the anguish which I cannot but feel from your unmanly attack.

I am very sorry I am obliged to speak of your nephew. I would fain impute to his youth, or to some other excusable cause, his unnatural, and I must say, criminal conduct. Had his relations rested only on your testimony, I should not have hesitated to have acquitted him of the charge, but a part of them at least, not fully detailed in your letter, was made in Mr. Ogden's presence.

On the 4th of August, a phaeton drove to the door with a led horse, and a person, appearing to be a servant, stepped out and enquired for Mr. Randolph. He was directed to the stable, and shortly after Mr. Randolph landed from the boat of a

Packet. His appearance bespoke severe illness. I showed him to his chamber, and venture to say from that time to the moment of his departure he was treated by me with the tenderness and kindness of a mother.

The injunction I have already mentioned restrains me from going into particulars. My health was injured by the fatigue to which I was exposed, the burthen of which I could not diminish without neglecting him; for I could not procure good nurses or servants. We were also under the disagreeable necessity of keeping a servant whom our friends had denounced as a thief. By the bye, I have reason to believe he is one of those 'ancient domestics,' you have taken under your protection. If so, I must in justice to myself inform you that your friend, Geo. Bevans, dismissed only two days before your arrival, was shortly after admitted to a lodging in the Bridewell of New York for theft.

And now, Sir, put the actual parties out of the question, and say what credit can be due to the calumnies of a person in your nephew's situation, soliciting and receiving favors to the very last moment.

Is it proper, or is it decent to found such calumnies on the suspicions of such a creature, even supposing them to have originated in his mind, and not been, as is too probable, instigated by you? Could anything but the most determined and inveterate malice induce any one above the level of an idiot to believe the only fact he pretended to articulate?

You cite as from him these words, 'How shocking she looks. I have not met her eyes three times since I have been in the house.' Can you believe this? Can you believe others to believe it? How happens it you did not cry out as anyone else would have done? 'Why did you stay in that house? Why did you submit to her kindness? Why did you accept her presents? Why did you pocket her money?' To such an apostrophe he might have replied perhaps, 'Uncle I could not help it. I was penniless, in daily expectation that you or my mother would bring relief. When at last she came, I found her almost as ill-off as myself. We were both detained until you arrived.'

To this excuse, which is a very lame one for a person who had a phaeton to sell or pledge, any one who feels a spark of generosity in his bosom would reply, 'Why, then, wretch, having from necessity or choice laid yourself under such a load of obligations, do you become the calumniator of your benefactress? Are you yet to learn what is due to the rites of hospitality, or have you, at the early age of nineteen, been taught to combine profound hypocrisy with deadly hate and assume the mask of love that you may more sure plant the assassin's dagger? Where did you learn these horrible lessons?' He might have replied and may yet reply, 'Uncle, I learned this from you.'

But to return to the wonderful circumstance that this young man had not met my eyes above once a month, though he saw me frequently every day. That he met them seldomer than I wished is true. I was sorry to observe what others had remarked, that he rarely looked any one in the face. I . . . tried to excuse it to others as a proof of uncommon modesty, of which nevertheless he gave no other proof . . . . I know not, and shall not pretend to guess, what heavy matter pressed on his conscience; perhaps it was only the disposition to be criminal. . . .

You make him say, 'my first impression as far back as I can remember is that she was an unchaste woman - my brother knew her better than I—she never could do anything with him.' - This too is admirable testimony to support your filthy accusations.

Pray, Mr. John Randolph of Roanoke, why did you not inform your audience that, when you turned me out of doors, this Mr. Tudor Randolph was but nine years old, and his brother, poor, deaf and dumb Saint George, just thirteen – Can it be necessary to add to your confusion by a single remark? It seems to be, if any one present at your wild declamation had noticed this fact, you would have been hissed even by a sisterhood of old maids.

Unluckily for you, I have letters from poor Saint George, one of which, written shortly before his late malady, is filled with assurances of attachment. I have a letter from my sister telling me the pleasure St. George manifested at the present of my portrait I made him. I have a letter also from her, shortly after her house was burnt, in which she tells me among the few things saved she was rejoiced to find my portrait which you brought out with your own.

By this act, you have some right to it, and . . . you may hang it up in your castle at Roanoke. I observe, Sir, in the course of your letter allusion to one of Shakespeare's best tragedies. I trust you are by this time convinced that you have clumsily performed the part of 'honest Iago.' Happily for my life, and for my husband's peace, you did not find in him a headlong, rash Othello. For a full and proper description of what you have written and spoken on this occasion, I refer you to the same admirable author. He will tell you it is a tale told by an idiot, full of sound and fury, signifying nothing.

Ann C. Morris

Nancy made six copies of the forty-page epistle and sent them, together with Jack's letter, to relatives and political associates. One went to William Giles whom she described as her defender long ago.

After Nancy and Morris celebrated their son's second birthday, Nancy followed up her original transmittal, "determined that (his) letter shall be seen in Virginia, with a copy of my answer," to her benefactor, Tucker.

"Could his heart experience one glow of parental or conjugal affection, he would afterward behold his own malignity with horror.

"It became my duty to state the mode in which this youth acquired money from my purse. When his mother reproved him for his extravagance and spoke of her inability to support it, I excused him by saying he was 'trained for making money and he had prospects.' Jack wrote my husband that I offered the children pecuniary reparations for their father's wrongs, adding he was told so or he should not have had the thought. I call a just God to witness that I never wronged Dick Randolph. Oh, had he never inflicted more misery on me than I did on him! His father's descendants seemed, and seem, destined to be wretched. . . ."

"Poor Dick's raving delirium and his torturing death" appeared to evoke an "unbelievable malice" from the family toward her.

❧

Nancy believed that Maria Ward Randolph, Gabriella Randolph Brockenbrough, and Nancy's sister Molly were among her strongest enemies in Virginia, but she wrote William Giles on March 22, "I really believe that Mrs. David Randolph would acquit me of 'associating with the players,' as Mr. R. states."

❧

When Jack reached Virginia he "found Tudor worse than I left him three months before and daily declining."

Saint wrote Nancy a sweet letter, "only ever did I receive such from him," but it would be the last one. Copies of her letter to Jack had been received in Virginia and were making the rounds. According to Jack, he never received Nancy's letter. Hearing of one in Giles's possession, he sent a venomous threat.

"I have from authority I cannot discredit that you have papers that I have never received."

He would not allow Giles to make himself "the vehicle of calumny against me or suffer my family history to be raked up with the ashes of the peaceful."

❧

When Judith protested to Morris the injustice done to Tudor, Morris responded, "It is only too true, my dear madam, that your son was a principal agent in those transactions which excite your indignation and abhorrence."

According to Judith, Saint had been completely restored "to his intellectual faculties but he has lost much of that cheerful content which he formerly employed, and, I greatly fear, forever."

Tudor was still ill in Richmond, in "an alarming state of health." Because of the "unusual rigors of winter and want of useful domestics," she was unable to bring him to Farmville.

❧

Martha despised Richard Hackley, Harriet's husband, for defrauding his creditors, his attachment to the "Spanish woman," and his lies to his wife. She termed him a "mean rascal and a fool!"

"Preeminent in wickedness" next to Hackley was "John Randolph and his conduct." She knew of his letter to Nancy and deplored the "morality of a district who can choose such a man to represent them." Martha thought of writing to contradict some of the charges, but Nancy's husband had taken up her defense so vigorously it was unnecessary.

Ellen had become Martha's nurse and companion and the "immediate jewel of his soul" to her father. Martha thought that Ellen was very much like Tom, without his temper, with "feelings too acute for her own happiness."

❧

With the war ended and no longer a divisive point between him and his constituents, Jack again ran against John Eppes for the House of Representatives. In elections where only white male property holders over twenty-one could vote, the voter announced the vote for his candidate to the county election officer. The votes were recorded by name of voter in the poll book, along with contested votes.

Saint voted for Jack while Randolph Harrison voted for John Eppes. Eppes won in the county but Jack carried the district. Two years later, Eppes was elected to the United States Senate. Informing Key of his election, Jack declared that it gave him no pleasure, except as a gratification to his friends. Key tactfully counseled him to "exhibit every grace and dignity of which this poor frail nature of ours is capable."

❧

Hopeful for a cure at mineral springs, Judith sent Tudor to Cheltenham in England. From here he would travel to Bordeaux, France. To pay for the trip, she borrowed money from Creed Taylor, giving her land as security. She accompanied Tudor to Norfolk in April, where he sailed on the *Benjamin Rush* for Liverpool, leaving Saint in Richmond.

When she returned to Farmville, Tucker had sent her ten of the twenty-three shares of New Virginia Bank stock that he had planned to leave her at his death. In acknowledging his generosity, which allowed her to discharge the debt to Taylor, she deplored "the injury done Tudor" by Nancy's implicating him in her attack.

⊱⊰

During the summer, Randolph Harrison and his daughter visited Morrisania. Afterward, Morris, concerned for his wife, beset by the animosity of his family, and abandoned by fair weather friends, took her on a long trip, traveling 1,200 miles, including along the "magnificent St. Lawrence River."

⊱⊰

Tudor wrote home encouragingly in June that the springs were benefiting him. However, a traveler told Jared Sparks, who had been at Harvard with Tudor, that he had been seen on the streets of London, seemingly past recovery. Tudor died in England on August 28.

⊱⊰

Jefferson had not found his final retirement to be the paradise he had sought so fiercely.

"Paris is the only place where a man . . . not obliged to do anything will always find something amusing to do," he wrote William Short.

⊱⊰

There was little amusement in his life these days. Now seventy-three, slow and unable to manage his properties, he felt compelled to place his grandson, Jeff, in charge of farm operations. Jeff had always adored his grandfather, and the new arrangement caused friction between father and son. It inured to Jefferson's benefit because Jeff became an outstanding farmer and manager. Tom, preoccupied with his own financial concerns, finally accepted Jefferson's advice to sell Varina.

Ann Cary Bankhead's husband, Charles, was a trial to her family. To save their farm at Port Royal, trustees, including her father, were named to manage it. Her grandfather gave her some property in Albemarle, also to be handled by the trustees, and she, her husband, and children moved back. In such close proximity, Martha learned that Charles was a wife-abusing alcoholic. The overseer reported seeing Ann hiding from her husband in a potato hole. Martha, knowing her husband's violent temper, said nothing to him, sharing her concern, instead, with her father.

❧

In October, Judith still awaiting encouraging news from Tudor in England, noted an injury done to Saint as being "very apparent" from being in the neighborhood of the plantation and negroes. She left the unpleasantness of Farmville and went to Richmond. Jack was shooting with Theodore Dudley when news of Tudor's death reached Dr. Brockenbrough, who was delegated to inform the family.

Judith asked Saint to inform Jack of the "funeral sermon to be preached at Cumberland tomorrow fortnight Sunday."

"I have declined setting out for Richmond yesterday because Mother was suffered. I know there was consequences to myself which I have been informed before this time . . . your afflicted but affectionate nephew JSGR."

❧

Judith had visited frequently at Bush Hill, the Coalter home just outside of Richmond, both before and after Fanny's death. She and Judge Coalter had always been on friendly terms. Men still found her attractive at age forty-two, and that winter Beverley and Harry discussed their understanding that their brother-in-law, John Coalter, now intended making Mrs. Judith Randolph his fourth wife.

1816

Judith, overcome by illness and mourning for Tudor, went to the Rices in Richmond. Jack, however, would not give up his efforts to ferret out details of Dick's death, and became even more convinced that Nancy had poisoned him.

"My brother came home very ill on the fifth and the disease terminated on the fourteenth, nine days later. Why was I not sent for until it was too late . . .?" he asked Judith in January.

"Did she mix or hand him the medicine?" . . . "Had she an opportunity of doing the deed?"

No mention was made of the 1796 rumors that Judith had poisoned Dick. Jessie Ball Thompson Krusen wrote in Tuckahoe Plantation in 1975, "Richard was murdered by his wife . . . but no charges were brought."

❧

This enigma of Dick's death has spanned two centuries. From the shroud of mystery emerged three possibilities—suicide, murder, or natural causes.

Loss of reputation and wounded pride following the scandal may have affected his desire for life. Hopelessly trapped in a loveless marriage and helpless to improve Nancy's situation, death may have seemed a welcome solution and which one senses from his will, written in 1796, four months before his death.

Many years later, Jack wrote his niece that "this vice . . . blasted the fair promise of his youth and rendered an untimely death a welcome and happy release from a blighted reputation."

The simplest explanation for Dick's death was a "bilious fever." Treatment with home remedies or the radical medical procedures may have made his agonizing death only more certain.

A mystery remains as to why both Judith and Tudor openly and maliciously accused Nancy of murdering Dick. And was there any connection when, in 1805, Saint blurted out, "My mother is guilty"? He was only four years old at the time of his father's death.

On February 23, Judith wrote her last letter to Tucker. She lived in solitude, except for visits to "my dear sister Fanny's children and their most excellent father . . . recollecting her tender affection and faithful friendship."

In the "midst of a busy city," she had visits from a few friends, and Saint was well and planned a visit to the Tuckers as soon as she had finished some linens he needed.

"This is an unpleasant life for me at my age and with my infirmities, both of mind and body. . . ."

❧

But Jack wrote a relative that she had "shaken off her remaining son almost entirely," after moving in with the Rices. She "flatly refused to make provisions . . . he is without home or credit." Jack was determined that Saint "should be abandoned to the underwriters before" he would interfere.

A few days later, John Coalter wrote Tucker that Mrs. Randolph was dangerously ill. She signed her will on March 9. The bulk of her estate went to Saint, with involved and lengthy provisions for his wife and children, if he should marry. The Rices received $1,000 for their friendship and help, as did a young woman under Judith's protection, and her sister Harriet Hackley, "free from the control of any present and future husband."

To Jack, she bequeathed all of Tudor's books and portfolio from Harvard, but his gold watch with the chain and seals she bequeathed to Saint in absolute perpetuity.

Judith strictly charged "that all the private papers of my son, Tudor Randolph, which are in his desk, be destroyed by the Reverend John

Rice without going into the hands of another person." Further, Mrs. Hackley was to have the "keys of my secretary to destroy all the letters found there before the keys are to be delivered to" her executor.

She died on March 10 and was interred in the cemetery at Tuckahoe, her choice of gravesite.

After writing the Rices to express his gratitude for their care of his "dear sister-in-law," Jack lashed out at Theodore Dudley, who was not as attentive as Jack demanded.

"How could you leave me for weeks, almost months, in such a situation?"

⤸

Dudley wrote of Jack, "He was a man endowed with two souls. In his dark days, when the evil genius predominated, the austere vindictiveness of his feeling towards those that a distempered fancy pictured as enemies, or as delinquent in truth, or honor, was horribly severe and remorseless."

⤸

Tucker assured Saint that his friends would comfort him. Nancy prayed that he would be protected, but Saint, homeless, anchorless, without close kin protection, slipped into madness. By November, he was in Philadelphia, where, two years earlier, Tucker had advised Judith to take him for treatment. This time, there was no treatment; he ended up in the "madhouse," where he would stay for many years. Jack visited him there in December and stayed overnight, sleeping with him.

⤸

The year 1816 began for Nancy with a New Year's Day sleigh ride with her son, now almost three years old. This year she hoped to put her problems behind her. When she heard the news from Virginia, she mourned more for Saint than she did for her sister. She and her husband planned a visit to Virginia, to the Harrisons at Clifton and a reunion with Tucker in Williamsburg.

In March, Morris wrote his friend John Parish in England, whom he had not seen since they parted on the Elbe River seventeen years earlier.

"I lead a quiet life . . . a happy life. The woman to whom I am married has much genius, has been well educated, and possesses, with an affectionate temper, industry and a love of order. Our little boy grows finely. . . . Behold your friend as he descends with tottering steps the bottom of life's hill supported by a kind companion, a tender female friend, and cheered by a little prattler. . . . I can reflect that I have not lived in vain."

Morris gave an elegant discourse to the Historical Society of New York in September, noted "a little frost last night" in October, and fell seriously ill. A few days later, in great pain and with diminishing strength, he made his new will, superseding the 1809 will that had favored his nieces and nephews.

Moss Kent and Nancy were executor and executrix. The will confirmed the ante-nuptial agreement, giving his wife $2,600 per annum. During her life, he gave her the estate of Morrisania, with plate, furnishings, and carriages. Then, in an extraordinary bequest, he stipulated that, in case his wife should remarry, she would receive "six hundred dollars more per annum, to defray the increased expenditures which may attend the connexion."

Morris left the whole of his estate to his son, except for some family bequests.

On November 6, Nancy's husband died. The last diary entry was hers: " . . . had I been told that this was to be the last morning we should leave our chamber together, the last night we should reenter it together – I should have thought my heart would burst."

⨯

After seeing Morris's death notice in the newspaper, Martha wrote to Nancy, "although we had not previously corresponded," she told Jefferson, then at Poplar Forest. The death of her husband had left Nancy "unprotected to the persecution by his heirs who have been disappointed by the birth of her child . . . she is surrounded by enemies and never is more in need of her family than at present."

After years of separation and little communication, Martha and Nancy found once again the rapport that they had shared in earlier, happier, and more prosperous times.

EPILOGUE

James Monroe was inaugurated as president on March 14, 1817 in the portico of the Hall of Congress. Grandiose plans for the inauguration in the House chamber hit a snag when Henry Clay, angry at not having been appointed secretary of state, refused to allow its use. James and Dolley Madison stayed on in the capital until April 8, attending dinners and balls in their honor. Ladies and gentlemen of the city were reluctant to bid farewell to Dolley, her elegant manners, and her drawing rooms. Secretary of the Navy Crowninshield accompanied the couple as far as Aquia Creek, where they boarded a recent invention, the steamboat, en route to their home, Montpelier.

Ground was broken for the Erie Canal in 1817, and it opened on October 26, 1825, by a telegraph of artillery five hundred miles long, from Lake Erie to the Atlantic Ocean. The *Seneca Chief* left Buffalo, traversing the canal and arriving in New York on November 4. Gouverneur Morris's name was included in the list of canal commissioners inscribed on a proscenium, the only recognition of his role in its inception.

Nancy learned that Ogden had mortgaged Morrisania in its entirety to his creditors, except for the burial vault enclosure. She filed suit against him, then worked to pay off the indebtedness. She sold property on the Susquehanna River and a house in Paris for $70,000, but kept

The Executive Mansion, Capitol Square, circa 1813, Richmond VA.
Thomas Mann Randolph lived here as governor, 1819-1822

the Tokay wine, given by Marie Louise to Marie Antoinette, brought from France. She finally cleared her "incomparable son's" property and land and ended a "twenty-one year trusteeship" for him.

"Six feet one inch tall, Gouverneur has all the manly virtue which adorns human nature."

Nancy never remarried and died on May 28, 1837. She was laid to rest beside her husband, "the best of men." Gouverneur Morris, Jr. donated land from Morrisania and money for construction of a church. In June 1841, St. Ann's Church was consecrated for the "Glory of God and in Memory of his Mother," built in what is now the Bronx slums. His mother was placed in a vault under a grating in the east wall, near her husband.

A stone was inscribed "And Here by Her Own Request/Repose the Remains/of the Wife and Mother/in Memory of Whom this Church was Created. To the God She Loved/by Filial Veneration."

Ann Cary Morris	Gouverneur Morris
May 28, 1837	November 6, 1816
In her 63rd Year	In his 65th Year

Randolph blood commingled again and the old tradition of cousin marrying cousin continued when Nancy's son married Martha Jefferson Cary, daughter of Nancy's beloved sister Virginia Randolph Cary, in 1842.

❧

Jefferson's great interest in his later years was the establishment of an "academical village," an institution that differed from his alma mater, William and Mary, both in physical appearance and instruction. Virginia's foremost statesmen and educators supported his efforts. He personally surveyed the site at Charlottesville and designed the rotunda and pavilions and squares, working closely with Benjamin Latrobe.

President James Monroe laid the cornerstone for the first building, known as Central College, in 1817, and the University of Virginia opened on March 7, 1825.

❧

In April 1819, Maria Cosway wrote her beloved of thirty years earlier, "In your Dialogue, Your Head would tell me 'that is enough.' Your

Heart, perhaps, will understand that I might wish for more." She wrote him of the "Establishment of Education," which she headed in Lodi, Italy. He described his mammoth undertaking and noted their mutual interest in education.

"The sympathies of our earlier days harmonize . . . in age also."

She decorated the grand salon of the college with murals representing the four corners of the globe. The wall intended to depict Monticello and the University of Virginia was left bare as a memorial to her friend who had been unable to send the descriptions.

Baroness Maria Cosway died in 1838. Her death received wide publicity, and members of the royal family attended her funeral.

Lafayette's return to America in 1825 as this country's guest included a two-week visit to Monticello and an emotional reunion, a highlight of Jefferson's last years.

⇜

Martha's and Tom's last child, George Wythe Randolph, was born on March 10, 1818, when Martha was forty-five years old. Described later as "one of the most popular men in Virginia," he served briefly as Confederate secretary of war. Tom assumed duties as governor of Virginia in March 1819. He participated little in Richmond's social life and, although his daughters visited him at the Governor's Mansion in Capitol Square, Martha came only twice, and legislators did not find her friendly. At the end of each week, Tom rode through the night to Monticello to be with Martha, returning on Sunday night.

Although unsuccessful in his proposal for the emancipation and deportation of slaves, as governor he created the Washington Monument Fund. This enabled the Commonwealth to have the monumental statue of George Washington and figures of Thomas Jefferson, Patrick Henry, Andrew Lewis, Thomas Nelson, George Mason, and John Marshall, which next to the Capitol itself, were to become the focal point of Capitol Square. The cornerstone was not laid, however, until many years later, in 1850.

After serving in the General Assembly, Tom returned to Albemarle and became a recluse.

Their eldest child, Ann, died in 1824, nearly breaking her grandfather's heart. After years of spousal abuse, however, Ellen felt that Ann accepted death as a welcome release.

Jefferson gave Martha a small jewelry box on July 2, 1826, to be opened after his death. He died on July 4, 1826. Inside the box was his verse:

"Then farewell, my dear, my lov'd daughter, adieu!
The last pang of life is in parting from you!
Two seraphs await me long shrouded in death;
I will bear them your love on my last parting breath."

❦

Martha took Septemia and George Wythe to Boston to live for a time with Ellen, now Mrs. Coolidge. Tom had a brief productive period when he surveyed the boundary between northern Florida and Georgia. Both he and Martha returned to Monticello, but he was never again a part of the family circle. He died in 1828.

Jefferson Randolph was unable to pay off the huge debts that had mounted over the years at Monticello, and it was sold to a Charlottesville druggist in 1831 for $9,000. Martha, mourning the loss of the place she loved, died in 1836 and was buried in the cemetery at her father's feet.

❦

Molly Randolph moved to Washington, and in 1820 published her cookbook, *The Virginia Housewife*. Virginia Randolph Cary's book, *Letters on Female Character*, was published in 1828. Tuckahoe Plantation was purchased by Tom's descendants through his daughter Ellen, around 1900.

❦

Dr. Theodore Dudley left Jack and the Roanoke plantation at the end of 1819. According to Jack, he had been disappointed in a love affair and moved to Richmond. Their friendship ended in 1822 when Jack "displayed the deepest malignity of feeling" toward Dudley. He moved to Louisiana and later compiled letters from Jack and published them under the title *Letters to a Young Relative*.

Jack's friendship with Nathaniel Macon remained intact; it was said to have lasted as long as they lived.

"In later years . . . when from advancing years and physical infirmity they were compelled to hug their firesides at Washington more closely than they had done in the past, they grew almost like husband and wife, who have shared the same thoughts and feelings so long that, from the ties of habit, if nothing else, they are indispensable to each other."

Title page of "Letters on Female Character,"
by Virginia Randolph Cary, 1828

In 1819, Jack wrote the first of three wills. The second one, written in December 1821, provided for emancipating his slaves.

In December 1822, Nancy wrote him, promising that he would know of Dick's true relationship to her. "When my most maligned son is a little older, he will write you a letter containing certificates from his two uncles – you will then know what passages were cut out of the bundle of Dick's letters conveyed to you . . . . I pitied Dick, I was his best friend. I was absolved by Tudor's death of my promises. His mother was then made acquainted with them."

Jack served in the Senate from 1825 to 1827. Jonathan Bryan, Jack's godson, lived at Roanoke from 1816 to 1820, along with John Randolph Clay. Bryan married Elizabeth Coalter, Fanny's daughter.

St. George Tucker, Jack's stepfather and Nancy's beloved guardian and friend, died in 1827.

Following another dispute with Henry Clay, Jack met his old adversary on the southern side of the Potomac in a duel in 1826. Jack did not fire and Clay's bullet pierced only the voluminous dressing gown that Jack wore.

The ongoing debt of more than fifty years was settled in 1829 when Jack made the final payment to what had been Hanbury's, then Hanbury and Lloyd and finally Lloyds of London.

The Virginia Constitutional Convention was held in 1829—1830 in Richmond to settle a controversy about the very low western representation in the General Assembly, and little money going into the region. John Marshall, James Madison, James Monroe, and Jack were all present at the capitol during the meetings, but it was John Randolph of Roanoke that the people wanted to hear.

Hugh Blair Grigsby, a young member, wrote, "The thrilling music of his speech fell upon the ear like the voice of a bird, singing in the pause of a storm."

Jack, appointed by President Andrew Jackson to serve as envoy to the Russian court, took John Randolph Clay and three slaves with him to St. Petersburg. An illness forced him to return after a very short period, and he left Clay to transact the necessary business. He billed and received from the United States government an exorbitant amount of money for his brief stay. In 1832, he made a third will, directing that his slaves be sold rather than freed.

In May 1833, while in a Philadelphia hotel before a planned departure for Europe, he became ill and attempted an oral manumission of his slaves before he died. A postmortem revealed that one testicle had never descended and the other was only as large as a pea, confirming the family reports of arrested sexual maturity. He was buried in the woods at Roanoke plantation, but in 1879 Tucker's great-grandson had his remains removed to Hollywood Cemetery in Richmond.

Litigation to determine which of the three wills was valid began in 1834 and continued for a decade. The will of 1821 was declared valid, and the slaves were freed and sent to Ohio for resettlement.

Perhaps the most tragic figure among the Randolphs was Saint, John St. George Randolph—handsome, gentle, talented, and doomed by his genetic defects. Nancy "thought often of poor Saint in the madhouse," where he spent many years, and information on his life after entering the insane asylum has been found only in bits and pieces.

By 1820, Jack found that he "refuses to write or spell on his fingers because he believes that a miracle has been wrought and he is restored to speech and hearing."

Wyatt Cardwell, of Charlotte County, became the agent for Jack's estate and accompanied his slaves to Ohio after their manumission. While in Philadelphia paying bills for Saint's care, he was dismayed by the deplorable circumstances of his life, and around 1850 arranged to take him to Charlotte Courthouse, into his home, and provided a horse and books in French, Latin, and English for him.

Author Marion Harland's husband was pastor of the church that Saint attended, and in her autobiography she wrote of him.

Saint bowed his head upon his hands in silent devotion in church and followed the service and sermon devoutly. His face lit up when he saw the minister, and, going to the front of the church, he held out one hand to the preacher, placing the other hand over his heart.

His hair had turned snow white, and he wore it long, to the collar of his coat. His eyes were still dark and piercing and his features finely chiseled. He was "erect as a Virginia pine" and "walked like an Indian, planting his feet straight forward, rising on his toes with a loping motion."

The people in the town thought highly of Saint, taking pride in the "relic of the heroic age." He adopted sign language again, and his comments were "repeated as bon mots." Saint died on February 1, 1858, a few weeks before his sixtieth-sixth birthday. The inventory of his personal property listed a carriage and harness, two grey horses, a rocking chair, spittoon, table and six chairs, lounge, washstand and bureau, with the total valued at $755.

His financial portfolio was more impressive. Stocks and bonds totaled $66,000, notes with interest were listed at $88,000, and land in Prince Edward and Cumberland counties was appraised at more than $50,000.

❧

The legacy of Frances Randolph Tucker's sons, half-blood kin to the Randolphs of Bizarre, was outstanding. Harry (Henry St. George Tucker) served two terms in the House of Representatives, was president of the Virginia Supreme Court of Appeals, and later became a professor of law at the College of William and Mary. He died in 1848. Beverley (Nathaniel Beverley Tucker) published *The Partisan Leader* and also served as professor of law at William and Mary. He died in 1851.

❧

Unlike Monticello and Tuckahoe, Bizarre is remembered only through a Virginia historical marker on Route 45, just outside of Farmville. It notes that "near here is the site of Bizarre, owned in 1742 by Richard Randolph of Curles. In 1781, his grandson, John Randolph of Roanoke, took refuge at Bizarre with his mother on account of Arnold's invasion. John Randolph lived here until 1810, when he moved to Roanoke in Charlotte County."

❧

Near the actual site of Bizarre, an iron fence surrounds a small graveyard and cows graze nearby. Perhaps Dick Randolph is buried here, and perhaps this is the graveyard where Nancy yearned to walk with her "dear boys," more than two hundred years ago.

THE RANDOLPHS OF VIRGINIA
LINE OF DESCENT

William Randolph of Turkey Island
1651-1711
M
Mary Isham of Bermuda Hundred

Richard of Curles
1690-1748
M
Jane Bolling

John Randolph of Matoax
1742-1775
M
Frances Bland of Cawsons
1752-1788

| Richard Randolph of Bizarre (Dick) 1770-1796 M | Theodorick Randolph (Theo) 1771-1792 | John Randolph of Roanoke (Jack) 1773-1833 |

Judith Randolph of Tuckahoe
1772-1816

John St. George Randolph
(Saint)
1792-1858
Tudor Theodorick Randolph
1795-1816

Frances Bland Randolph
M
St. George Tucker
1752-1827

| Ann Frances Bland Tucker (Fanny) 1779-1813 M Judge John Coalter | Henry St. George Tucker 1780-1848 | Nathaniel Beverley Tucker 1784-1851 |

Isham Randolph of Dungeness
1685-1742
M
Jane Rogers

Jane
M
Peter Jefferson
1707-1757

Thomas
1743-1826
President of United States
M
Martha W. Skelton

Martha
1772-1836
M
Thomas Mann Randolph, Jr.
1768-1828
Governor of Virginia

Mary (Maria)
1778-1804
M
John Wayles Eppes

Ann Randolph
Thomas Jefferson Randolph
Ellen Randolph
Cornelia Randolph
Virginia Randolph
Mary Randolph
James Madison Randolph
Benjamin Franklin Randolph
Meriwether Lewis Randolph
Septemia Randolph
George Wythe Randolph
(Confederate Secretary of War)

Francis Wayles Eppes

Thomas Randolph of Tuckahoe
1683-1729
M
Judith Fleming

William Randolph   Mary Randolph
1713-1746   M
M   James Keith
Maria Judith Page

                                           Mary Randolph Keith
Thomas Mann Randolph   M
1741-1793   Thomas Marshall
M
1. Ann Cary of Ampthill   John Marshall
   (cousins)   1755-1835
                                           Chief Justice of U.S.

Mary Randolph (Molly) married David Meade Randolph (cousins)
Elizabeth Randolph married Robert Pleasants
Thomas Mann Randolph Jr. married Martha Jefferson (cousins)
William Randolph married Lucy Bolling Randolph (cousins)
Judith Randolph married Richard Randolph of Bizarre (cousins)
Ann Randolph (Nancy) (1774-1837) married Gouverneur Morris
   (1752-1816)
Jane Randolph married Thomas Eston Randolph (cousins)
John Randolph married Judith Lewis
Harriet Randolph married Richard Hackley
Virginia Randolph married Wilson Jefferson Cary (cousins)

2. Gabriella Harvie
   Thomas Mann Randolph II

John Randolph of Matoax
M
Frances Bland of Cawsons
(cousins)

Richard Randolph of Bizarre   Theodorick   John Randolph of Roanoke
M
Judith Randolph of Tuckahoe
(cousins)

John St. George
Tudor Theodorick

ABBREVIATIONS

DLC	Library of Congress
LVA	Library of Virginia
RC	Randolph College
VHS	Virginia Historical Society
ViU	University of Virginia
W&M	College of William and Mary

BC	Brown Coleman Collection
BR Papers	Bruce Randolph Personal Papers
BTC	Brown Tucker Coalter Collection
CT	Creed Taylor Papers
JR	John Randolph Collection
JR Papers	John Randolph Papers
NR	Nancy Randolph Collection
RF Papers	Randolph Family Papers
RKR	Richard Kidder Randolph Collection
TC	Tucker Coleman Collection
VMH&B	Virginia Magazine of History and Biography
W&M Qtrly	William and Mary Quarterly

END NOTES

The Trial, April 29, 1793

This chapter is based on *John Marshall's Notes of Evidence,* copied by John Randolph, Williamsburg, Virginia, June 1793, VHS.

"God Himself," Daniels, *Randolphs of Virginia,* 145.

"Great personal beauty," Bruce, *Randolph of Roanoke,* 2:506.

"A beautiful woman," *VMH&B* 48:238-242.

The minutes of this proceeding, Bloom, *Generation of Leaves,* 620; Shepherd, *Statutes at Large of Virginia,* 20-21.

"Did you send enough?" Henry, *Patrick Henry,* 2:491.

Gum guaicum, Cullen and Johnson, *John Marshall,* 168-169.

"Thrust a dagger," Daniels, *Randolphs of Virginia,* 96.

The gentlemen justices ruled, *Cumberland County Order Book,* 1792-1797, 217.

Jack rode postilion, *John Randolph Diary,* BR Papers, LVA.

"They have been tried and acquitted," Martha Randolph to Thomas Jefferson, May 16, 1793, Betts and Bear, *Family Letters,* 117-118.

1787

"**Storm the citadel,**" *VMH&B* 48:238.

Judith complained to her second cousin, Judith Randolph to Martha Jefferson, Feb. 12, 1785, *Trist film*, Viu.

Tuckahoe, Krusen, *Tuckahoe Plantation*, 13.

"**An apartment all done in velvet and gold,**" Ibid, 21.

Tom Jones, **a titillating novel,** Daniels, *Randolphs of Virginia*, 125.

Mary of Tuckahoe, *Ibid.*, 50-51.

"**Conceal every circumstance,**" Frances Tucker to St. George Tucker, Sept. 27, 1787, *T/C*, W&M.

"**Charm a bird out of a tree,**" Daniels, *Randolphs of Virginia*, 97.

Matoax Plantation, Coleman, *Citizen*, 52.

"**Lose no time,**" St. George Tucker to Frances Tucker, June 1781, Ibid, 59.

"**My son,**" **she replied,** John Randolph to Tudor Randolph, December 13, 1813, Grinnan, ViU.

"**I wish I had a tutor,**" Theodorick Randolph to St. George Tucker, July 9, 1781, *TC*, W&M.

"**My lips have not been touched,**" Frances Tucker to St. George Tucker, Coleman, *Citizen*, 49.

"**He embraced George Washington,**" St. George Tucker to Frances Tucker, Sept. 15, 1781, Ibid, 70.

"**We were never so glad,**" Theodorick Randolph to St. George Tucker, July 17, 1781, *TC*, W&M.

Tucker spoke French fluently, Thomas Nelson, Jr. to St. George Tucker, Sept. 16, 1781, *VMH&B* 102:2, 170.

Yankee Doodle, Gottschalk, *Lafayette in America*, 326; Wibberley, *Man of Liberty*, 173.

Walker Maury's School, Dawidoff, *Education of John Randolph*, 116.

"**Return on a long, boisterous journey,**" John Randolph to Tudor Randolph, Dec. 13, 1813, *Grinnan*, ViU.

Maury made a violent attack, John Banister to St. George Tucker, Sept. 1784, *TC,* W&M.

"Shocking barbarity," John Randolph to Tudor Randolph, Dec. 13, 1813, *Grinnan,* ViU.

"Rope of sand, wanting energy," McGee, *Framers of the Constitution,* 13.

"Still more on guard," *VMH&B* 102:2, 179.

"Anarchy reigns," Frances Tucker to St. George Tucker, Sept. 27, 1787, Coleman, *Virginia Silhouettes,* 3-4.

Fall off porch, Richard Randolph to Frances Tucker, Sept. 10, 1787, *B/C,* W&M.

"Remedy suggested was a pediluvium," Theodorick Bland to St. George Tucker, Dec. 1787, *T/C,* W&M.

"Till court rises," Frances Tucker to St. George Tucker, Dec. 2, 1787, *T/C,* W&M.

"Ever dear boys," St. George Tucker to Randolph brothers, Dec. 17, 1787, *Bryan,* ViU.

"We had gone to New York," John Randolph to Tudor Randolph, Dec. 13, 1813, Grinnan, ViU.

Red frock; students called her Jeffy, Randall, *Thomas Jefferson,* 370.

"A sweet girl," Nabby Adams; McCullough, *John Adams,* 322.

"If in the House of Hades," Brodie, *Intimate History,* 150.

Deaths among women and infants, Clinton, *Plantation Mistress,* 139.

They arrived by channel boat at Le Havre, Dos Passos, *Head and Heart,* 254-255.

"Pretty statues and windows," Martha Jefferson to Elizabeth Trist, Dos Passos, *Head and Heart, ibid.*

"We were obliged to send immediately," Martha Jefferson to Elizabeth Trist; Fleming, *Man from Monticello,* 122.

"Conjugal love," Thomas Jefferson to Charles Bellini, Sept. 30, 1785; Brodie, *Intimate History,* 97.

Lucy had died, Brodie, Ibid, 190.

"Very elegant, even for Paris," Fleming, *Man from Monticello,* 130.

"A Dialogue Between my Head and my Heart," Thomas Jefferson to Maria Cosway, Oct. 12, 1786, Brodie, *Intimate History*, 483.

"Night thoughts, the pain of separation," Maria Cosway to Thomas Jefferson, Nov. 17, 1786, Ibid, 214.

The Eppes family finally arranged, S. N. Randolph, Domestic Life, 125, Wibberley, *Man of Liberty*, 203.

"Come and we will breakfast," Thomas Jefferson to Maria Cosway, Feb. 1, 1787, Peterson, *Jefferson's Writings*, 899-900.

"To bid you adieu," Maria Cosway to Thomas Jefferson, Dec. 7, 1787, Brodie, *Intimate History*, 224.

Some kind of failure, *Ibid.*, 225.

"Popularity with women," Bowen, *Miracle in Philadelphia*, 42

Madison later wrote, McGee, *Framers of the Constitution*, 284-285; Bowen, *Miracle in Philadelphia*, 242.

1788

"Quis desiderio sit modu?" Ode of Horace, Odes 1:24; Coleman, *Citizen*, 93.

"Where a body could meet a body," Sanford, *Richmond*, 107.

Young men were as careful, Hill, *Evolution of Fashion*, 45.

Two to four musicians played, Stoutamire, *Music of the Old South*, 41; Kierner, *Beyond the Household*, 52.

"Roman god," Anna Dudley, *Randolph Will Litigation*, LVA.

His second cousin, John Randolph to Tudor Randolph, Dec 13, 1813, *Grinnan*, ViU

Thirty per cent of taxpayers, *VMH&B* 61: 313.

"They have taken Virginia," "A James River Planter," *Virginia Independent Chronicle*, Dec. 9, 1786.

"The splendid maintenance," Garland, *Life of John Randolph*, 1:30.

Henry stood and apologized, Henry, *Patrick Henry Life*, 2:372.

Leslie urged him not to withdraw, Gaines, *Thomas Mann Randolph,* 21.

A woman's power as absolute monarch, Fox-Genovese, *Within Plantation Household,* 206.

Gouverneur Morris accepted Colonel Randolph's invitation, Swiggett, *Extraordinary Mr. Morris,* 136-37.

Leslie arrived in August, Gaines, *Thomas Mann Randolph,* 22.

"A grand processional wound," John Randolph to St. George Tucker, July 30, 1788, New York Public Library.

"You will have heard," St. George Tucker to Richard, John, and Theodorick Randolph, Aug. 12, 1788, *Bryan,* ViU.

Back to college in New York by packet, St. George Tucker to Theodorick Randolph, Sept. 1788, *TC,* W&M.

"As young people cannot," Ann Randolph to St. George Tucker, Sept. 23, 1788, Coleman, *Citizen,* 109-110.

Tucker left Matoax, Ibid., 97-98.

The children called it Fort St. George, *VMH&B,* 102:2, 178.

John Coalter came with St. George Tucker, John Coalter to his father, Jan. 30, 1789, *W&M Quarterly,* I, 8:57.

"That manly and most elegant youth," Swiggett, *Extraordinary Mr. Morris,* 81.

"At Dusseldorf I wished for you much," Thomas Jefferson to Maria Cosway, April 24, 1788, Page Smith, *Jefferson Revealing Biography,* 197; Bullock, *Head and Heart,* 90-92.

Martha's growing interest in the Catholic religion, S. N. Randolph, *Domestic Life,* 146.

Miniature copies of his portrait, Brodie, *Intimate History,* 236.

A bad harvest and severe famine, Wibberley, *Man of Liberty,* 206.

1789

He met Adele de Flahaut, Swiggett, *Extraordinary Mr. Morri,* 157.

He rode to the convent, Brodie, *Intimate History,* 240.

Seven hundred francs, Ibid.

"A matter of natural curiosity," Swiggett, *Extraordinary Mr. Morris*, 219.

"Gracious God, what a people," Ibid., 172.

Jefferson spent 216 francs within a few weeks, Brodie, *Intimate History*, 240.

"Spring might give us a meeting in Paris," Thomas Jefferson to Maria Cosway, Oct. 14, 1789, Bullock, *Head and Heart*, 125.

Judith, Nancy and Jenny scratched the date, March 17, 1789, Krusen, *Tuckahoe Plantation*, 58.

"Although tall and commanding," *American Heritage*, October 1974, 48.

"Burning affection tinctured with sadness," John Leslie to Thomas Mann Randolph, June 6, 1789, Gaines, *Thomas Mann Randolph*, 21.

Sir John Leslie, *Ency. Britannica* 40, 7:295.

Tucker gave him an allowance, St. George. Tucker to Theodorick Randolph, Jan. 2, 1789, *TC*, W&M.

He reminded his stepson, St. George Tucker to Theodorick Randolph, Feb. 20, 1789, Ibid.

The ship caught fire, Wibberley, *Man of Liberty*, 212.

Stopped over at Tuckahoe, Daniels, *Randolphs of Virginia*, 129.

Tucker's satirical description, The Cynic, Jan. 1, 1790, TC, W&M., Kierner, *Scandal at Bizarre*, 24.

"To shew her power," Nancy Morris to St. George Tucker, Mar. 2, 1815, *TC*, W&M.

1790

He and Judith entertained lavishly, Richard Randolph to Neill Buchannan, Feb. 24, 1790, *TC*, W&M.

Tucker devised various errands, St. George Tucker to Theodorick Randolph, Jan. 18, 1790, Ibid.

In two years, Garland, *Life of John Randolph*, 1:24.

"He, ever indulgent to my wishes," Judith Randolph to Mary Harrison, Nov. 11, 1790, *Harrison,* VHS.

Martha Jefferson's wedding, Gaines, *Thomas Mann Randolph,* 29.

"Continue to love me," Thomas Jefferson to Martha Randolph, Jan. 16, 1781, Betts and Bear, *Family Letters.*

Gabriella Harvie, Gaines, *Thomas Mann Randolph,* 32.

They visited Aunt Polly, Nancy Morris to St. George Tucker, Mar. 2, 1815, *TC,* W&M.

"Love and cherish what is good," Betts and Bear, *Family Letters,* 61.

"Perhaps you think," Thomas Jefferson to Martha Randolph, Dec. 23, 1790, S. N. Randolph, *Domestic Life,* 193.

1791

"Unlike the North, where women in labor," Ulrich, *A Midwife's Tale,* 177.

"She is very well now," Maria Jefferson to Thomas Jefferson, Feb. 13, 1791, S. N. Randolph, *Domestic Life,* 194.

"One announced you are become," Thomas Jefferson to Martha Randolph, Feb. 9, 1791, Ibid., 192.

"A pin for existence without her," John Randolph to Henry Rutledge, Feb. 24, 1791, *BR Papers,* LVA.

"You made many accusations," Nancy Morris to John Randolph, Jan. 16, 1815, *Spicy Correspondence,* RC.

Lelia and Tucker were married, *Lancaster County Marriage Register* 10, 74.

"Dick had one fault of great magnitude," Nancy Morris to St. Geo. Tucker, Mar. 2, 1815, *TC,* W&M.

The British debts case was heard, Cullen and Johnson, *John Marshall,* 293-294.

1792

"Your abilities were asserted," Swiggett, *Extraordinary Mr. Morris,* 225.

"The two years which followed," Lodge, *Historical and Political Essays,* 103.

"Sweet Lelia's power to supply," Beverley Randolph to St. George Tucker, Jan. 7, 1792, *TC,* W&M.

"The same, poor fellow," Judith Randolph to St. George Tucker, Jan. 10. 1792, *BTC,* W&M.

"Disagreeable journey," Martha Randolph to Thomas Jefferson, Feb. 20, 1792, Betts and Bear, *Family Letters,* 95.

"Poor Dick possessed," Nancy Morris to St. George Tucker, Mar. 2, 1815, *TC,* W&M.

Judith gave birth, John Randolph to Tudor Randolph, Dec. 13, 1813, *Grinnan,* ViU.

The Randolphs visit to Glentivar, *Notes of Evidence,* June 1793, VHS.

"It is painful . . . to be obliged," Martha Randolph to Thomas Jefferson, May 16, 1793, Betts and Bear, *Family Letters,* 118.

"The first intelligence," John Randolph Diary, *B/R Papers,* LVA.

"If passion had not diverted your aim," Nancy Morris to John Randolph, Jan. 16, 1815, *Spicy Correspondence.* RC.

1793

"Villainy of traducers," VGGA: *To the Public,* Apr. 3, 1793.

"Vile wretch," Judith Randolph to Elizabeth Pleasants, Mar. 12, 1793, *BR Papers,* LVA.

Recommended a novel approach, Bloom, *Generation of Leaves,* 620.

Alexander Campbell, Mordecai, *Richmond Bygone Days,* 83.

"What have I not suffered," Judith Randolph to Mary Harrison, Apr. 7, 1793, *Harrison,* VHS.

Offer a 70-pound retainer, Meade, *Patrick Henry,* 417-420; *Cumberland County Order Book 18,* 1792-1797; 217.

Marshall's records show, Cullen and Johnson, *John Marshall,* 459.

"Wash out with blood," Nancy Randolph Morris to St. George Tucker, Feb. 14, 1815, *TC,* W&M.

Jack rode Star, John Randolph Diary, *BR Papers, LVA.*

The gentlemen justices ruled, *Cumberland County Order Book 18,* 1792-1797, 217.

"Dick sent sixteen yellow jasmine," Fanny Tucker to St. George Tucker, April 29, 1793, *TC,* W&M.

"Everyone stands on their merit," Thomas Jefferson to Martha Randolph, April 1,1793, Betts and Bear, *Family Letters,* 115-116.

"Infinite anxiety, both to Mr. Randolph and myself," Martha Randolph to Thomas Jefferson, May 16, 1793, Ibid., 117-118.

"Scenes of greater tranquility," Thomas Jefferson to George Washington, Simmons, *Mr. Jefferson's Ladies,* 129.

"Thought that enthusiasm," Thomas Jefferson to Angelica Church, Nov. 21,1793, Bullock, *Head and Heart,* 138.

"The ardor of his feelings," Nancy Morris to John Randolph, Dec. 17, 1822, *TC,* W&M.

"The blasterer of my happiness," Nancy Morris to St. George Tucker, Nov. 1814, *TC,* W&M.

"The charge was very public," John Marshall to Gouverneur Morris, Dec. 12, 1809, Baker, *Life in Law,* 153.

"The little boy named Alexander," John Randolph Diary, *BR Papers,* LVA.

"He is the link," Martha Randolph to Thomas Jefferson, May 16, 1793, Betts and Bear, *Family Letters,* 119.

Made a will for him, *Goochland County Will Book* 16:334.

"My arm was between the pillow," Nancy Randolph to Mary Johnston, Feb. 21, 1805, *NR,* W&M.

St. George Tucker applied to Henrico County, Henry Banks to St. George Tucker, Jan. 8, 1794, *BC,* W&M.

He rented ministerial quarters, Whittredge, *American Heritage, 1976,* 89.

"Her pubic hair cut off," Faderman, *Surpassing the Love*, 93.

"He has spent his fortune," Lodge, *Historical and Political Essays*, 107.

"She was tossed out," Asquith, *Marie Antoinette*, 222.

1794

Smallpox epidemic, Nancy Randolph to St. George Tucker, Mar. 1794, *TC*, W&M.

Cowpox vaccinations as soon as they were old enough, Gaines, *Thomas Mann Randolph*, 41.

"Cruelly disappointed," Martha Randolph to Thomas Jefferson, Feb. 27, 1793, Betts and Bear, *Family Letters*, 112

"Good riddance of bad ware," John Adams to John Quincy Adams, Jan. 6, 1794, McCullough, *John Adams*, 448.

Hester Hargrave, Dr. St. George Grinnan to William Cabell Bruce, letter nd, *BR Papers*, LVA.

Jack described such an incident, John Randolph to Elizabeth C. Bryan, Mar. 27, 1828, *Bryan*, ViU.

"The vilest of reports," Judith Randolph to Mary Harrison, May 23, 1794, *Harrison*, VHS.

The sale brought 1600 pounds, Lutz, *Chesterfield, Old Virginia County*, 147.

Rearing her sister Virginia, Judith Randolph to Mary Harrison, June 5, 1794, Harrison, VHS.

"Two at once! God forbid," Judith Randolph to Mary *Harrison,* Ibid.

"Returning from a morning ride," Nancy Morris to John Randolph, Jan. 16, 1815, *Spicy Correspondence*, RC.

"I have seen," John Randolph to Fanny Coalter, Nov. 21, 1813, *Bryan*, ViU.

Martha worried about Tom, Simmons, *Mr. Jefferson's Ladies*, 132.

Requested two or three guineas, Nancy Randolph to St. George Tucker, Dec. 5, 1794, *TC*, W&M.

1795

She explained to Tucker from Rocky Mills, Nancy Randolph to St. George Tucker, Feb. 23, 1795, *TC,* W&M.

"In a ruinous condition," Martha Randolph to Thomas Jefferson, Jan. 5, 1795, Betts and Bear, *Family Letters,* 131.

Virginians who were financially able, Reniers, *Life and Death,* 12-13.

Nancy's homeless situation, Thomas Jefferson to Martha Randolph, July 31, 1795, Betts & Bear, *Family Letters,* 134.

"I long ardently to see you all," Nancy Randolph to St. George Tucker, July 12, 1795, *TC,* W&M.

Nancy replenished her wardrobe, Nancy Randolph to St. Geo. Tucker, Ibid.

"A reasonable amount of spiritous liquor," Richard Randolph to Creed Taylor, Jan. 28, 1795, *BR Papers,* LVA.

"When are we to promise ourselves," Richard Randolph to Creed Taylor, Jan. 18, 1795, Ibid.

"A pleasure long denied," Richard Randolph to Creed Taylor, June 6, 1795, Ibid.

Forcing or bearing pains, Ulrich, *Midwife's Tale,* 175.

"When they said 'push,'" Tillyard, *Aristocrats,* 239.

"A mere lounger," John Randolph to Tudor Randolph, Dec. 13, 1813, *Grinnan,* ViU..

"You have seen the sad relic," John Randolph to Henry Rutledge, Jan. 28, 1795, Bruce, *Randolph of Roanoke,* 1:93.

"Where I hope to embrace," Garland, *Life of John Randolph,* 1:65.

1796

Sir John Nesbit, Ibid., 1:65.

Yazoo frauds, Ibid., 1:66-67.

"A planter's support of family," Clinton, *Plantation Mistress,* 45.

With Bizarre as an example, Harland, *Autobiography,* 110.

Dick wrote his will, *Prince Edward County Will Book 1,* 4-7.

Jacobin died, John Randolph to St. George Tucker, Aug. 6, 1796, *JR,* RC.

Jack became ill, John Randolph to Judith Randolph, Jan. 20, 1816, *RF Papers,* VHS.

Nancy alone would see her, Nancy Randolph to St. George Tucker, May 18, 1796, *TC,* W&M.

A stranger arrived at Bizarre, Carter, *Latrobe Journal,* June 12, 1796.

"From memory of Miss Nancy Randolph," Carter, *Latrobe View of America,* 48-49.

"He seemed very unhappy," Nancy Randolph to St. George Tucker, Feb. 9, 1815, *TC,* W&M.

"This is a scene," Nancy Randolph to St. George Tucker, June, 1796, *TC,* W&M.

"My dear Jack," Nancy Randolph to John Randolph, June, 1796, Ibid.

"Your goodness can never be effaced," Nancy Randolph to Mary Johnston, letter nd, *NR,* W&M.

"I have no body," John Randolph to St. Geo. Tucker, July 12, 1796, *JR,* W&M.

"The only rag of comfort," Judith Randolph to Mary Harrison, Sept. 17, 1796, Harrison, *VHS.*

There were rumors that Dick died, Biddle, *A Casual Past,* 40.

Tartar emetic is a poison, Weider, *Murder of Napoleon,* 220.

Alexander Campbell's suicide, Mordecai, *Richmond Bygone Days,* 111.

"Sympathies on loss of Elizabeth," Judith Randolph to St. George Tucker, Aug. 2, 1796, *TC,* W&M.

"Much time was spent in amusement," Carter, *Latrobe Journal,* Aug. 24, 1796, 193.

"The whirl of gaieties," Sale, *Mansions of Virginia,* 122.

Madison began campaigning, Wibberley, *Man of Liberty,* 294.

"Every sentiment of tenderness," Martha Randolph to Thomas Jefferson, Jan. 22, 1798, Betts and Bear, *Family Letters,* 154.

1797

"**Health and spirits are somewhat recruited,**" Judith Randolph to Mary Harrison, Feb. 15, 1797, *Harrison, VHS.*

On April 18, 1797, she, as executrix, filed, *Prince Edward County Will Book 1,* 9-12.

"**A flying trip to Petersburg,**" Judith Randolph to Mary Harrison, Apr. 30, 1797, *Harrison, VHS.*

"**I was turned out of the house,**" Nancy Randolph to Sally Taylor, Nov. 11, 1798, *TC,* W&M.

"**Macbeth hath murdered sleep,**" Randolph Will Litigation; Garland, *Life of John Randolph,* 1:70.

Inventory of Dick's estate, July, 1797, *Prince Edward County Will Book 1,* 9.

"**Why do we not see you at Bizarre?**" Judith Randolph to Creed Taylor, Nov. 18, 1797, *BR Papers,* LVA.

"**It is scarcely possible to wield my pen,**" Nancy Randolph to Sally Taylor, letter nd, CT, ViU.

"**He is as he was,**" John Adams to Abigail Adams, Mar. 13, 1797, McCullough, *John Adams,* 476.

Lidderdale v. Randolph, Daniels, *Randolphs of Virginia,* 148.

Have the children vaccinated against smallpox, Martha Randolph to Thomas Jefferson, Jan. 31, 1797, Betts and Bear, *Family Letters,* 143.

As having a harelip, McLaughlin, *Jefferson, Biography of Builder,* 264.

He viewed Eppes as the joining link, Simmons, *Mr. Jefferson's Ladies,* 161.

At the wedding on October 13, Bober, *Jefferson, Man on Mountain,* 29.

"**From the frenzy of a monster,**" Simmons, *Mr. Jefferson's Ladies,* 128.

1798

"**I have not been to a ball yet,**" Judith Randolph to Mary Harrison, Feb. 16, 1798, *Harrison, VHS.*

"I have witnessed the mutual animosities," Nancy Randolph to St. George Tucker, May 29, 1798, *TC, W&M.*

"The obligation to seek asylum," Nancy Randolph to St. George Tucker, Nov. 11, 1798, Ibid.

"Nancy has at length reached Bizarre," Judith Randolph to Sally Taylor, letter nd, *BR Papers,* LVA.

He urged Jack to run, John Randolph to Creed Taylor, Sept. 16, 1798, *CT,* ViU.

There she had met Mr. and Mrs. John Walker, Maria Eppes to Thomas Jefferson, May 27, 1798, Betts and Bear, *Family Letters,* 163.

"The heart swelling with which I address you," Martha Jefferson to Thomas Jefferson, July 1, 1798, Ibid., 166.

"The south pavilion, parlor and study," Thomas Jefferson to Martha Randolph, Feb. 2, 1798, S. N. Randolph, *Domestic Life,* 156.

Adams sent John Marshall and Elbridge Gerry, McCullough, *John Adams,* 485.

XYZ affair, Ibid, 494-496.

The Alien and Sedition Acts, Wibberley, *Man of Liberty,* 301.

Gouverneur Morris returned to America, Swiggett, *Extraordinary Mr. Morris,* 237.

1799

"The state had quitted the sphere," Garland, *Life of John Randolph,* 1:131.

"The sun has set," Henry, *Patrick Henry,* 2:610.

Smartly attired in a blue coat, Garland, *Life of John Randolph,* 1:129.

"Maria has completely riveted," Judith Randolph to St. George Tucker, Apr. 22, 1799, *BCT,* W&M.

"Low spirits, the most terrible," Fanny Tucker to St. George Tucker, Aug. 11, 1799, *TC,* W&M.

Jack and William had taken a trip, Randolph Will Litigation, *BR Papers,* LVA.

His affinity for women and alcohol, Bruce, *Randolph of Roanoke,* 2:547.

It was two-storied, with a gallery, Gaines, *Thomas Mann Randolph,* 44.

"Mr. J's presence imposes upon me," Nancy Randolph to St. George Tucker, Sept. 12, 1799, *TC,* W&M.

Molly Randolph became a local personage, Mordecai, *Richmond Bygone Days,* 128-130.

Gouverneur Morris delivered the funeral oration, Swiggett, *Extraordinary Mr. Morris,* 342.

1800

"A genius otherwise capable," Judith Randolph to Mary Harrison, Apr. 29, 1800, *Harrison,* VHS.

She sold part of the Bizarre plantation, *Farmville Herald,* 227.

"I forgot yesterday to say something," Judith Randolph to Creed Taylor, Nov. 27, 1799, *CT,* ViU.

"On Sunday, Judy and William Thompson left me," Nancy Randolph to Sally Taylor, letter nd, *BR* Papers, LVA.

"Our sister is now asleep," William Thompson to John Randolph, Garland, *Life of John Randolph,* 1:74.

"The lady's husband is a beast," William Thompson to John Randolph, Ibid., 1:171.

"The report which you have heard," Judith Randolph to Mary Harrison, Feb. 23, 1800, *Harrison,* VHS.

"Heed not the shafts," William Thompson to John Randolph, Garland, *Life of John Randolph,* 1:182.

Jack galloped up, *W&M Quarterly, Series 2,* 8:259-60.

"Would you suppose, my dearest brother?" William Thompson to John Randolph, Garland, *Life of John Randolph,* 1:175.

"Consult your own heart," Ibid.

"Judy bestows all the displeasure," Nancy Randolph to St. George Tucker, Sept. 12, 1800, *TC,* W&M.

"Hundreds of large ships," Gouverneur Morris diary Sept. 12, 1803; Bloom, *Generation of Leaves,* 330.

"I shall endeavor to be satisfied," Maria Eppes to Thomas Jefferson, Dec. 28, 1800, *Family Letters*, 189.

1801

"No such usurpation," Cresson, *James Monroe*, 178-79.

"His election can only promote," Mitchell, *Alexander Hamilton*, 353-5.

Jack sent a report on February 12, John Randolph to James Monroe, Feb. 12, 1801, *JR*, RC.

"Ten states for Jefferson," John Randolph to St. George Tucker, Feb. 17, 1801, Ibid.

"Panted to be away," Thomas Jefferson to Maria Eppes, S. N. Randolph, *Domestic Life*, 274.

There was no rush to appoint midnight judges, McCullough, *John Adams*, 563.

"The loss of that intelligent attention," Swiggett, *Extraordinary Mr. Morris*, 351.

"Escorted by a body of militia," Hildreth, *History of United States*, 5:420.

Jefferson removed David Meade Randolph . . . as Federal Marshall, Betts and Bear, *Family Letters*, 318.

Applauded his fine continental cuisine and superior wines, Brodie, *Intimate History*, 364.

She dipped snuff, Swiggett, *Extraordinary Mr. Morris*, 375.

"The mind calling forth every energy," Martha Randolph to Thomas Jefferson, Nov. 10, 1801, Betts and Bear, *Family Letters*, 213.

"Judy is so thin and looks so badly," John Randolph to St. George Tucker, May 9, 1801, *JR*, RC.

"The health of my family," John Randolph to Joseph Nicholson, July 18, 1801, *BR Papers*, LVA.

"Don't you think it rather in the romantic way?" Lelia Ann Byrd to Fanny Tucker, Apr. 12, 1801, *BCT*, W&M.

"Since you left us I have consented," Judith Randolph to Mary Harrison, June 18, 1801, *Harrison*, VHS.

"Sitting down to dinner," Judith Randolph to Mary Harrison, Aug. 7, 1801, *Grinnan*, VHS.

"The slaves are entitled to their freedom," Judith Randolph to St. George Tucker, Oct. 18, 1801, *TC*, W&M.

Jack became chairman, Mapp, *Jefferson Passionate Pilgrim*, 40.

1802-1804

"Breckinridge and Stone . . . Morris and Tracy have been the Achilles and Ajax . . .," John Randolph to St. George Tucker, Jan. 15, 1802, *JR*, RC.

"The object of her choice," John Randolph to St. George Tucker, Feb. 23, 1802, *JR*, RC.

In July, The Portfolio, a Philadelphia newspaper, *PP,* Jan. 22, 1803.

John Marshall praised the Recorder, Brodie, *Intimate History,* 355.

"Black Venus," Mapp, *Jefferson Passionate Pilgrim*, 34.

"Wrathful and venomous at the attacks," Brodie, *Intimate History*, 370.

The house was in its almost perpetual state, McLaughlin, *Biography of a Builder,* 232.

A "Sunday pudding," Ibid.

"Exquisite features, all good . . .," Mapp, *Jefferson Passionate Pilgrim*, 38.

140. **"Rather homely, a delicate likeness of her father,"** Ibid., 39.

"Poor Nancy cannot be less satisfied," Judith Randolph to John Randolph, Apr. 12, 1803, *Bryan*, ViU.

"Often involved a mature woman and younger woman," Smith-Rosenberg, *Female World of Love*, 125.

He told his father-in-law, Gaines, *Thomas Mann Randolph*, 48.

"One of the most generous, disinterested and high-minded men," Mapp, *Jefferson Passionate Pilgrim*, 337.

Even though Jefferson acted without Constitutional authority, John Randolph to St. George Tucker, Jan. 15, 1803, *JR*, RC.

"Doing as well as can be expected," Martha Randolph to Thomas Jefferson, Jan. 14, 1804, Betts & Bear, *Family Letters*, 252.

"A band of sharpers," Gaines, *Thomas Mann Randolph*, 55.

"Had swaggered back into Congress," Brown, *William Plumer*, 249.

"Almost incesssant employment of my pen," John Randolph to St. George Tucker, Nov. 23, 1803, *JR*, RC.

"Adieu once more, best beloved of my soul," Maria Eppes to John Eppes, Feb. 6, 1804, McLaughlin, *Jefferson, Biography of Builder*, 205.

"The fairest flower which my eyes ever beheld," Thomas Mann Randolph, Ibid., 206.

"A gloom in unison with my feelings," Nancy Randolph to St. George Tucker, May 28, 1804, *TC*, W&M.

"I charge you to protect his fame," Hildreth, *History of United States*, 5:526.

"His gentle manner made me quite easy," Nancy Randolph to St. George Tucker, Sept. 11, 1804, *TC*, W&M.

John Briggs, from Dinwiddie County, maintained a detailed diary, *A Trip to the Sweet Springs*, VHS.

"I hope my sister will become free," Nancy Randolph to St. George Tucker, July 7, 1804, *TC*, W&M.

"Reasons for not allowing the visit," Fanny Coalter, to Lelia Tucker, Apr. 11, 1805, *TC*, W&M.

"You may conceive the state of my feelings, Nancy Randolph to St. George Tucker, 11/25/1804, *TC*, W&M.

Judith ate nothing but lettuce, Mary Harrison to Nancy Randolph, Sept. 4, 1804, *TC*, W&M.

1805

"The Yazoo claims – Louisiana and the impeachment," John Randolph to St. George Tucker, Jan. 30, 1805, *JR*, RC.

"Emotions were excited . . .," Brown, *William Plumer*, 311.

"The torments of the damned," John Randolph to Joseph Nicholson, Feb. 1805, *BR Papers,* LVA.

"We are indeed fallen on evil times," Bruce, *Randolph of Roanoke,* 1:203.

"The Chief Justice appeared to be frightened," *Plumer Memorandum,* 291; Isenberg, Fallen Founder, 366.

"Today, I crawl out to the Senate," John Randolph to St. George Tucker, Feb. 22, 1805, *JR,* RC.

"The fellow cried like a baby," Bruce, *Randolph of Roanoke,* 1:210.

"Follow the respondent then," *Abridgement of Debates,* 280.

"Yazoo and Judge Chase making a devilish noise," John Randolph to St. George Tucker, letter nd, *JR,* RC.

"Without fire, my feet under me," Nancy Randolph to Mary Johnston, Feb. 21, 1805, *NR,* W&M.

"Since my return from Albemarle," Nancy Randolph to Mary Johnston, Ibid.

"He never closed an eye," John Randolph to Joseph Nicholson, Mar. 17, 1805, *JR,* RC.

"Nancy, when do you leave this house," Nancy Morris to John Randolph, Jan. 16, 1815, *Spicy Correspondence. RC.*

They left Bizarre in mid-November, John Randolph to St. George Tucker, Nov. 12, 1805, *TC,* W&M.

"Every member of your family is remembered," Nancy Randolph to Mary Johnston, letter nd, *NR,* W&M.

She ordered a trunk of "wedding cloaths," Martha Randolph to Thomas Jefferson, Betts and Bear, *Family Letters,* 277.

"My courage shrinks," Martha Randolph to Thomas Jefferson, Oct. 26, 1805, Ibid., 280.

Judith answered with a lengthy letter, Judith Randolph to Mary Harrison, Nov. 22, 1805, *Harrison,* VHS.

"This old house is not habitable," Judith Randolph to Fanny Coalter, Dec. 1805, *BCT,* W&M.

Jack traveled to Baltimore, John Randolph to St. George Tucker, Dec. 17, 1805, *JR*, RC.

1806

Martha had the option, Smith, M. B., *First Forty Years*, 404-405.

On Jan. 16, 1806, she gave birth, Gaines, *Thomas Mann Randolph*, 59.

"An unconstitutional suggestion," Bruce, *Randolph of Roanoke*, 1:223.

"The foreign business . . . from first to last," Cresson, *James Monroe*, 220.

"You have passed the Rubicon," Joseph Bryan to John Randolph, Apr. 23, 1806, *BR Papers*, LVA.

"What has thrown us into this heat?" *Annals of Congress, 1805.07*:1104.

"Made more noise than had been useful," Gaines, *Thomas Mann Randolph*, 61.

"On his side . . . a single life," Thomas Jefferson to Thomas Randolph, June 23, 1806, Brodie, *Intimate History*, 394.

"Maria Ward is to be married on March 22," Judith Randolph to Mary Harrison, Feb. 25, 1806, *Harrison*, VHS.

"I fear that I ought not to," Edmund Randolph to Maria Ward, Mar. 15, 1806, Conway, *Omitted Chapters of History*, 386.

"All was cards, dancing and merriment," Beverley Tucker to St. George Tucker, Mar. 24, 1806, *TC*, W&M.

"Maria's marriage has taken . . . ," Fanny Coalter to St. George Tucker, April 11, 1806, ibid.

"Leave the president alone," Joseph Bryan to John Randolph, June 24, 1806, *BR Papers*, LVA.

"For relieving the infirmity," John Randolph to John St. George Randolph, July 3, 1806, *JR Papers, Spec. Coll.*, Duke.

George Wythe was poisoned, Mordecai, *Richmond Bygone Days*, 106.

"I would have you taught to dance and fence," John Randolph to John St. George Randolph, Sept. 6, 1806, *JR Papers, Spec. Colls*, Duke.

"I have spent two miserable months," Nancy Randolph to St. George Tucker, Nov. 1806, *TC*, W&M.

1807

"I cannot think of leaving my seat," John Randolph to St. George Tucker, Nov. 24, 1806, *JR*, W&M.

"During the horrible visit," Nancy Morris to St. George Tucker, letter nd, *TC*, W&M.

David Meade Randolph proposed that she rent larger quarters, Nancy Morris to St. George Tucker, Kierner, *Scandal at Bizarre*, 114.

The Haymarket gardens were large, Mordecai, *Richmond Bygone Days*, 219-220.

"Ryland Randolph will convey my affection," Nancy Randolph to St. George Tucker, Mar.18, 1807. *TC*, W&M.

Apparently, Tom and John Eppes had a disagreement, Thomas Jefferson to Martha Randolph, Mar. 18, 1807, Beran, *Jefferson's Demons*, 179.

"I am absolutely enchanted with Richmond," Irving, *Life and Letters*, 1:196; Duke and Daniel, Richmond Reader, 44.

They planned to invade Mexico, McDonald, *Presidency of Thomas Jefferson*, 124-127.

Burr's capture, Ibid.

Beverley Tucker saw them pass Charlotte Courthouse, Beverley Tucker to St. George Tucker, Apr. 12, 1807, *TC*, W&M.

Jack reported seeing them near Bizarre, John Randolph to Joseph Nicholson, Mar. 25,1807, *Nicholson*, DLC.

Marshall interrogating Burr two days later, Scott, *Old Richmond Neighborhoods*, 131.

The doctrine of "constructive treason," Isenberg, *Fallen Founder*, 385.

Colonel Robert Gamble and Robert Taylor, Dabney, *Richmond, Story of a City*, 71-72.

"Exclude this letter and nothing remains," Lomask, *Aaron Burr*, 231.

Riding Brunette, he came down from Farmville, John Randolph Diary, *BR Papers,* LVA.

"Treason rejoicing dinner," *Richmond Inquirer, Apr. 10, 1807.*

"Let me inform the conscience of the Chief Justice," Ibid.

"The dogs of war, the hell hounds of persecution," Brodie, *Intimate History,* 409.

"Leave the nation without an executive branch," Thomas Jefferson to George Hay, June 20, 1807, Lomask, *Aaron Burr,* 249.

"To see their wives, get their clothes washed," Irving, *Life and Letters,* 192.

"Swelling like a turkey cock," Isenberg, *Fallen Founder,* 348.

"Yesterday the grand jury found bills for treason," Wheelan, *Jefferson's Vendetta,* 170; Daniels, *Randolphs of Virginia,* 365.

Visitors who brought various delicacies, Fleming, *Man from Monticello,* 318.

"Jupiter might invisibly elude the guards of Danae," Blennerhasset Papers, Brodie, *Intimate History,* 410.

"Ridiculed the experiment of a republic," Daniels, *Randolphs of Virginia,* 367.

Rumors soon flew about Theodosia and men, Ibid., 366.

"I shant be able to hang Burr," Brodie, *Intimate History,* 410.

"Burr stood . . . on the brink of danger . . . ." Winfield Scott; Wheelan, *Jefferson's Vendetta,* 95.

"Directed and animated the proceedings," Ibid., 102.

In three hours of instruction to the jury, Fleming, *Man from Monticello,* 318.

"We of the jury say . . ." Ibid.

"Judicial opinions are like changeable silks," Anderson, *William Branch Giles,* 119.

"Habited for execution," Severn, *Man Who Made Court Supreme,* 161.

"None laid so profound a plot," Nancy Randolph to St. George Tucker, Jan. 9, 1808, *TC,* W&M.

He found her and her quarters fastidiously neat, John Randolph to Nancy Morris, Oct. 31, 1814, *Spicy Correspondence,* RC.

"Brave all dangers rather than remain," Nancy Randolph to St. George Tucker, 1807, *TC,* W&M.

Penniless and desperate, asked him to lend her $50, Nancy Randolph to John Randolph, Dec. 11, 1807, *TC,* W&M.

"I united them all for awhile . . ." John Randolph to Kidder Randolph, Feb. 2, 1816, *BR Papers,* LVA.

"She is not *in the way,"* Coleman, *Citizen,* 145.

"Tudor has seen his mother's difficulties," Judith Randolph to John Randolph, Aug. 22, 1807, *Bryan,* ViU.

"A milk and water bill," Caffrey, *Twilight's Last Gleaming,* 84.

"The embargo seriously afflicted," Ellen Randolph to Thomas Jefferson, Jan. 29, 1798, Betts and Bear, *Family Letters,* 324.

1808-1809

Martha found Jeff's inherited traits, Martha Randolph to Thomas Jefferson, Ibid., 360.

Jefferson urged Martha and Tom to live with them, Thomas Jefferson to Martha Randolph, Jan. 5, 1808, Ibid., 319.

The Tirtium Quids, Bruce, *Randolph of Roanoke,* 1:331-341.

"Scenes of rural retirement," Thomas Jefferson to Charles Willson Peale, Feb. 6, 1809, Brodie, *Intimate History,* 424.

She wore a champagne-colored . . . dress with a long train, Ketcham, *James Madison, a Biography,* 475.

He trembled, perspiring, during the inaugural ceremony, Caffrey, *Twilight's Last Gleaming,* 119; Moore, *Madisons, a Biography,* 221.

He attended a ball and danced, Brodie, *Intimate History,* 425.

179. He was guest of honor at a dinner, Scott, *Old Richmond Neighborhoods,* 131.

Richmonders attested to her "festive boards," Mordecai, *Richmond Bygone Days,* 130.

A standard for "southern fried chicken," Randolph, *Virginia Housewife,* 253.

His "engravings on stone," Judith Randolph to St. George Tucker, 1808, *TC,* W&M.

The "human desert" the House of Representatives, John Randolph to St. George Tucker, letter nd 1808, *JR* RC.

The "play house and the animals" in London, John St. George Randolph to St. George Tucker, *TC,* W&M.

"One of the handsomest young men I ever saw," Harland, *Autobiography,* 321.

"Judgment and feelings equally revolt," John Randolph to St. George Tucker, Nov. 3, 1809, *JR,* RC.

Little calculated to enliven us," John Randolph to St. George Tucker, Nov. 14, 1809, Ibid.

Saying she had "fled from justice," Nancy Randolph to St. George Tucker, Nov. 9, 1808, *BTC,* W&M.

Turned upon Molly for spreading the stories, Ibid.

He replied, suggesting a meeting, Nancy Morris to Joseph Cabell, Aug. 1831, *Cabell Papers,* ViU.

Her "refrigerator" had not yet reached the freezing point, Nancy Randolph to St. George Tucker, Dec. 19, 1808, *TC,* W&M.

"You shall tell me your tale of sorrow," Swiggett, *Extraordinary Mr. Morris,* 316-317.

"Tho' perishing from want," Gouverneur Morris to St. George Tucker, Dec. 26, 1814, *TC,* W&M.

Morris had spent over $50,000 since his return from Europe, Swiggett, *Extraordinary Mr. Morris,* 359.

185. **Marshall felt the rumors were spread and magnified,** Cullen and Johnson, *Papers of John Marshall,* 2:222-223; Baker, *John Marshall, a Life,* 153.

"Brown gown patched at the elbows," Nancy Morris to Joseph Cabell, May 30, 1828, *BR Papers,* LVA.

"I marry this day Ann Cary Randolph," Biddle, *Casual Life,* 43.

"Yesterday, I became the wife of Gouverneur Morris," Nancy Morris to St. GeorgeTucker, Dec. 26, 1809, *TC,* W&M.

1810-1811

He asked pardon, Gouverneur Morris to Gertrude Meredith, Jan. 1810, Hist. Soc. Pa; Swiggett, *Extraordinary Mr. Morris*, 403.

He took his bride with him, June 21, 1810, RF Papers, VHS.

They visited the Falls of Niagara, Ibid.

On a "fine January day," John Randolph to St. George Tucker, Jan. 17, 1810, John Randolph Diary, *BR Papers*, LVA.

"Which I can compare to nothing," John Randolph to St. George Tucker, Mar. 13, 1810, *JR*, RC.

"I have had much reflection," Judith Randolph to Creed Taylor, Mar. 17, 1810, *BR*, LVA.

More than ninety slaves were freed, Ely, *Israel on Appomattox*, 51.

"From as many headaches," John Randolph to Theodore Dudley, Nov. 30, 1810, Dudley. *Letters.*

"Used to explain everything," John St. George Randolph to St. George Tucker, Mar. 7, 1810, *BTC*, W&M.

"Wolves in sheep's clothing," Harland, *Autobiography*, 319.

A heavy rain fell through Albemarle, Gaines, *Thomas Mann Randolph*, 73-74.

He passed the door without speaking, Judith Randolph to St. George Tucker, Mar. 9, 1811, *TC*, W&M.

"Took care to throw himself in my way," Bruce, *Randolph of Roanoke*, 2:363.

"I dined here yesterday," John Randolph to John St. George Randolph, July 29, 1811, *JR Papers*, Spec. Coll. Duke.194.

"I received your very kind letter," John Randolph to John St. George Randolph, Nov. 4, 1811, *JR Papers*, Spec. Coll. Duke.

"More like the love of a woman for a man," Bruce, *John Randolph*, 2:592.

"Jack's public speaking," delighted her, Nancy Morris to St. George Tucker, Dec. 24, 1811, *TC*, W&M.

"When Mr. Morris brought you to Washington," John Randolph to Nancy Morris, Oct. 31, 1814, *Spicy Correspondence*, RC.

"I have always loved Jefferson," McCullough, *John Adams*, 602-603.

1812

Jefferson responded promptly, Thomas Jefferson to John Adams, Jan. 21, 1812, Brodie, *Intimate History*, 446.

In Congress, the War Hawks, Caffrey, *Twilight's Last Gleaming*, 40; Anderson, *William Branch Giles*, 175-176.

"Agrarian cupidity, not maritime rights," John Randolph, *Annals of Congress*, *Dec. 1811;* Caffrey, *Twilight's Last Gleaming*, 140.

"Expecting to be confined in February," Nancy Morris to St. George Tucker, Sept. 9, 1812, *TC*, W&M.

"Perhaps some wind may yet waft you," Sparks, *Life Gouverneur Morris*, 494-495.

Quincy escorted Tudor on to Cambridge, Bruce, *Randolph of Roanoke*, 2:603.

"A very peculiar character," Ibid., 2:491-92.

"I am lonesome by myself," John St. George Randolph to John Randolph, Nov. 8, 1812, *Bryan*, ViU.

"I think you do not write your English," John Randolph to John St. George Randolph, Dec. 13, 1812, *Curry Collection*, DLC.

"If Virginia should persist . . ." Mahon, *War of 1812*, 97.

1813

Saint flooded his uncle with minutiae, John St. George Randolph to John Randolph, Jan. 8, 1813, Jan. 20, 1813, *Bryan*, ViU.

"My wife was delivered of a son," Gouverneur Morris to St. George Tucker, Feb. 10, 1813, *TC*, W&M.

"Preserving for a relic," Judith Randolph to St. George Tucker, Apr. 4, 1813, *TC*, W&M.

"The grapes are not sour," John Randolph to Francis Scott Key, Garland, *Life of John Randolph*, 2:12.

"Agga is not even able to bring us water," John Coalter to St. George Tucker, Coleman, *Citizen*, 159.

"I do not mean to speak," John St. George Randolph to John Randolph, July 9, 1813, *Bryan*, ViU.

"I am afraid it will give you grief," John St. George Randolph to John Randolph, July 1813, Ibid.

"I am more mortified than you should think," John St. George Randolph to John Randolph, Oct. 8, 1813, Ibid.

"And you, my darling, my most beloved child," St. George Tucker to Fanny Coalter, Aug. 27, 1813, Coleman, *Citizen*, 163.

He received an odd letter from his uncle, December 13, 1813, *Grinnan*, ViU..

In command of the 20th Regiment of Infantry, Gaines, *Thomas Mann Randolph*, 86-87.

1814

"The arrows from his quiver," Bruce, *Randolph of Roanoke*, 2:94.

"I am so easy of it," John St. George Randolph to John Randolph, April 19, 1814, *BR Papers*. LVA.

"This county has none of the gold rings," ibid.

"The high road, the tavern opposite," Judith Randolph to John Randolph, June 28, 1814, ibid.

"Incurably alienated from his mother," John Randolph to Francis Scott Key, June 3, 1814, Swiggettt, *Extraordinary Mr. Morris*, 422.

210. **"It has not escaped our attention,"** John Randolph to Gouverneur Morris, Aug. 13, 1814, ibid.

His "earnest wish to come home," Judith Randolph to John Randolph, Aug. 1, 1814, *Randolph*, ViU.

"It will be more convenient," Moore, *The Madisons, A Biography*, 313.

"Flying at full speed," ibid, 317.

One officer appropriated a clean shirt, Mahon, *War of 1812*, 301.

"**In a few hours I became a wanderer,**" Thomas Tudor Tucker to St. George Tucker, Sept. 9, 1814, Coleman, *Citizen*, 166.

"**The lower country between the York and James Rivers,**" John Randolph Diary, *BR Papers*, LVA.

"**In truth, I can think of nothing but you,**" John Randolph to Theodore Dudley, Sept. 7, 1814, Dudley, *Letters*, 159-160.

"**His gloomy, guilty look,**" Nancy Morris to St. George Tucker, Dec. 1814, *TC*, W&M.

With funds provided by Tucker, St. George Tucker to Judith Randolph, July 1, 1814, *ibid.*

"**The fourth letter that I have addressed to you,**" John Randolph to Theodore Dudley, Oct. 8, 1814, Dudley, *Letters*, 160-61.

Someone had tried to smother him, Nancy Morris to William Giles, Feb. 17, 1815, *RF Papers*, VHS.

"**I am like one broken on the wheel,**" John Randolph to Richard Kidder Randolph, Oct. 24, 1814, *BR Papers*, LVA.

"**When, at my departure,**" John Randolph to Nancy Morris, Oct. 31, 1814, *"Spicy Correspondence,"* RC.

"**Wound that has been inflicted,**" St. George Tucker to Nancy Morris, Dec. 16, 1814, *TC*, W&M.

"**Can you account for all,**" Nancy Morris to St. George Tucker, Dec. 1814, *TC*, W&M.

"**Embittered every crumb,**" ibid.

"**Innocence, my dear Nancy,**" St. George Tucker to Nancy Morris, Dec. 16, 1814, ibid.

"**Your goodness cannot persuade me,**" Gouverneur Morris to St. George Tucker, Dec. 26, 1814. ibid.

1815

One went to William Giles, Nancy Morris to William Giles, Feb. 17, 1815, *William Branch Giles Papers*, VHS.

"**I really believe,**" Nancy Morris to William Giles, Mar. 22, 1815, *RF Papers*, VHS.

"I have from authority," John Randolph to William Giles, Mar. 22, 1815, film, NU, ViU.

"Mean rascal and a fool," Martha Randolph to Elizabeth Trist, May 31, /1815, *Trist,* VHS.

Saint voted for Jack, *Cumberland County Deed Book 13,* 123.

"Paris is the only place," Thomas Jefferson to William Short, Mar. 25, 1815, Brodie, *Intimate History,* 443.

The overseer reported seeing Ann, ibid, 458.

"I have declined setting out for Richmond," John St. George Randolph to John Randolph, Mar. 10, 1815, *Bryan,* ViU.

1816

"My brother came home very ill," John Randolph to Judith Randolph, Jan. 20, 1816, *RF Papers,* VHS.

"This vice ... blasted," John Randolph to Elizabeth Coalter Bryan, *BR Papers,* LVA.

In the "midst of a busy city," Judith Randolph to St. George Tucker, Feb. 22, 1816, *TC,* W&M.

"Shaken off her remaining son," John Randolph to Richard Kidder Randolph, Feb. 2, 1816, *BR Papers,* LVA.

She signed her will, *Prince Edward County Will Book* 35, 98.

"How could you leave me?" John Randolph to Theodore Dudley, Dec. 26, 1816, Dudley, *Letters,* 175.

"A Man endowed with two souls," ibid, 221.

"I lead a quiet life," Gouverneur Morris to John Parish, July 26, 1816, Sparks, *Life of Gouverneur Morris,* 495.

"Although we have not previously corresponded," Martha Randolph to Thomas Jefferson, Nov, 20, 1816, Betts & Bear, *Family Letters,* 416-417.

Epilogue

Ended a twenty-one year trusteeship, Swiggett, *Extraordinary Mr. Morris,* 406.

"In your Dialogue," Maria Cosway to Thomas Jefferson, Apr. 18, 1819, S. N. Randolph, *Domestic Life*, 369.

"The sympathies of our earlier days," Thomas Jefferson to Maria Cosway, Bullock, *My Head and My Heart*, 182.

"Then, farewell, my dear," Thomas Jefferson to Martha Randolph, Mapp, *Passionate Pilgrim*, 354.

"When my most maligned son," Nancy Morris to John Randolph, Dec. 17, 1822, *TC*, W&M.

"The thrilling music of his speech, *BR Papers*, LVA.

"Refuses to write or spell," John Randolph to *Richard Kidder Randolph*, Richard Kidder Randolph, Aug. 14, 1820. DLC

"Erect as a Virginia pine," Harland, *Autobiography*, 320-322.

Inventory of his personal property, *Charlotte County Will Book 9*, 413, *Will Book 12*, 93. Estate worth over $200,000.

BIBLIOGRAPHY

Abadie, Ann J., Hart, Mary L. *Encyclopedia of Southern Culture.*
    Chapel Hill: University of North Carolina Press, 1989.

Allgor, Catherine. *Parlor Politics – In Which the Ladies of Washington
    Help Build a City and a Government.* Charlottesville: University
    Press of Virginia, 2000.

Anderson, Dice Robins. *William Branch Giles.* Gloucester, MA:
    P. Smith, 1965.

Andrews, Matthew Page. *Virginia the Old Dominion.* Volume 1.
    Richmond, VA: Dietz Press, 1949.

Asquith, Annunziata. *Marie Antoinette.* New York: McMillan, 1974.

Baker, Leonard. *John Marshall – A Life in Law.* New York: Collins
    Books, 1974.

Beran, Michael Knox. *Jefferson's Demons.* New York: Free Press, 2003.

Betts, Edwin Morris and Bear, James Adam, Jr. eds. *The Family Letters
    of Thomas Jefferson.* Columbia, University of Missouri Press,
    1966.
Beveridge, Albert J. *The Life of John Marshall.* vol. 2. Boston:
    Houghton Mifflin, 1916.

Biddle, Francis. *A Casual Past*. New York: Doubleday, 1961.

Blackburn, Joyce. *George Wythe of Williamsburg*. New York: Harper & Rowe, 1975.

Blanton, Wyndham, M. D. *Medicine in Virginia in the Eighteenth Century*. Richmond, VA: Garrett Massie, 1931.

Bloom, Robert S. *A Generation of Leaves*. New York: Ballantine Books, 1992.

Bober, Natalie S. *Thomas Jefferson, Man on a Mountain*. New York: Atheneum, 1988.

Botkin, B. A. ed. *A Treasury of Southern Folklore*. New York: Bonanza Books, 1980.

Bouldin, Powhatan. *Home Reminiscences of John Randolph of Roanoke*. Richmond, VA: Clement & Jones, 1876.

Bowen, Catherine Drinker. *Miracle in Philadelphia*. New York: Little Brown, 1966 and 1986.

Brady, Patricia. *George Washington's Beautiful Nelly: The Letters of Eleanor Parke Custis Lewis to Elizabeth Borden Gibson, 1794-1851*. Columbia: University of South Carolina Press, 1991.

Brodie, Fawn. *Thomas Jefferson, An Intimate History*. New York: W. W. Norton, 1974.

Brookhiser, Richard. *Gentleman Revolutionary: Gouverneur Morris, The Rake Who Wrote the Constitution*. New York: Free Press, 2003.

Brown, Everett S. ed. *William Plumer's Memorandum of Proceedings in the United States Senate, 1803-1807*. New York: The MacMillan Company. 1923.

Bruce, William Cabell. *John Randolph of Roanoke*. 2 vols. New York: G. P. Putnam, 1922.

Bullock, Helen D. *My Head and My Heart: A Little History of Thomas Jefferson and Maria Cosway*. New York and Virginia: Putnam and Company, 1945.

Burt, Nathanial. *First Families of America*. Boston: Little, Brown & Co., 1977.

Caffrey, Kate. *The Twilight's Last Gleaming*. New York: Stern & Day, 1977.

Carter, Edward C. II, Van Horn, John C., and Brownell, Charles, eds. *Latrobe's View of America, 1795-1820*. New Haven: Yale University Press, 1985.

Carter, Edward C. II. and Polites, Angeline eds. *Virginia Journal of Benjamin H. Latrobe – 1796-1798*. 2 vols. New Haven: Yale University Press, 1977.

Cary, Virginia. *Letters on Female Character*. Richmond, VA: A. Works, 1828.

Clinton, Catherine. *Plantation Mistress – Woman's World in the Old South*. New York: Pantheon Books, 1982.

Coleman, Mary Haldane. *Citizen of No Mean City*. Richmond, VA: Dietz Press, 1938. *Virginia Silhouttes*. Richmond, VA: Dietz Press, 1934.

Contini, Mila. *Fashion: From Ancient Egypt to the Present Day*. New York: Odyssey Press, 1965.

Conway, Moncure Daniel. *Omitted Chapters of History Disclosed in the Life and Papers of Edmund Randolph*. New York: G. P. Putnam's Sons, 1888.

Corson, Richard. *Fashions in Hair: The First 5000 Years.* New York: Hastings, 1965.

Cott, Nancy F. *The Bonds of Womanhood.* New Haven, CT: Yale University Press, 1997.

Courtwright, David. *Dark Paradise, Study of Opiates in America before 1940.* Cambridge, MA: Harvard University Press, 1982.

Cresson, W. P. *James Monroe.* Chapel Hill: University of North Carolina Press, 1946.

Cullen, Charles T. and Johnson, Herbert A., eds. *Papers of John Marshall.* vol. 2. Chapel Hill: University of North Carolina Press, 1977.

Dabney, Richard Heath. *John Randolph A Character Sketch.* Chicago: H. C. Campbell Co. 1898.

Dabney, Virginius. *Richmond, The Story of a City.* New York: Doubleday, 1976.

Daniels, Jonathan. *The Randolphs of Virginia.* New York: Doubleday, 1972. *Ordeal of Ambition, Jefferson, Hamilton, Burr.* New York: Doubleday, 1970.

Dawidoff, Robert. *The Education of John Randolph.* New York: W. W. Norton, 1979.

D'Emilio, John & Freedman, Esther B. *Intimate Matters: A History of Sexuality in America.* Second edition. Chicago: University of Chicago Press, 1997.

Dos Passos, John. *Head and Heart of Thomas Jefferson.* New York: Doubleday, 1954.

Dudley, Theodore. *Letters of John Randolph to a Young Relative.* Philadelphia: Cary, Lea and Blanchard, 1834.

Duke, Maurice and Jordan, Daniel P. eds. *A Richmond Reader, 1733–1983.* Chapel Hill: University of North Carolina Press, 1983.

Eckenrode, H. J. *The Randolphs: The Story of a Virginia Family.* Indianapolis, In: Bobbs, Merrill, 1946.

Elkins, Stanley and Eric McKitrick. *The Age of Federalism.* New York: Oxford University Press, 1993.

Ely, Melvin Patrick. *Israel on the Appomattox.* New York: Alfred A. Knopf, 2004.

Faderman, Lillian. *Surpassing the Love of Men, Romantic Friendship and Love Between Women from the Renaissance to the Present.* New York: William Morrow, 1981.

Fishwick, Marshall W. *Gentlemen of Virginia.* New York: Dodd Mead, 1961.

Fleming, Thomas. *Thomas Jefferson, Man from Monticello.* New York: Morrow, 1969.

Flexnor, Eleanor. *Mary Wollstonecraft.* New York: Penguin Books, 1972.

Fox-Genovese, Elizabeth. *Within the Plantation Household: Black and White Women of the Old South.* Chapel Hill: University of North Carolina Press, 1988.

Gaines, William H. Jr. *Thomas Mann Randolph - Jefferson's Son-in-law.* Baton Rouge: University of Louisiana Press, 1966.

Garland, Hugh A. *Life of John Randolph of Roanoke.* 2 vols. New York: D. Appleton, 1850 and 1856.

Gleason, David King. *Virginia Plantation Homes.* Baton Rouge: Louisiana State University Press, 1989.

Gottschalk, Louis R. *Lafayette in America, 1777-1783.* Arveyres, France: L'Esprit de Lafayette Society, 1975.

Gunderson, Joan. *To Be Useful to the World: Women in Revolutionary America.* New York: Prentice-Hall, 1996.

Hall, Gordon Langley. *Mr. Jefferson's Ladies.* Boston: Beacon Press, 1966.

Hamlin, Talbot. *Benjamin Henry Latrobe.* New York: Oxford University Press, 1955.

Handlin, Oscar and Lilian Handlin, *Liberty in Expansion 1760-1800.* New York: Harper & Row, 1989.

Harland, Marion. *Marion Harland's Autobiography.* New York: Harper Bros., 1910.

Headley, Robert K. *Genealogical Abstracts from Eighteenth Century Virginia Newspapers.* Baltimore, MD: Genealogical Publishing Company, 1987.

Henry, William Wirt. *Patrick Henry: Life, Correspondence, and Speeches.* vol. 3. Harrisonburg, VA: Sprinkle Publishing Company, 1993.

Hildreth, Richard. *History of the United States.* vol. 5. New York: Harper & Bros., 1856.

Hill, Margot H. *Evolution of Fashion.* New York: Reinhold, 1967.

Holton, Woody. *Unruly Americans and the origins of the Constitution.* New York: Hill & Wang, 2007.

Irving, Washington. *Life and Letters.* New York: Putnam, 1862.

Isenberg, Nancy. *Fallen Founder, the Life of Aaron Burr.* New York: The Viking Penguin Group, 2007.

Ketcham, Ralph. *James Madison - A Biography.* Charlottesville, University of Virginia Press, 1970.

Kierner, Cynthia A. *Beyond the Household: Woman's Place in the Early South 1700-1835.* Ithaca, NY: Cornell University Press, 1998. *Scandal at Bizarre.* New York: Palgrave-MacMillan, 2004.

Kozol, Jonathon. *Amazing Grace.* New York: Harper Collins, 1996.

Krusen, Jessie Ball Thompson. *Tuckahoe Plantation.* Richmond, VA: Whittet & Shepperson, 1975.

Kukla, Jon. *Mr. Jefferson's Women.* New York: Alfred A. Knopf, 2007.

Langhorne, Elizabeth. *Monticello: A Family Story.* Chapel Hill, NC: Algonquin Press, 1987.

Lebsock, Suzanne. *The Free Women of Petersburg.* New York: W. W. Norton, 1984.

Lipscomb, Andrew A., ed. *Writings of Thomas Jefferson.* vol. 2. Washington DC: Jefferson Memorial Association, 1903.

Lodge, Henry Cabot. *Historical and Political Essays.* Boston and New York: Houghton Mifflin and Company, 1898.

Lomask, Milton. *Aaron Burr, The Conspiracy and Years of Exile 1805-1836.* New York: Farrar, Straus & Giroux, 1982.

Lutz, Francis Earle. *Chesterfield, an Old Virginia County.* Richmond, VA, Byrd Press, 1954. *A Richmond Album.* Richmond, VA: Byrd Press, 1937.

Mahon, John K. *War of 1812*. Gainesville: University of Florida Press, 1972.

Malone, Dumas. *Jefferson and the Ordeal of Liberty*. Boston: Little, Brown, 1962.

Mapp, Alf J. Jr. *Thomas Jefferson Passionate Pilgrim*. Lanham, MD: Madison, Brady, 1991.

Maury, Anne Fontaine, ed. *Intimate Virginiana*. Richmond, VA: Dietz Press, 1941.

McCullough, David. *John Adams*. New York: Simon & Shuster, 2001.

McDonald, Forrest. *The Presidency of Thomas Jefferson*. Kansas City: University of Kansas Press, 1976.

McGee, Dorothy Horton. *Framers of the Constitution*. New York: Dodd, Mead, 1968.

McLaughlin, Jack. *Jefferson and Monticello: The Biography of a Builder*. New York: Henry Holt, 1988.

Meade, Robert Douthat. *Patrick Henry, Practical Revolutionary*. New York: Lippincott, 1969.

Mitchell, Broaddus. *Alexander Hamilton, A Concise Biography*. New York: Oxford Press, 1976.

Mintz, Max M. *Gouverneur Morris and the American Revolution*. Norman: University of Oklahoma Press, 1970.

Moore, Virginia. *The Madisons: A Biography*. New York: McGraw Hill, 1979.

Mordecai, Samuel. *Richmond in Bygone Days*. Richmond, VA: George M. West, 1856 and 1946.

Morgan, Edmond S. *Virginians at Home – Family Life in 18th Century.* Colonial Williamsburg, VA: 1952.

Peterson, Merrill D. *Thomas Jefferson's Writings.* Selections. New York: Library of America, 1984.

Randall, William I. *Thomas Jefferson.* New York: Henry Holt, 1993.

Randolph, Mary. *The Virginia Housewife.* Edited by Karen Hess. Columbia: University of South Carolina Press, 1984.

Randolph, S. N. *The Domestic Life of Thomas Jefferson.* Charlottesville, University of Virginia Press, 1975.

Rehnquist, William H. *Grand Inquests.* New York: William Morrow, 1992.

Reniers, Percival. *Life and Death at the Springs of Virginia.* Chapel Hill: University of North Carolina Press, 1941.

Rogow, Arnold A. *A Fatal Friendship: Alexander Hamilton and Aaron Burr.* New York: Hill & Wang, 1998.

Sale, Edith Tunis. *Mansions of Virginia in Colonial Times.* Philadelphia: J. R. Lippincott, 1909.

Sanford, James K. *Richmond, Her Triumph, Tragedies and Growth.* Richmond, VA: Richmond Metro Chamber of Commerce, 1975.

Scott, Mary Wingfield. *Old Richmond Neighborhoods.* Richmond, VA: Valentine Museum, 1950.

Severn, William. *John Marshall, The Man who Made the Court Supreme.* New York: McCoy Co., 1969.

Shepherd, Samuel. *Statutes at Large of Virginia.* New York: AMS Press, 1970.

Smith, Jean Edward. *John Marshall, Definer of a Nation.* New York: Henry Holt, 1996.

Smith, Page. *Jefferson: a Revealing Biography.* New York: American Heritage Publishing Co., 1976.

Smith-Rosenberg. Carroll. *The Female World of Love and Ritual: Relations Between Women in Nineteenth Century America.* Signs: Journal of Women in Culture and Society, 1975, 1 (1) 1-30.

Sparks, Jared. *Life of Gouverneur Morris.* Boston: Gray, 1832.

Stites, Francis N. *John Marshall, Defender of the Constitution.* Boston: Little Brown & Co., 1981.

Stokes, William T. Jr. and Francis L. Berkely, Jr. *Papers of John Randolph of Roanoke.* Charlottesville VA: University of Virginia Press, 1950.

The Early Life of John Randolph of Roanoke 1773-1794. Charlottesville, VA: University of Virginia Press, 1950.

Randolph of Roanoke - a Virginia Patriot Early Years 1773-1805, Charlottesville, VA: University of Virginia Press, 1955.

Stoutamire, Albert. *Music of the Old South.* Rutherford, NJ: Dickinson University Press, 1972.

Swiggett, Howard. *The Extraordinary Mr. Morris.* New York: Doubleday, 1952.

Tillyard, Stella. *Aristocrats- Caroline, Emily, Louise and Sarah Lennox 1740-1832.* New York: Farrar, Straus and Giroux. 1994.

Ulrich, Laurel Thatcher. *A Midwife's Tale.* New York: A. A. Knopf, 1990.

Vidal, Gore. *Burr.* New York: Random House, 1973.

Walach, Nancy. *Women and the American Experience.* New York: Dual, Sloane and Pearce, 1981.

Walz, Jay and Audrey. *The Bizarre Sisters.* New York: Dual, Sloane and Pearce, 1950.

Weider, Ben and Hapgood, David. *The Murder of Napoleon.* New York: Congdon & Lottes, 1982.

Wheelan, Joseph. *Jefferson's Vendetta: The Pursuit of Aaron Burr and the Judiciary.* New York: Carroll & Graf Publishers, 2005.

Whittredge, Arnold. American Heritage, 1976.

Wibberley, Leonard. *Man of Liberty: A Life of Thomas Jefferson.* New York: Farrar, Giroux & Straus, 1968.

Wilson, Eunice. *A History of Shoe Fashions.* London: Pitman Publishing, 1972.

Zehmer, John G. *Old Richmond Today.* Richmond: Council of Historic Richmond, 1988

Collections

Alderman Library, University of Virginia, Charlottesville, Virginia:

Edgehill/Randolph Papers

Carr-Cary papers

Joseph Bryan Collection

Grinnan Mss.

Randolph Papers

Creed Taylor Mss.

Trist Papers

Cabell Family Papers

Swem Library, College of William and Mary, Williamsburg, Virginia:

Brown-Tucker-Coalter Collection

Nancy Randolph Papers

Tucker-Coleman Collection

Virginia Historical Society, Richmond, Virginia:

Grinnan Family Papers

Harrison Family Papers

Randolph Family Papers

Elizabeth House Trist Papers

William Branch Giles Papers

John Briggs: *A Diary of a Trip to Sweet Springs*

John Marshall's Notes of Evidence: *Republica v. Randolph, April 29, 1793*. Copied by John Randolph, Williamsburg, VA, June 1793.

Lipscomb Library, Randolph College, Lynchburg, Virginia:

John Randolph Papers

A Spicy Correspondence Between John Randolph of Roanoke and His Cousin Nancy. Special Edition, 1888.

State Archives, Library of Virginia, Richmond, Virginia:

Bruce-Randolph Personal Papers

Creed Taylor Papers

Library of Congress, Washington, DC:

John Randolph Mss.

Richard Kidder Randolph Collection

Duke University, Durham, North Carolina:

John Randolph Papers, Special Collections.

COURT RECORDS

Charlotte County Will Book, Charlotte Courthouse, VA

Chesterfield County Deed Books, Chesterfield Courthouse, VA

Cumberland County Deed Books, Cumberland Courthouse, VA

Cumberland County Order Books, Cumberland Courthouse, VA

Cumberland County Will Books, Cumberland Courthouse, VA

Goochland County Will Book, Goochland Courthouse, VA

Lancaster County Marriage Register, 1715-1852, October 1791, Lancaster Courthouse, VA

Lancaster County Order Books, Lancaster Courthouse, VA

Prince Edward County Order Books, Prince Edward Courthouse, VA

Prince Edward County Will Books, Prince Edward Courthouse, VA

Powhatan County Marriages, Powhatan Courthouse, VA

Miscellaneous

Abridgement of Debates of Congress, 1780-1856, Volume 3, New York, 1857

Amelia County, Virginia Buildings Survey, Kathleen Hadfield, 1982.

American Heritage, October 1974 and April 1976.

Annals of Congress, 1805-1807, John Appleton, Massachusetts Historical Society Library

Encyclopedia Britannica, 40, Volume VII

History of Prince Edward County

Today and Yesterday in the Heart of Virginia – Farmville Herald 1935

Virginia Gazette and General Advertiser. Library of Virginia

Virginia Independent Chronicle, 12/9/1786. Virginia Historical
Society

Virginia Magazine of History and Biography, Virginia Historical
Society, volumes 2, 25, and 61
Volume 48, 238-42, "Letters From Old Trunks," Randolph-
Carr letter courtesy of Mrs. Anna Dean Carr David

William and Mary Quarterly, Series I, II, and III

Works Progress Administration of Virginia – Historical Inventory 1936

INDEX

ABOUT THE AUTHOR

Ruth Doumlele lives in Powhatan County, Virginia, a few miles from the Randolph family plantations. She is a member of the National Society Daughters of the American Revolution and her Hailey ancestors fought in the same battles as the Randolphs. She holds a bachelor's degree from Mary Baldwin College in Staunton, Virginia, and a master's degree from the University of Richmond. Ruth writes local and regional history, and is a docent at Virginia's circa 1813 Executive Mansion in Richmond, where Thomas Mann Randolph lived as governor, 1819-1822.